A WORMS EYE VIEW FROM A BIRD'S BEAK

Raven Chacon

A Worm's Eye View from a Bird's Beak

Published by Sternberg Press

Swiss Institute, New York
Nordnorsk Kunstmuseum, Northern Norway/Sápmi

Katya García-Antón
and Stefanie Hessler

A Worm's Eye View from a Bird's Beak

In Navajo/Diné creation myths, Raven Chacon recounts, there are four different worlds below this one. Above this world, there are other ones, too. But rather than conceiving of the worlds below as the past and the worlds above as the future in the linear way that Western narratives might suggest, in Navajo cosmogony those multiple worlds still, or already, exist. In Chacon's sound installation *Still Life No. 3* (2015), a woman tells this Navajo story of origins through a series of speakers installed in a vertical half circle. Parts of the narrative repeat and overlap, blurring its forward progression and allowing different times to coexist and co-affect one another.

It is in between bygone and yet to come, between Western and Navajo worldviews, between score and performance, between the political and the spiritual, that Chacon's notational, sonic, performative, collaborative, filmic, and sculptural practice unfolds. This book is the first monograph dedicated to his practice, accompanying his first solo exhibition in New York and Europe, *A Worm's Eye View from a Bird's Beak* at Swiss Institute (SI) in New York and Nordnorsk Kunstmuseum in Northern Norway/Sápmi. The exhibition spans diverse geographical contexts: Sápmi (the Sámi homeland traversed by the present-day nation-states of Norway, Sweden, Finland, and Russia) and Lenapehoking, or New York, in Turtle Island. Both locations, however, share Indigenous histories that colonialism has attempted to eradicate for centuries, where resilience, or, in the words of cultural theorist Gerald Vizenor, survivance,[1] continues to thrive.

Weaving connections between these geographies, Chacon traveled to Tromsø/Romsa on three occasions, including a residency in the home of legendary Sámi figure Nils Aslak Valkeapää/Áillohaš, to collaborate with local Sámi artists, joikers, reindeer herders, and activists. Several new works emerged from this time: *For Four (River Valley)* (2024), a video installation featuring joikers singing to the four compass points in Skibotn/Ivgubahta, in northernmost

1 Vizenor defines survivance as "an active sense of presence, the continuance of native stories, not a mere reaction, [...] renunciations of dominance, tragedy, and victimry." Gerald Vizenor, *Manifest Manners: Narratives on Postindian Survivance* (Lincoln, NE: Bison Books, 1999), vii.

Norway/Sápmi, where the recurring threat of windmill parks in sacred and reindeer-herding areas has been met over the last decades with (so far) successful resistance, and later, a sister piece, *For Four (Caldera)* (2024), showing four women standing on the volcanic caldera in the Jemez Mountains of New Mexico, singing and reading to their natural surroundings. Also commissioned for the exhibition is the sculptural and video installation ... *the sky ladder* (2024), emerging from a collaboration with members of the Bål Nango family (reindeer herders and land guardians), some of whom are also contributors to this book, as they share intergenerational stories and site-specific knowledges in the process of drilling holes into wooden planks that trace (and notate, score-like) the outlines of mountain ranges and other significant landscapes.

Chacon is an artist deeply engaged in the struggle for sovereignty and justice. Questions of politics, from centering alternatives to settler-colonialist narratives and appropriation of land and people, to strengthening community, imagining more direct forms of democratic representation and collective resistance, and protecting land, water, and air, emerge from many of his works. *Silent Choir* captures a moment during the No Dakota Access Pipeline (NoDAPL) protests near Standing Rock Indian Reservation in 2016–17 against the building of a pipeline that would affect the Lakota tribe's sovereignty and livelihood. During the women-led social and environmental justice movement, a group of hundreds of water protectors gathered at the site and silently stared at the pipeline security and North Dakota state police. *Voiceless Mass* (2021), for which Chacon was awarded the Pulitzer Prize as the first Native American musician in 2022, was written for the pipe organ at the Cathedral of St. John the Evangelist in Milwaukee, Wisconsin, alongside a flute, a clarinet, percussion, strings, and other instruments. Unlike a traditional mass, the sound of the organ replaces what would be human voices. The piece is both a powerful reflection on the silencing of Indigenous populations by state and Church, and on the repurposing of colonial architectures that were tooled to the task.

One of the core questions guiding Chacon is how to relink political affect and change, or, put differently, how can we imagine and put into practice new systems beyond those reliant on extraction, accumulation, and dispossession? To broach this issue, Chacon remembers and reimagines, listens carefully and powerfully speaks out, with the aim to build relations between registers of knowing and doing that might produce change. In this spirit, the score *American Ledger No. 1* (2018) recounts the founding of the United States in chronological descending order. Shown as a flag, billboard, or blanket, as in the exhibition at SI, the performers use percussion and woodwinds as well as coins thrown in a metal can, an axe to chop wood, a police whistle blown for a sustained period of time, and a struck match to remember this violent history:

a history that encompasses the diasporic Indigenous communities living in today's urban metropolises on traditional land, the attempts to excise Indigenous epistemologies, and stretches back in time to the introduction of colonial law, land appropriation, enslavement of Black people, economic inequity, and Christian religion—and protest—to first moments of contact. Similarly, *Report* (2001/2015), composed and scored for an ensemble of firearms, punctuates so-called silence through a cacophony of both power and resistance, whereas *Field Recordings* (1999) from the American Southwest counters what settler imaginaries envisioned as a silent *terra nullius* (empty land), honoring the sovereign vibrational patterns of these locations. It is in these in-between spaces, or through creating connections where they might be hard to imagine, that new as well as ancient ways of relating, and of politics, may be glimpsed.

Many of these concerns and more are developed further by the contributors to this publication. In Eric-Paul Riege's contribution, the Diné/Navajo artist explores the permanence and impermanence of home through what Chacon via Sámi law professor, joiker, and artist, Ánde Somby, calls vertical neighbors—those who have lived before us yet are still here and who we, as Riege writes, bury not only below but also around and above. Keeping with the in-between of Chacon's work, with past, present, and future coexisting in nonlinear ways, Chacon asks Riege of insects entering a house: "Is it clockwise for the bugs that enter from below and when they look up?" As the title of this publication and the exhibition, *A Worm's Eye View from a Bird's Beak*, suggests, this reversal of perspectives in their redressing of power imbalances, or rather their coexistence, guides the texts and visual contributions.

A conversation between Chacon and Ánde Somby, who participated in the new video installation *For Four (River Valley)* (2024), reflects upon Sámi and Navajo epistemologies. Refashioned by Chacon into the form of scripts and scattered throughout the book, their dialogue addresses the multiplicity of dimensions that characterize their respective worldviews and across which knowledge transfers and changes over time. Chacon and Somby find common ground in the notion of living in a world delineated by relations that occur from the earth to the sky and back, as well as from ancestors to future generations and back. They highlight the potential of sound to channel and empower those relations, as well as to counter silenced Indigenous voices across generations and build community across time and place.

In "Notational Relations," musicologist Patrick Nickleson and (Stó:lō/Skwah) artist, curator, and writer Dylan Robinson highlight the critical and generative dynamics at play in Chacon's practice. Leveraging a deep understanding of music epistemologies belonging to Western and Indigenous traditions, Chacon samples from both, be it the adaptation of Western tools to serve Indigenous communities, the adaptation of Western notation to express Indigenous values and stories, or countering Indigenous taboos. In doing so, he neither rescinds his Indigenous sovereignty nor does he exacerbate, as Robinson and Nickleson so aptly describe, "the pernicious settler syndrome of mutual exclusivity, that takes us out of relationship."[2] The authors go on to argue that Chacon's concern with the social actions and the relationality that result from his practice hollow out the positionality and individuality (read universalism) of modernism. In this sense Chacon is critical of both John Cage's position on silence (for its exclusion of bodily relations) and Pauline Oliveros's deep listening (for the privilege that ability entails). His scored music and performances, music institutions, and music pedagogies nourish the relation between music, families, neighborhoods, and lands, as much as they push for diversification of the field and performer equity. As Robinson and Nickleson argue, Chacon offers us "a decolonial theory [and practice] for change."[3]

Writer and critic Aruna D'Souza's essay considers how Chacon continuously reimagines what a score might be while holding in disruptive and productive tension the classical music of European musical conventions and notational systems, and Indigenous traditions. Those systems, D'Souza writes, not only vary sonically, but also embody different epistemologies. Chacon's scores exist in these tensions; they are deeply relational. D'Souza, like Nickleson and Robinson, suggests that various works central to Chacon's practice are subversions of Cage's Duchampian gesture of silence. *Duet* (2000) is premised upon collaboration, brought together in silence, albeit one rich with the push and pull that constitutes relationships. The installation *Silent Choir* (2016/2022) goes further beyond the silence of the individual musician, documenting the sounds deflected back to the listener. The recording garners strength from the intentional withholding of the sounds of a group, where the innumerable relationships, tensions, and attention to other bodies creates a loaded, almost electric, multiplicity of sounds produced not by bodies, but by the physical and psychological relations between them.

Invoking the late curator Okwui Enwezor's use of the Igbo proverb *ife kwulu, ife akwuso ya*, curator Anthony Huberman homes in on the many *withs* that emerge from the relational spaces that comprise Chacon's art. The proverb suggests that wherever and whenever someone stands, something or someone else is always standing nearby. This is true for ancestors and descendants, for a river or wind, and for music, too. Nothing, and no one, exists outside of these relations; we are all beholden to those who came before us and those who will come after. Huberman traces these relations through Chacon's practice close to the land and in relation with musicians, friends, and students, through collectivity, teaching, and learning, through sleeping on a collaborator's sofa,

2 See Dylan Robinson and Patrick Nickleson, "Notational Relations," in this volume, p. 85.

3 Ibid., 91.

through including voices of Navajo and Hopi students, through programming noise musicians and poets or queer/feminist, Black, and Indigenous platforms. And, indeed, Huberman suggests, music always has something happening right next to it, standing nearby or with it.

In the poem "Stolen," Sámi filmmaker and reindeer herder Marja Bål Nango (sister of Smávot Ingir, who also contributed to the book, and both of whom collaborated on Chacon's new installation ... *the sky ladder*) presents a critical perspective on the justifications used to prop up Nordic colonization strategies past and present. As dark as it is defiant, the poem calls out the inherent colonial inequity within the notion of democratic equality that Nordic governments identify with, and which is hailed globally. By highlighting the land and water inhabited by Sámi people as an indivisible part of their culture, Bål Nango reveals the current wave of green colonialism (in this case, aeolic energy parks) as a further form of epistemic aggression against the Sámi people. In "The Map," Sámi filmmaker and reindeer herder Smávot Ingir addresses the epistemological ignorance of the settler-colonial Nordic regime and the weight of its genocidal impact. The age-old tropes of *terra nullius* that underpinned the early conquest of the North in Europe and the Americas linger still in today's colonial apparatus. However, without the holistic knowledge to read that land, to apprehend the interconnectedness of its biome and the Sámi people living on it, extinction is bound to happen. And yet, there is one element the genocidal apparatus didn't (and doesn't) count upon: Indigenous survivance.

In their speculative fiction short story, Diné/Bilagáana writer and scholar Lou Cornum imagines a world in the not so far future where billionaire venture capitalists' attempts to colonize and artwash the moon have failed. The moon, now again a lone rock seen from afar in the night sky, can exist in its alterity without attempts led by hubris to know and possess. The story closes with a reminder of Navajo protocols for lunar eclipses: rather than watch, people are meant to avert their gaze from the astronomical phenomenon. Earth and moon may be distant but they are nonetheless in relation, and this relationship to a stranger must be valued beyond seeking mastery.

Poet Sigbjørn Skåden's contribution can be read in a similar vein. Transcribing bird sounds by ear and according to English orthography, Skåden creates a subjective map of human–bird relations, and of his own perception in relation to a sonic space—a place otherwise known as Láŋtdievvá/Planterhaug (N 68.537, E 16.753). The Sámi and English ornithological names of the birds he hears are listed, but next to the rhythmic, uncontainable exuberance of their voicings, these names feel like reductions that are lacking. The transcriptions are invitations, too, for readers to voice these bird songs, to embody them.

Finally, Candice Hopkins's "An archive of sound" draws from

years of thinking, being, hearing, and making sound with Chacon. Punctuated by seven sections ("Howl.," "Hiss.," "Scrape.," "Song.," "Roar.," "Trill.," "Gust.") Hopkins's contribution leverages the musicality and emotional tonality of words, drawing deep from a journey across time and site. Earth, flesh, and wind bring memories long gone and just made, settler-enforced disalignments, the layering of beauty astride beauty. Her thoughts linger around each other, in rise and fall, portrait and process of a practice dedicated to a life of sound.

The design of this book by Santiago da Silva and Ana Cecilia Brena, developed closely with Chacon, weaves relationships between his works through a notational system. A lexicon, composed of elements used by Chacon in his scores, prompts various readings of the texts. Readers may find visual signs distributed throughout the book, and in the "Lexicon" at the back, Chacon includes instructions or questions for readers to reference, creating different layers for interpretation, and modes for interacting with the book. These prompts encourage embodied perusal or even performance, and function similarly to how Chacon works with performers.

Concluding with an extended list of works, this book brings together for the first time a comprehensive selection of Chacon's solo and collaborative projects from 1990 to 2023.

We express our profound gratitude to Raven Chacon for his trust to organize the exhibition and book, and for the generous inspiration he has offered us throughout the process. Thanks to Santiago da Silva and Ana Cecilia Brena's ingenious design, the publication closely mirrors Chacon's notational practice and layered ways of engaging with his work. We are specially indebted to all the writers and contributors for their perspectives on Chacon's work.

We wish to thank all those who contributed to the new production of works: Joar Nango, the Lásságami Foundation, the Bål Nango family, joikers Risten Anine Gaup, Ingá-Máret Gaup-Juuso, Ánde Somby, and Niko Valkeapää, filmmakers Christine Cynn and Sondre Sandbakken, sound recorders Valentin Manz and Rune Hansen, Charlotte Heatherington at Artica Svalbard, Rebecca Head Trautmann and the Smithsonian National Museum of the American Indian, and Anna Zepp at the Metropolitan Museum of Art. Our deepest gratitude to Stavia Grimani, Robbie Wing, and Martin D. Fowler at Chacon's studio.

Lastly, the teams at Nordnorsk Kunstmuseum and Swiss Institute have worked enthusiastically on bringing the exhibition to life. A heartfelt thank-you to Ylva Foss Valde, Mathilde Stubmark, Kim Skytte, Øystein Oldervoll, Rebecca Bayram, Stella Kessler, Marc Lüedi, and Oliver Graney at NNKM, and, at SI, Patrick Reynolds, KJ Abudu, and especially Alison Coplan, our co-editor and co-curator extraordinaire.

Raven Chacon

Being in a position

My music does not focus on melody. It is not a priority at all. It does not care about pitches or keys or tuning. In most cases, the first note can start from any position.

Nor does it concern itself with rhythm. Instead, it concerns itself with patterns over a long period of time; personal time or collective. One cannot escape time.

There is consideration of volume in acknowledgment of the edges of its spectrum, the inaudible in either direction. Of what has been silenced and what happens when it is not.

And often, my music does not care about timbre or tone. Or, I should clarify, the consistency of replicating a specific sound. What is important is from who or from what the tone originates.

The musical parameter that is most important to me is counterpoint. Not in the sense of its Baroque and classical meaning, that being, "the relationship between two or more melody lines that are played at the same time, resulting in harmony."

Instead, I am speaking about the contrary motion of navigating a world that assumes where you are going because of where you come from. Before that contrary motion is discovered, the switching of course, running parallel with whatever is chasing you or whatever you are chasing, at a dissonant interval and distance.

It is the zigzagging into crevices where you are not allowed, maybe you bring a friend with you, another species, and you zigzag together. And you gather more, changing forms and formations, mimicking each other's voices to confuse the listeners who want to trap you in your position.

It is also the questioning of your traditions and protocols. It is the walking of a path with respect and knowledge of the previous time you cannot escape. Or perhaps it's a future time.

To practice counterpoint is to be a teacher and forever a student, to find your location in the universe, a humble yet oscillating position, somewhere between the inside of the earth and the middle of the sky.

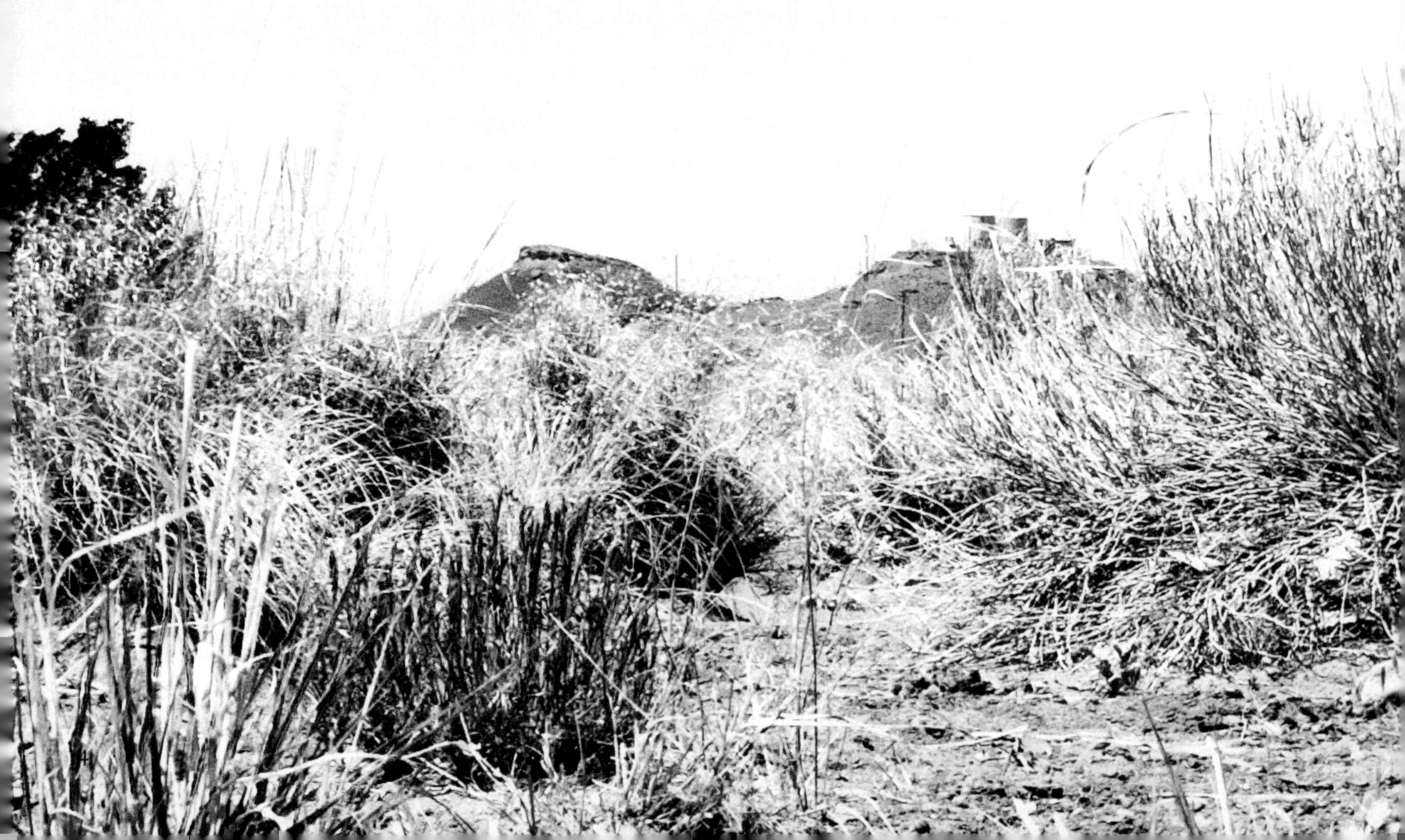

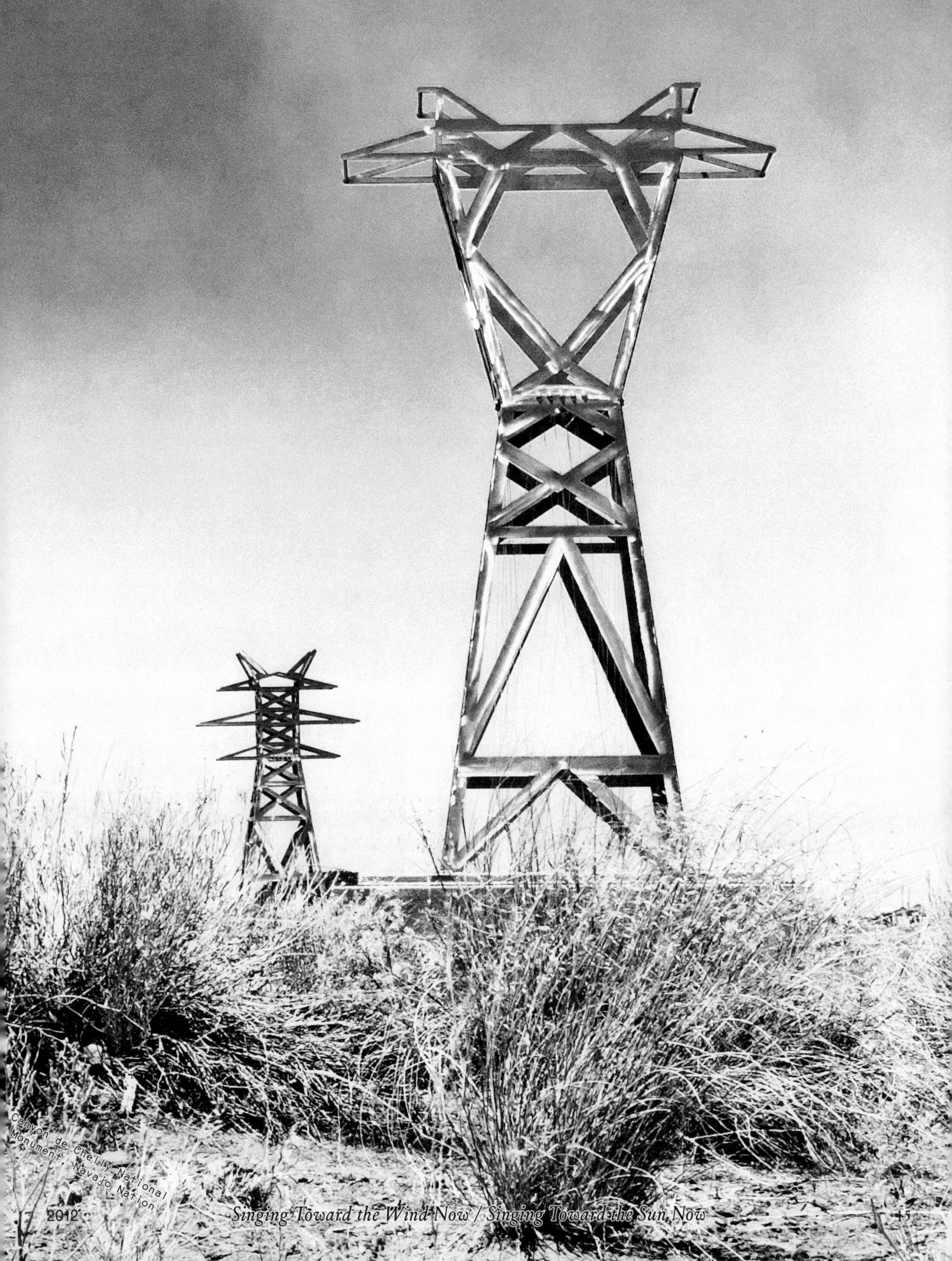
Canyon de Chelly National
Monument, Navajo Nation

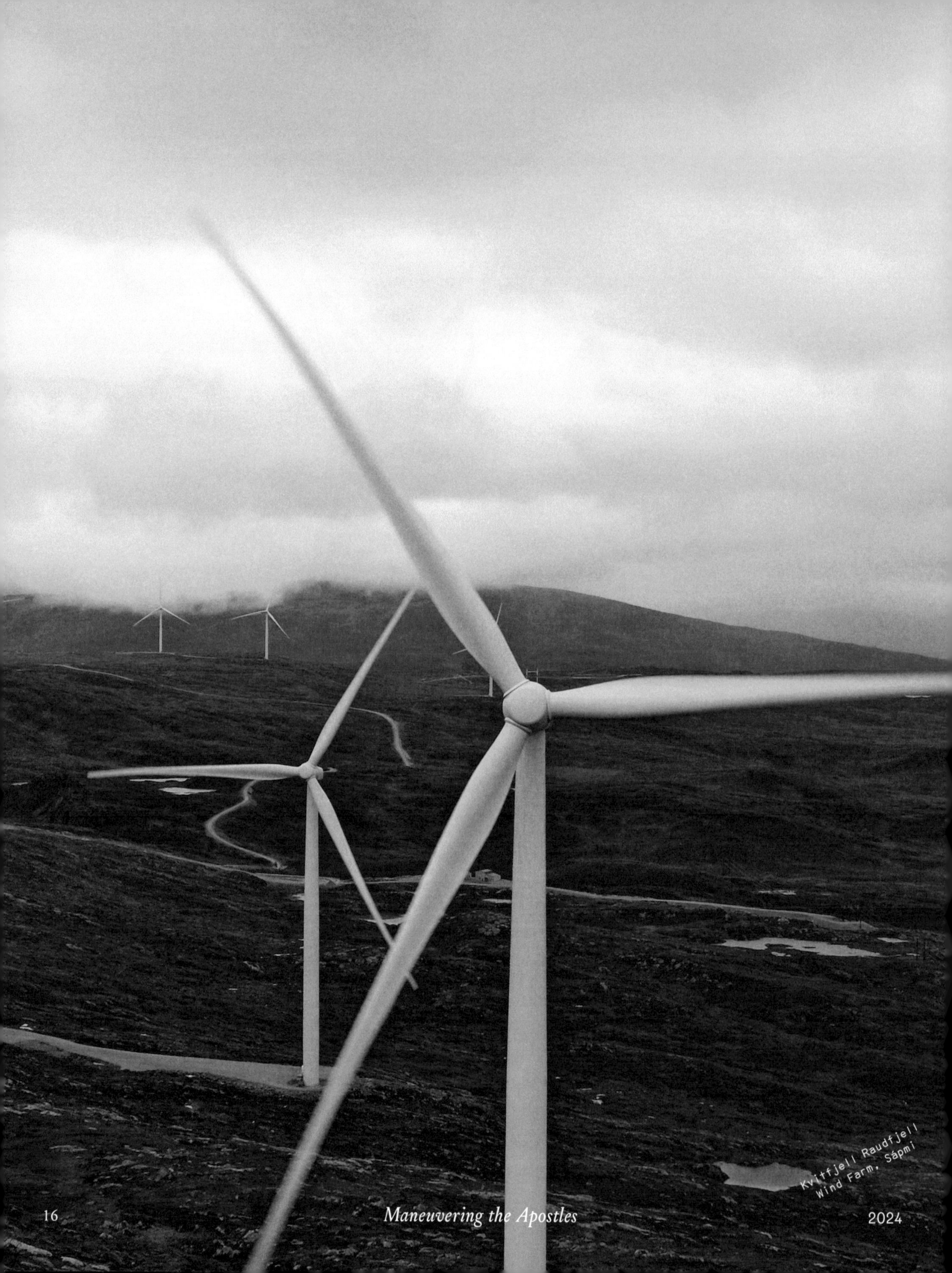
Kvitfjell Raudfjell
Wind Farm, Sápmi

FADE IN:

INT/EXT. - DAY

RAVEN

Last time we spoke, we talked a lot about stories of coming from the ground into the sky. What I shared with you last time was that in Diné ways, in our stories, there are four different worlds below this world. I wonder if they're also talking about different past moments of migrations. Starting with a time when everyone was living in a darkness. In these other worlds we were more closely related to insects. They guided us up into the next world above that first one, and we continued up together. And all these different worlds have different colors. And as we emerged into these new worlds, we started becoming other animals, or were encountering other new animals. And as these animals migrate too, we had to go and follow them into the next world.

And then there's other stories, of monsters and conflict. And eventually, we arrive in this world where we are today, and we acknowledge there's further worlds above us. And whether that's speaking allegorically about what happens when we pass on, or we talk about the next generations, we're still thinking that above can mean the future. But at the same time it's not the future. We call it the place where everything melts into one, is eventually where we end up. But I acknowledge too, that those other below and above worlds are not the past or future; they still or already exist.

ÁNDE SOMBY

You know, the origin story of joik is that they got joik from the underground people. And even today, when you hear a really good joik, then you would characterize that the joik, that she joiks like an underground, or he joiks like an underground. And it's such an interesting contrast, if you characterize somebody singing saying that he sings like an angel, she sings like an angel. So therefore we always used to say the greatest that can happen to you, music-wise, is that you are sort of in a place where you get to hear an underground when the underground is joiks. I actually heard one that I was almost characterized like underground. From the people who live under the ground.

ÁNDE

Here's the poem there: Where neither the sun nor the moon shines, there I can be the light. Where the sun does not shine, there I can be the sun. Where the moon doesn't shine, I can be the moon.

Aruna D'Souza

The Score

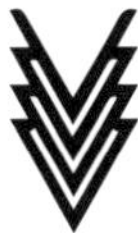

What is a score for you?

A score for me is the document that's going to allow me to collaborate with people who are going to make the sound. I realized early on that there's a potential for metaphor inside of the score.

Epigraph: unless otherwise noted, all quotes by Raven Chacon derive from a conversation with the author on April 19, 2023.

For the past twenty-five years, Raven Chacon has been working with multiple—often contradictory—conceptions of sound: the European-origin, classical music tradition in which he was trained, brought to the Americas by settler colonists, heavy with philosophical and ideological baggage; avant-garde deconstructions and challenges to that classical authority, including noise; and a variety of Indigenous traditions, ranging from the Navajo music ways he inherited to those of the Sámi people of what is now Northern Europe, to which he was introduced by collaborators and friends. These systems are not simply sonically different—they represent different worldviews. Chacon's work holds them in tension, sometimes puts them at odds, and often attempts to reverse or upend ossified hierarchies among them, asking us to see a new world by singing it, playing it, or hearing it into being.

In the same way, Chacon works in a variety of mediums—musical composition and performance, but also video, installation, and other forms of sound-based art. These too exist in relation to each other (tension, harmony, mute coexistence) and to their sites.

At the heart of Chacon's practice is the score: both in its conventional sense (the documentation of a piece of music in written format showing how different parts of a composition work together) and in the sense of the metaphorical possibilities opened up by its visual and conceptual form. If the traditional Western score is a set of instructions for musicians, telling them what to do and when, Chacon's scores are propositions for togetherness—an ethics of how we can interact with each other and the world. They are ways of putting people into relationships and allowing them to form and reform those relationships as long as the score lasts—in which each interpreter of the score retains a sense of responsibility to the other.

Silence

In 2000, Chacon created a score titled *Duet*, intended for two musicians. Marked in 4/4 time, it is filled not with notes but with rests—an indication of the absence of sound. It is a homage to, or perhaps a subversion of, or merely a variation on, John Cage's *4′33″*, composed in 1952, which famously asked its performers—one person or many people using any instrument or combination of instruments—to refrain from playing for the time in question.

Perhaps counterintuitively, Cage resisted the idea that *4′33″* was about silence. In a later interview, he said of his interpreters, "They missed the point. There's no such thing as silence. What they thought was silence, because they didn't know how to listen, was full of accidental sounds. You could hear the wind stirring outside during the first movement. During the second, raindrops began pattering the roof, and during the third the people themselves made all kinds of interesting sounds as they talked or walked out."[1]

Cage's work was a Duchampian gesture: it made use of readymade sonic phenomena instead of creating it anew. It was tied to Cage's interest in Buddhism. It was also a response to a 1951 series of white paintings by his friend and sometime collaborator Robert Rauschenberg, in which pictorial incident was supplied by the shadows and light that happened to fall across the surface of the canvas as it was hung in a gallery.

But with *Duet*, Chacon came at Cage differently: the two musicians who perform the piece are not just there to create an opportunity for listeners to hear the silence, but also to shape a relationship between the performers. A score, for Chacon, is an invitation to collaboration—What forms of collaboration can silence supply? "I was thinking about what kinds of nonverbal, nonvisual alignments two people could have—and how these could be ways to organize not only musicians, but people," Chacon says.

The idea reaches an apotheosis of sorts in *Silent Choir* (2016/2022), a piece he presented at the 2022 Whitney Biennial.[2] There is nothing to see here: the piece consists only of a soundtrack of recordings the artist made at the No Dakota Access Pipeline demonstrations at Standing Rock in 2016 and 2017.[3] He captured an event that took place just after Thanksgiving, known to many by its alternative name, the National Day of Mourning, in recognition of the centuries of genocide that this celebration of the Pilgrim holiday entirely elides. The event was a silent resistance, led by the elder women in

1 John Cage, in Richard Kostelanetz, *Conversing with Cage*, 2nd ed. (New York: Routledge, 2002), 70.

2 Aruna D'Souza, "Whitney Biennial 2022," *4Columns*, May 15, 2002, https://4columns.org/d-souza-aruna/whitney-biennial-2022.

3 At the Whitney, a photograph Chacon took of the protest—a thick crowd of people, seen from the back, entirely still—was displayed on a billboard outside the museum, on the High Line.

the encampment—five or six hundred people facing down state police and the pipeline's security forces. Instead of the expected din of protest, we hear the respiration of the crowds, the occasional surveillance helicopter whirring overhead, the rustling of bodies. This might seem like the interval before or after action—a recouping of energy, perhaps, or a moment of deciding how to proceed, calm and tense by turns. But it is also an action itself.

This is not just a congregation of silent individuals—it is a silent choir: an ensemble, a group in which multiple people may share a voice, in which multiple voices build a composition.

Sounding the Site

Chacon had engaged with the Cagean idea of (non)silence in his first artwork, *Field Recordings* (1999), which was made at three significant sites in the Southwest—Window Rock, Arizona (known in Navajo as Tségháhoodzání, which serves as the seat of the Navajo Nation); the Sandia Mountains, just east of Albuquerque, New Mexico; and Canyon de Chelly, now a national monument that lies within the boundaries of the Navajo Nation in northeastern Arizona. (The artist spent his early childhood down the road from Canyon de Chelly before moving to Albuquerque, where he grew up.) Chacon chose them, he told me, because they were "the quietest places that I knew." In each of these sites, Chacon set up recording instruments for thirty minutes at different times of day (4 a.m., 11 p.m., and 10 a.m., respectively); back in the studio, he "turned it all the way up to its maximum."

Where Cage's piece relied on the idea of accidental sound—wind, raindrops, bodies moving—that intrudes into the performance space, the noise captured by Chacon's recording devices seems to point to a different kind of aural experience altogether: it is as if we are hearing not the sounds produced *within* the natural setting but *by* it. But we hear them at an angle, as it were: the high-fidelity recordings are overamplified, so that while we may not be able to identify any individual noise from the sites, we can hear what are, in effect, sonic landscapes—each recording consists of a different "color" of noise, becoming, in the process, a form of landscape.[4]

Chacon's approach in *Field Recordings* initiated a methodology that has recurred throughout his practice over the years. If it calls to mind Pauline Oliveros's notion of "deep listening," a practice that encouraged both musicians and nonmusicians to enhance their sensory perceptions by retreating to different environments in Europe and North America, including New Mexico, it's not quite: "deep listening" seems to leave out the historical contestations adhering to the landscapes in which it takes place, especially when it comes to settler-colonial histories.

The differences become apparent when considering works like *Dispatch*. Chacon made the work with his wife

4 The idea of the color of noise is not merely metaphorical in this context: in audio engineering and other scientific fields, the color of noise refers to the power spectrum of a sound; it is akin to the notion of musical timbre.

and frequent collaborator, the curator and writer Candice Hopkins, in 2020, published as part of "Unsettling Scores," a series curated by Liquid Architecture for Monash University Museum of Art in Melbourne, Australia. The conceptual score is a transcription (or perhaps transposition?) of events surrounding the protests at Standing Rock in 2016, write Chacon and Hopkins: "The players, the prompts, and the schematics are derived from an analysis of the surface dynamics and organization of the Water Protectors in defense of Standing Rock during the #noDAPL movement, not glossing over the miscommunication, profiteering, and injustices."[5] Instead of merely asking "What do you hear?" as Cage and Oliveros might, Chacon and Hopkins ask a different set of questions:

> What does the land need?
> What do the hosts want?
> Do you belong here?
> Who do you look to for guidance?
> What are your skills/strengths?
> What are the threats?
> Who do you trust?
> What are you willing to risk?
> Who is in charge?
> What is the model of leadership?
> How do we maintain focus?[6]

Hopkins and Chacon's notion of deep listening, in other words, is not just about the landscape in a Western sense—rather, it insists that land is inextricable from its occupants and stewards, and from the history that the land is witness to. To listen to the land is to listen to each other, to the past, to the future.

The field recordings approach is apparent, too, in Chacon's work with the collective Postcommodity. He was a member from 2009 to 2018 and contributed greatly to the group's approach to working within intersecting communities and among different stakeholders over time, as with *Repellent Fence* (2015). The project achieved the seemingly impossible—building a fence that didn't run along the US–Mexico border but rather ran right through it. (This was the only work without a sound component that Chacon has undertaken.) But it is another piece—*Do You Remember When?* (2012), a site-specific, multimedia installation—that most clearly upends the anthropological and ethnographical use of the audio recording as a form of data collection or evidence.[7] To the extent that such disciplines were linked to colonial expansion and consolidation, field recordings were often made to preserve cultures that were in the process of being "lost," often through genocidal violence and assimilation. In *Do You Remember When?* a hole is cut in the floor of a museum that sits on top of tribal lands; above the hole—which now acts as a kind of portal—hangs a speaker which broadcasts a Pee Posh social dance song that speaks of sustaining the earth. In this piece, the field recording interrupts the Western scientific worldview by introducing Indigenous forms of knowledge.[8]

5 "Candice Hopkins and Raven Chacon: Dispatch" (*Unsettling Scores*), accessed September 27, 2023, https://disclaimer.org.au/contents/unsettling-scores/dispatch.

6 Candice Hopkins and Raven Chacon, "Dispatch," in this volume, 65.

7 The piece was installed twice: in 2012 at the Arizona State University Museum and in 2018 at the Sydney Biennial.

8 The piece is documented at https://postcommodity.com/DoYouRememberWhen.html, accessed September 27, 2023.

To sing, in many Indigenous cultures, is to conjure the world into existence—the land, its inhabitants (human and non), ancestors, family and relations, and histories. *Still Life No. 3* (2015) hinges on this practice. It consists of a series of speakers that rises from the floor of the gallery and traverses its length along the ceiling, a series of text panels, and colored lights. From the speakers a woman's voice recounts the Diné Bahane'—the Navajo story of creation, of the emergence of people from the lower worlds into the earth, at each stage learning a different lesson. "A lot of them are allegories for how we've moved and ended up in the homelands that we call our homelands today, but also how we became aware of our own traditions, how we developed the protocols we still honor," Chacon says.

In *Still Life No. 3*, however, this creation story is not recounted in a simply linear way, as a tale with a beginning, middle, and end. Rather, each speaker plays the same recording of the same woman telling the same story, but using timed audio and delay systems they emit different parts simultaneously. Past and future overlap, blur, and, importantly, repeat.

This is a vision of recursive time, of time that circles and circles around itself without finding a resolution. It is the opposite of Christian eschatology (a movement from Genesis to the Second Coming), and therefore of Euro-American, settler-colonial notions of temporality. But thanks to both the narrative and the physical form of the piece, here time also reaches upward, from earth to sky.

In two recent works, made in collaboration with Sámi musicians and land guardians in Sámpi, an area bounded by Northern Norway, Chacon continues to explore this idea of an Indigenous, nonlinear time. *For Four* (2024) is a round: a composition in which multiple singers perform the same melody, each starting at a different point, repeating the song over and over again, their voices overlapping to create harmonies ("Row, Row, Row Your Boat" is a familiar example). In *For Four*, which was filmed in the Alta River valley, the site of historic protests between 1978 and 1982 over plans to build a massive hydroelectric plant on traditional Sámi territories, four Sámi singers—*yoikers*[9]—face one of the four cardinal directions and turn clockwise, singing the land as it existed before their peoples' displacement and as it exists now. Here, in a sense, the landscape itself

9 A *yoik* or *joik* is a traditional Sámi song, meant to reflect or evoke a person, animal, or place. Often, people adopt or are conferred a yoik as a sort of signature; significantly, in relation to Chacon's thinking, the yoik also has a circular structure.

For Four (River Valley), 2024

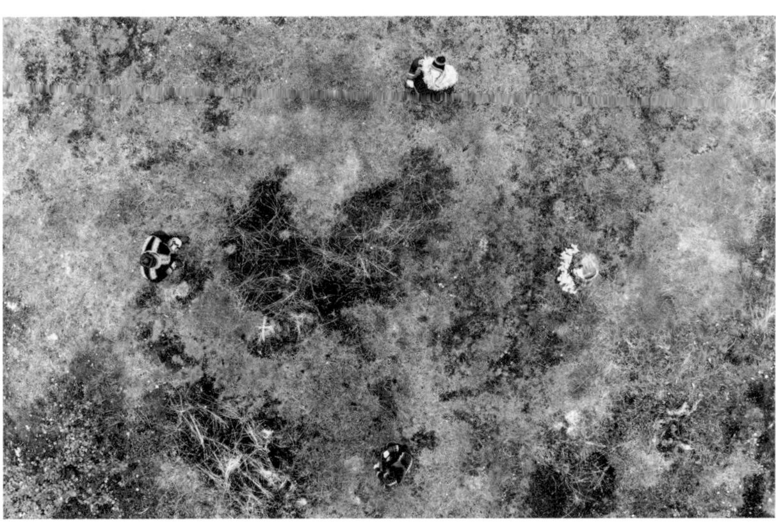

10 *Still Life No. 4* was first performed at the Colorado Springs Fine Arts Center in 2017.

is the score, and thus the composition—the round—could go on forever. It is an acknowledgment of constant struggle and a testament to survival and endurance, a promise that time will never end.

Similarly, ... *the sky ladder* (2024) proposes a notion of never-endingness, of perpetuity. It was inspired by an artwork by the Sámi multimedia artist Nils-Aslak Valkeapää (1943–2001), otherwise known as Áillohaš, in which he collected pieces of driftwood along the fjords and sawed them in half to reveal wormholes. When Chacon saw these, he thought they looked like scores.

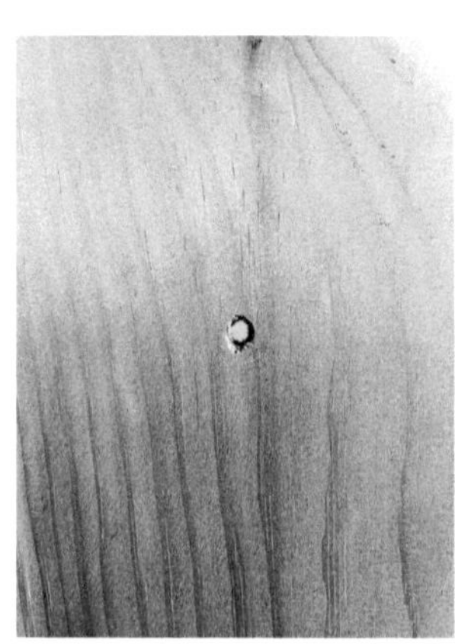

Detail from ... *the sky ladder*, 2024

Chacon's piece consists of thirteen pine planks hanging from floor to ceiling, each pockmarked with tiny holes made with a handheld power drill by members of the Bål Nango family—traditional reindeer herders, the younger generation of whom are activists. The group gathered at Lásságámmi, Áillohaš's former home, and, starting with the eldest among them, shared stories about a particular mountain, each making holes in a plank with a spiral bore to represent the landscape. Arranged in this order of age from floor to ceiling in the gallery, the planks become a score for a solo musician playing any instrument—the song both sings the land and recognizes the importance of generational memory.

In all these works, time is not a straight line, but nor is it merely circular. Rather, it has a vertical dimension, even as it recurs and folds back on itself. Time is a spiral, like a drill's movement, snaking in both directions, backward and forward.

Siting the Sound

When Chacon's work is installed in a museum, it often pushes against the institution: both the history of its form/formation (the rise of the museum is more or less directly tied to European, then American, empire building along with the colonial violence that resulted), and the contemporary contradictions by which it is still riven. Among these is the continued presence of "artifacts" of still-living cultures in its collection—objects which, for many of those cultures across many continents, are considered, if not exactly sentient, then still animate in some way. To be held in a museum, away from the life of their people, is a form of incarceration; to sit, unused, unperformed, unactivated through ritual, is a form of death. These objects are victims of colonialism, too.

Still Life No. 4 (2017–) is an ongoing sound installation composed of what Chacon calls "reclaimed sound": for each exhibition of the piece, the institution supplies (from its own collection, or borrowed from another museum) a drum that has not been struck for an extended period of time, but is not so fragile that it couldn't be struck again.[10] Chacon (or, on occasion, depending on the origin of the artifact, a collaborator) beats the drum once, recording and looping the resulting reverberation, which

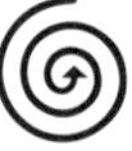

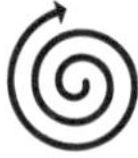

he then plays at different "listening stations," some inside the museum and some beyond its doors. The repeated drumbeat is faster or slower depending on the listening station's proximity to the object itself—the reverberation dies as you move from the drum into the world around it. The conceit might remind you of a metal detector—the sound gets faster as you get closer to the "treasure," which certainly conforms to the museum's logic of value. But it might also remind you of a mournful loss—the way you might feel when the voice of a loved one gets fainter and fainter as it's taken away from you.

Though *Mouth Piece* also mines the museum, it works in a different way. Commissioned by the Los Angeles County Museum of Art in 2020, the piece is composed of seven songs that Chacon composed for a variety of instruments in the museum's collection of pre-Columbian art—ocarinas, flutes, whistles, and so on. (The songs were performed by Alethia Lozano, principal flautist of the National Symphony Orchestra of Mexico.) Each composition was meant not only to revive—bring back to life—the instruments that are played, but to represent, animate, and sing other objects in the collection: to allow the screams of the Gritóns (ancient mouth-shaped jars made in Colombia in the first and second millennia BCE) to be heard, say, or to allow for Marcel Duchamp's *Chocolate Grinder* (made in France in 1914) to converse with *Tripod Vessel with Supernatural Palace Scene and Cacao Tree* (made by Maya peoples in Guatemala, 750–850 CE), perhaps about where chocolate came from in the first place.

The Shape of Sound

The score for *Plainsong* (2020), when it was first performed in Saskatoon, Saskatchewan, was displayed on the side of a building. Visually, it doesn't look much like a musical score in any traditional sense: it recalls, rather, the geometric designs used by different Native American cultures, with nested triangles arrayed across a rectangle like bent staves, punctuated by small, black triangles that function as noteheads.

The title of the piece—*Plainsong*—reaches out in two, perhaps opposing, directions: the songs of Plains Indians, the first people to dwell on the land in that part of Saskatchewan, and plainsong, liturgical chants used in the early Catholic church, exclusively so until the ninth century. The latter were monophonic, consisting of a single melody, sung or played without harmony or counterpoint.

In Chacon's piece, each of the multiple musicians plays the same score, the same tune, but out of sync—they can start on different notes, and each triangular notehead points to a possible next note to play. As they move on to the next note, they must move their body to that position in relation to the painted score, but with the following caveat: they must keep a distance from other players, and so they might have to

11 *Plainsong* was first performed during the COVID-19 shutdown—when the idea of coexisting in space (in terms of social distancing) and codependence was on people's minds.

wait before choosing and moving to a new note. They might have to play the note they are on for a longer duration in order to make space for others, so as not to take up a position that is not theirs—in order not to displace anyone, that is to say. Among other things, the piece asks us to imagine a form of spatial coexistence, and thereby refuse the idea of the occupation of a territory.[11]

Plainsong asks: How can we exist in relation to each other in both space and time? (a score, after all, uses time as much as sound as its medium). The question becomes especially crucial when one considers the overlapping struggles for justice in the United States, a settler-colonial nation founded on two original sins: the genocide of Native Americans, and the enslavement of people of African descent. Chacon's *American Ledgers*—a series of three scores that tell the story of this country's history—don't imagine solidarity as a naive form of harmony, but as a complex coming together in and out of space, in which individuals participate in a form of collective music-making within which there is the opportunity for individual agency and variation.

American Ledger No. 1 (2018) is meant to be displayed as a flag, a wall, a blanket, a billboard, or a door, and is modeled on the American flag—if you look closely at its abstract notations, you will discern stars and stripes. From the land unsullied by people at the top, to the arrival of Europeans, to the exploitation of resources and the policing (and killing) of people, to the building of cities, to the assassinations of John F. Kennedy and Martin Luther King Jr., to the seeming

Raven Chacon
Score for *Plainsong*, 2020

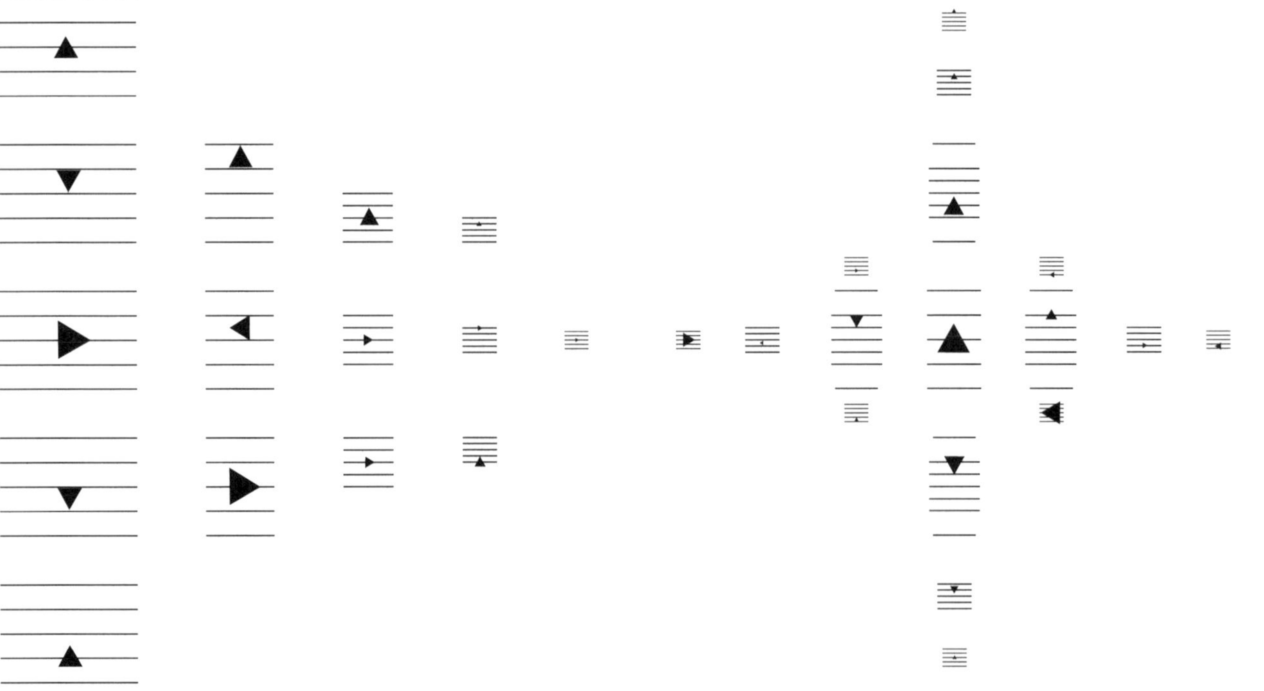

cacophony and chaos of our current political moment—all these are translated visually via musical language, and sonically through a variety of sound-making techniques: musical instruments, police whistles, the casting of coins into buckets, the chopping of wood, the striking of a match.

American Ledger No. 2 (2019) can be presented as a flag, a billboard, railroad debris, or a pyrographed object sourced from the area around Tulsa, Oklahoma, where it was commissioned and performed in 2019. It is based on the Oklahoma state flag, which adopts an Osage warrior's shield overlaid with a peace pipe and olive branch to symbolize peace between the white settlers and Native Americans. Chacon complicates this too-easy symbolic narration of Tulsa's history in his score by structuring it around displacement—musicians walking a circular path are required to move in and out of the ring. The action evokes the resettlement of Indian tribes from all over the country to a designated "Indian Territory" in what is now Oklahoma in the mid-nineteenth century, and the coerced removal of a long-standing Black community as a result of the Tulsa race massacre in 1921. But it also, in its form—which is akin to musical chairs, a competitive game of claiming space—suggests the complexities of finding common purpose in the struggle against white supremacy. Chacon describes the score as a "crabs in a bucket" scenario—the idea, derived from observing trapped crustaceans, that anytime an individual crab tries to free itself, the others will prevent it from escaping. But in *American Ledger No. 2*, the score challenges its interpreters to break this cycle, eventually finding a way out of the circle.

American Ledger No. 3, made in 2020 as the protests sparked by the murders of George Floyd and Breonna Taylor unfolded across the country, pays homage to Ida B. Wells, the journalist, suffragist, and—crucially—anti-lynching activist. The score is performed from top to middle by one women's choir, and from bottom to middle by another; both are accompanied by glockenspiels, drums, and coins. The bidirectional movement of the parts evokes the past and present meeting in a sort of cacophonous middle, but the words the singers repeat there—"onward, skyward," a phrase drawn from Wells's famous text, "Lynch Law and the Color Line"—exhort us to keep moving, not just forward but upward, as history repeats itself, a resistance to the inevitability of historical repetition, a breaking of cycles.

Time, Chacon reminds us, is a spiral, like a drill's movement. It goes onward and upward. Is it possible to reverse the direction of time's spin? To undo history, to go back to a before? What happens to the wounds, the holes, the absences, the occlusions, the losses, that history has wrought? Is the point of struggle to reverse the violent history of colonization, or transcend it, or simply to make space for healing? And in this struggle, how will we find the music that allows us to be together?

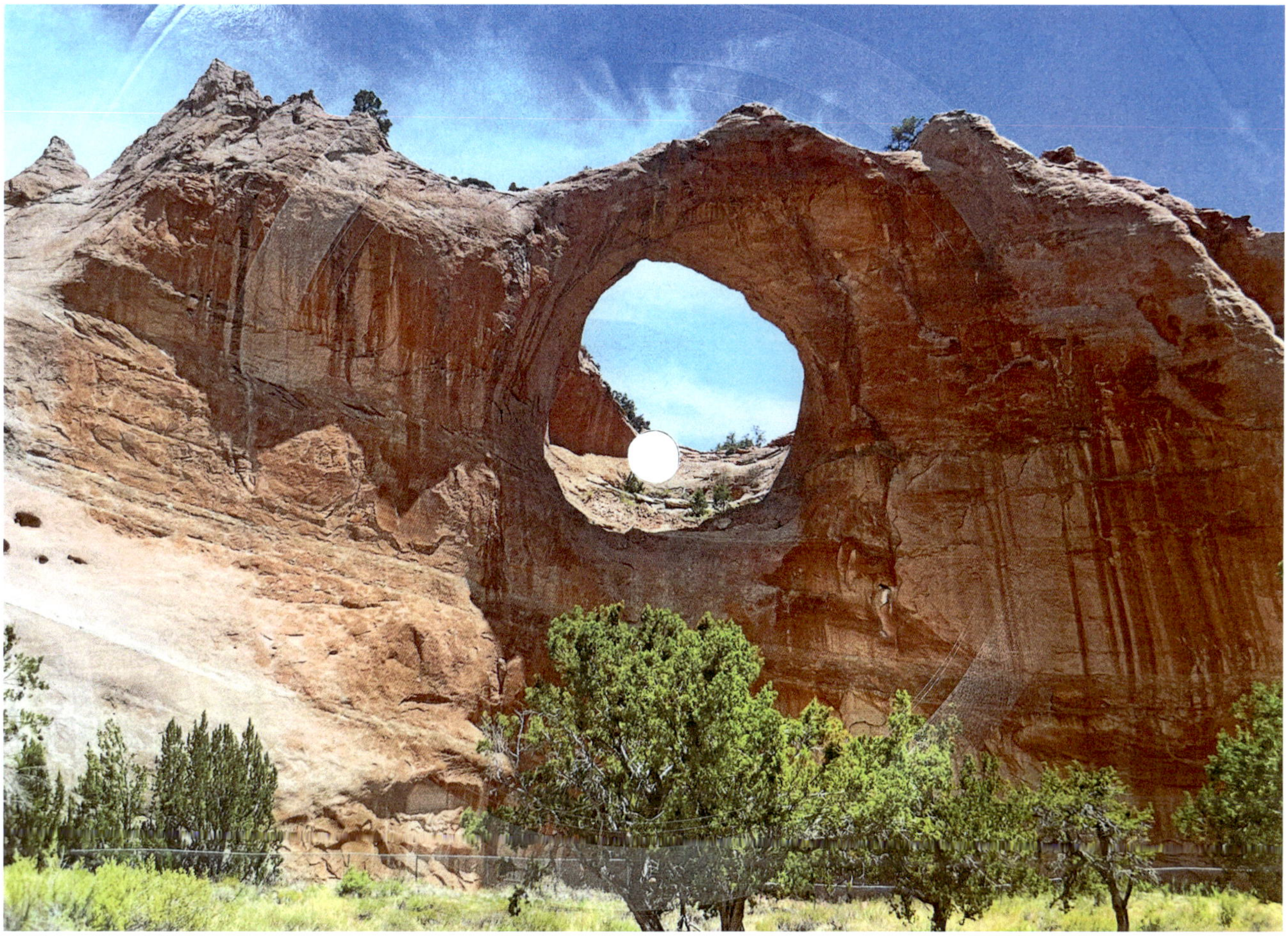

Window Rock, 4:00 a.m.

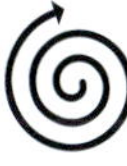

1999

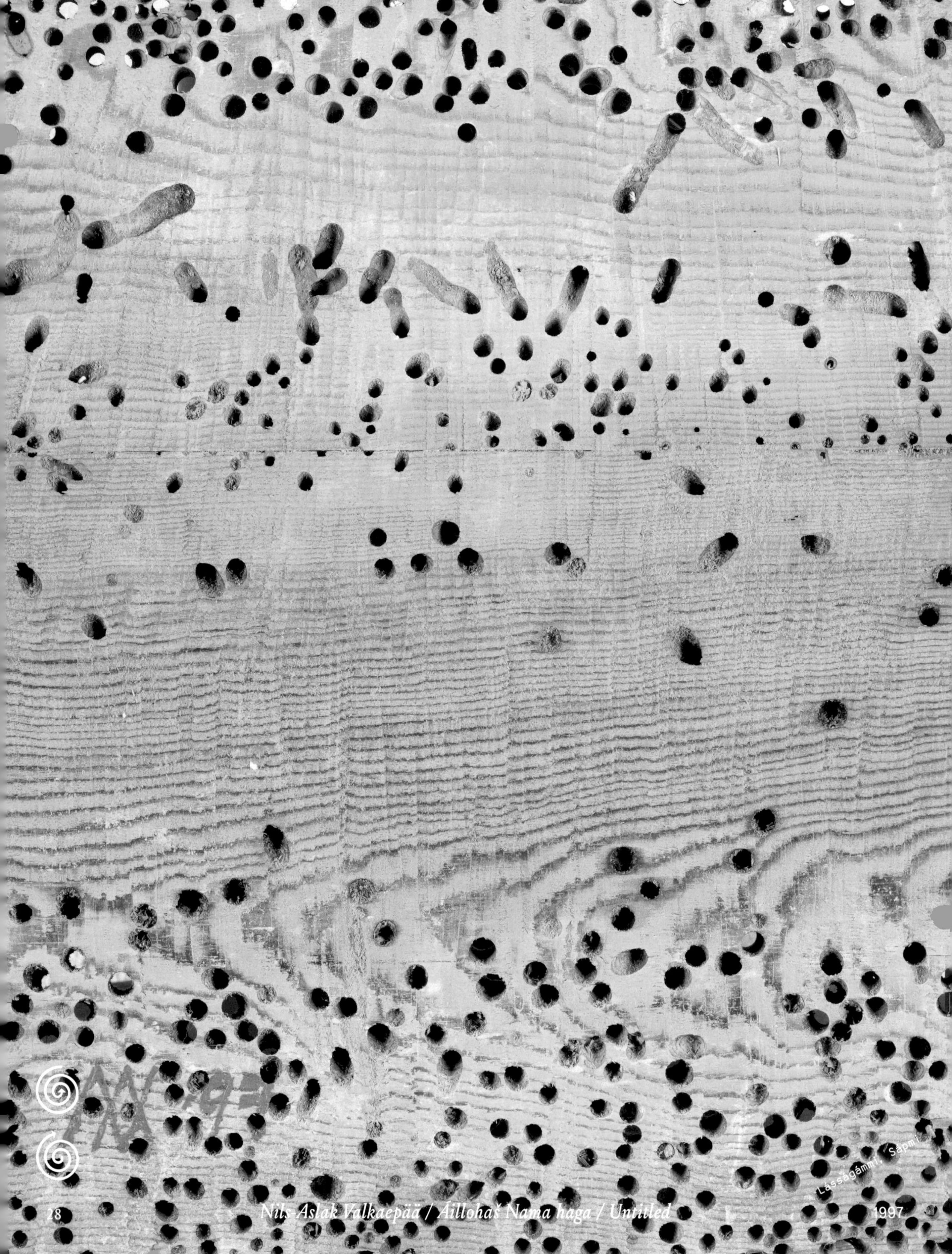

Nils-Aslak Valkeapää / Áillohaš Nama haga / Untitled 1997

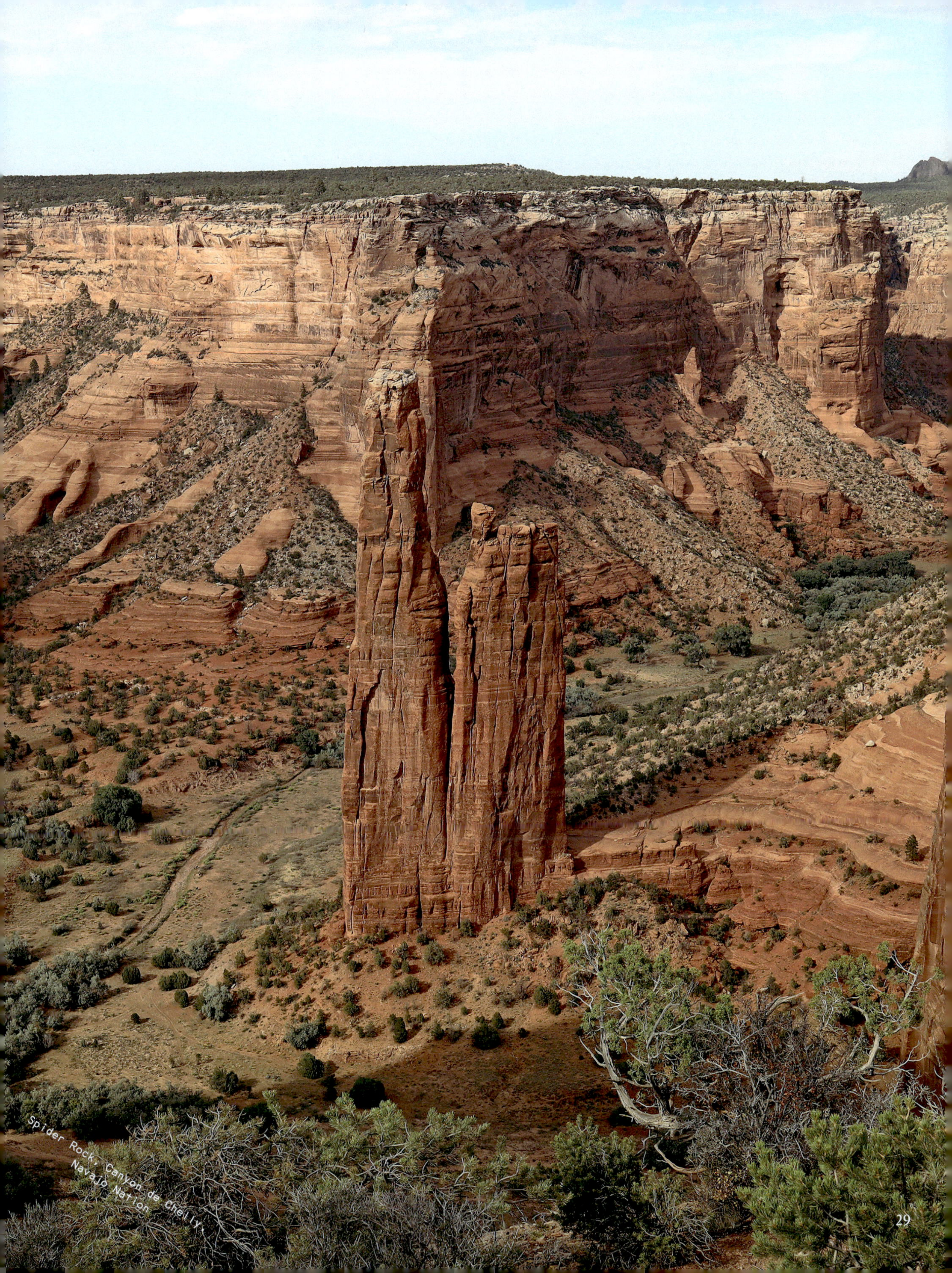

Spider Rock, Canyon de Chelly, Navajo Nation

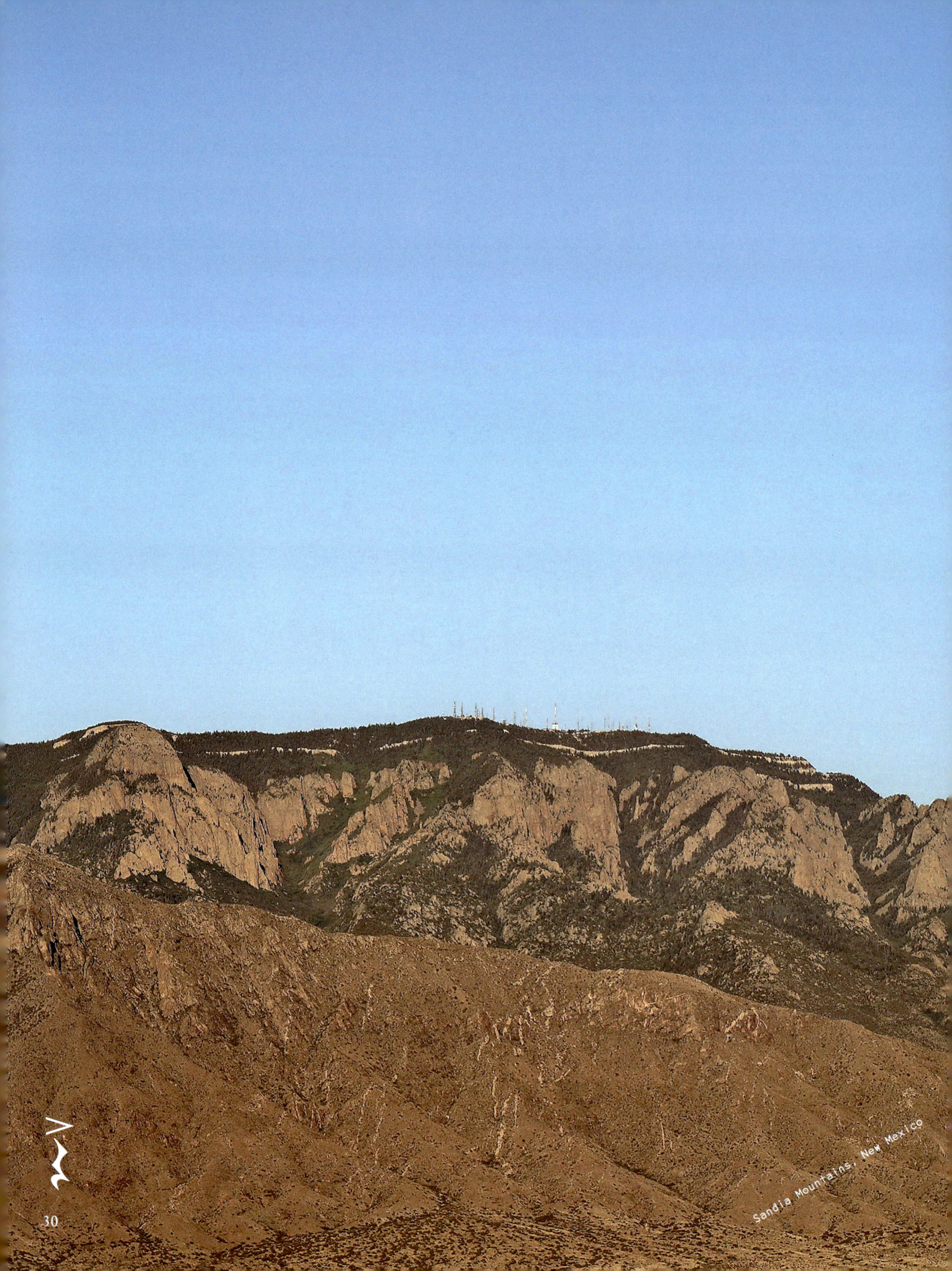

Sandia Mountains, New Mexico

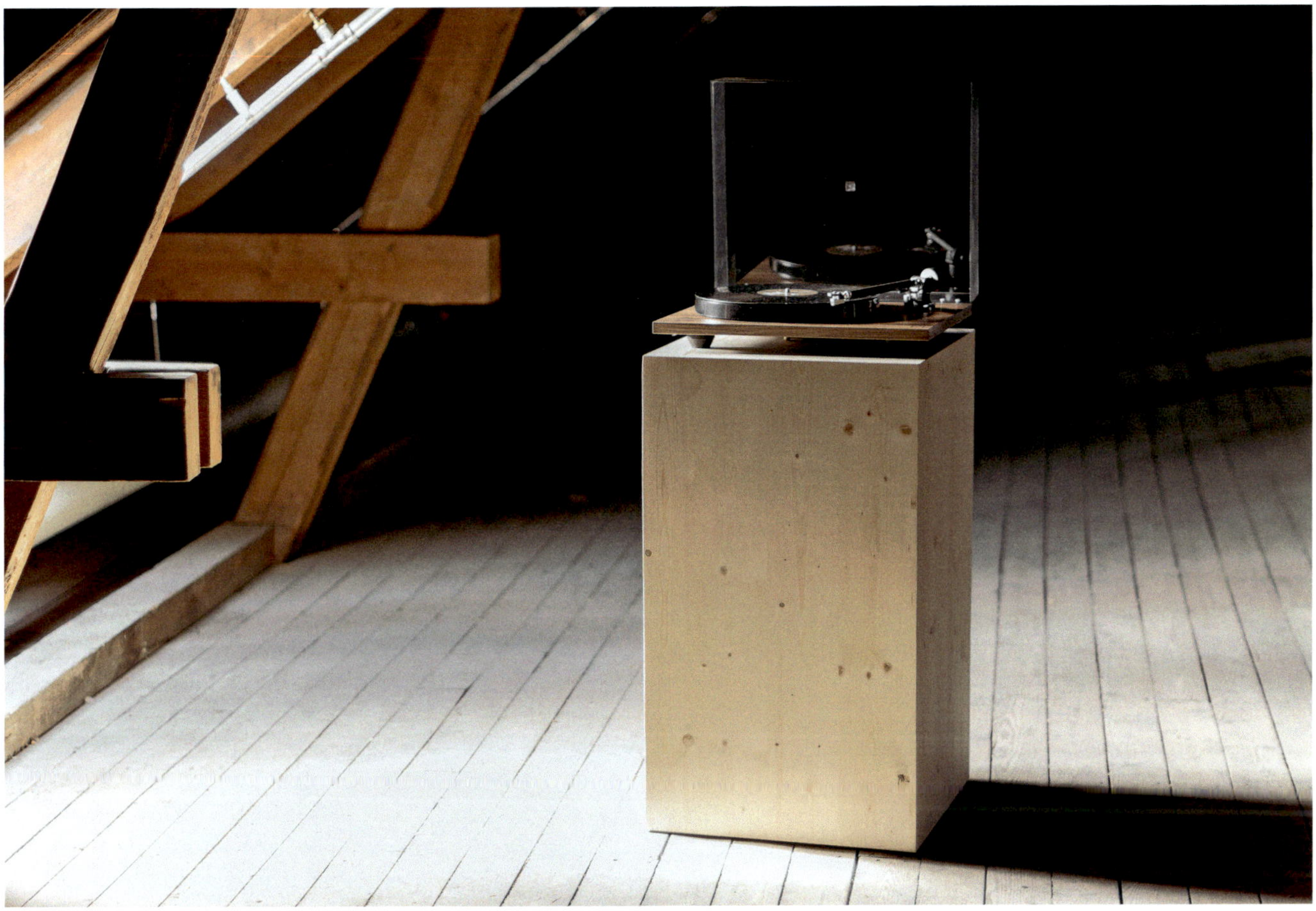

Nordnorsk Kunstmuseum,
Northern Norway/Sápmi

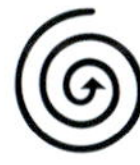

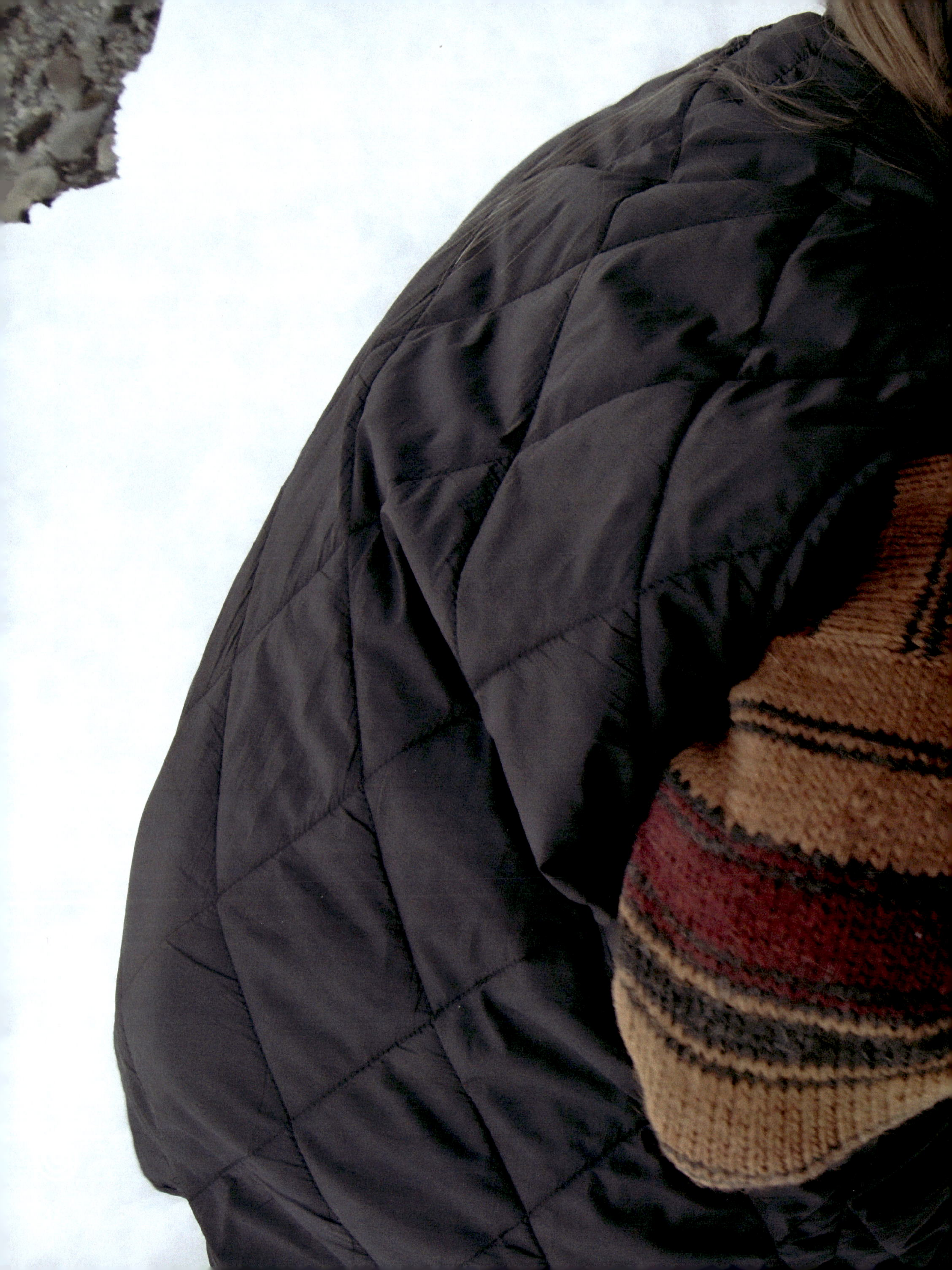

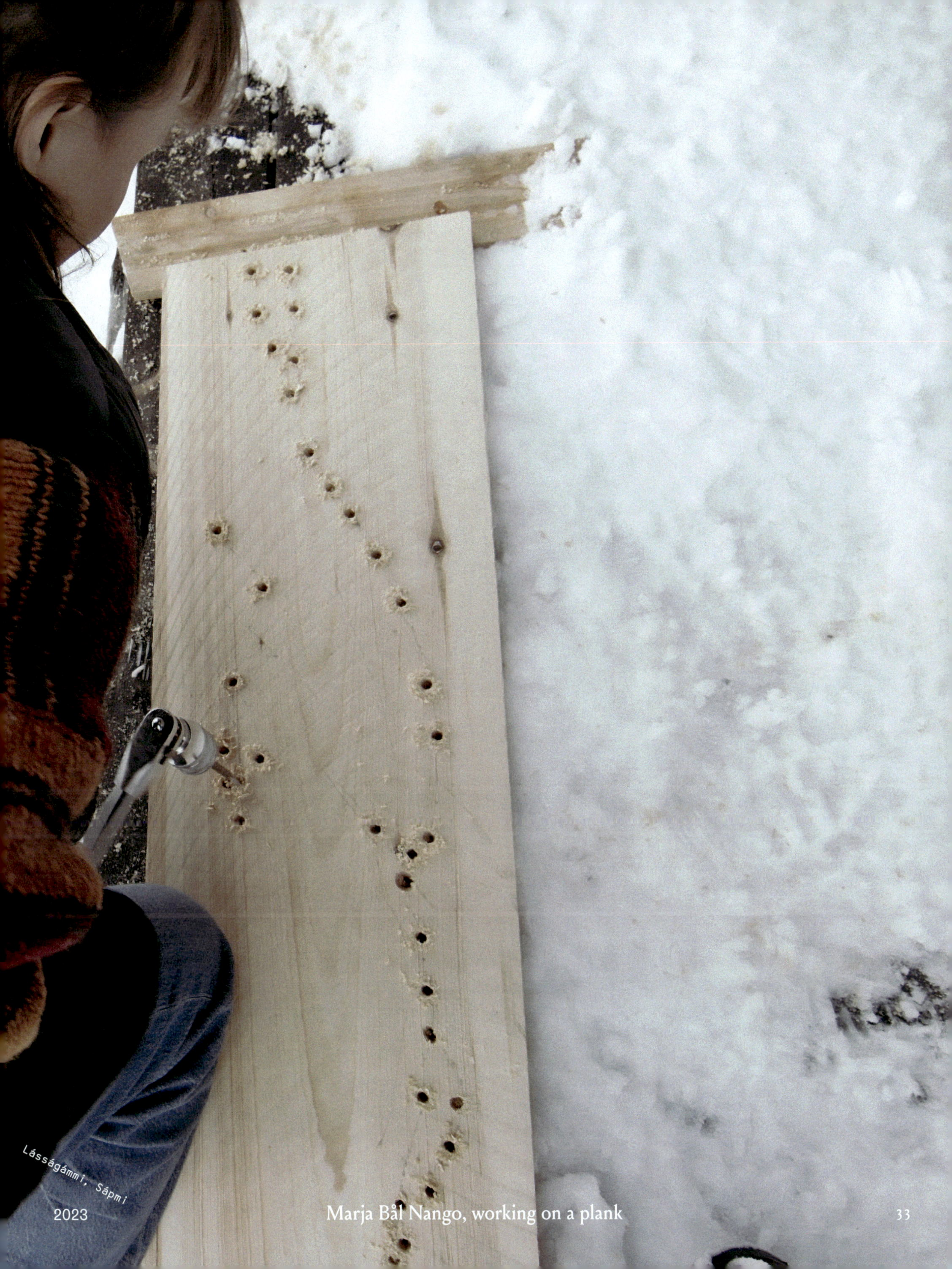

2023

Marja Bål Nango, working on a plank

High Hall

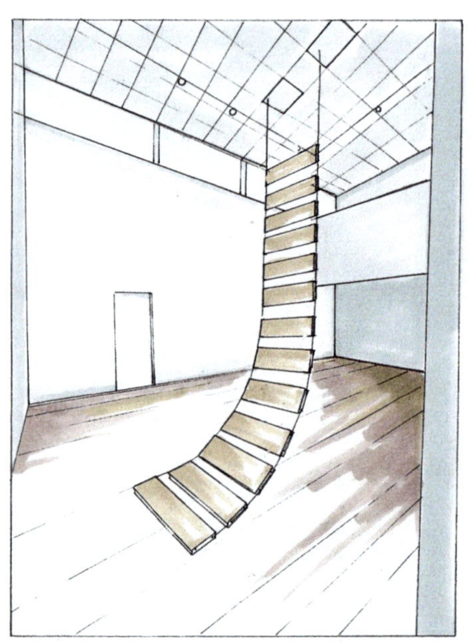

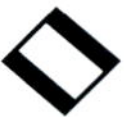

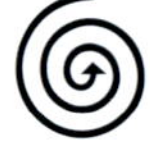

Sketch for ... the sky ladder

2024

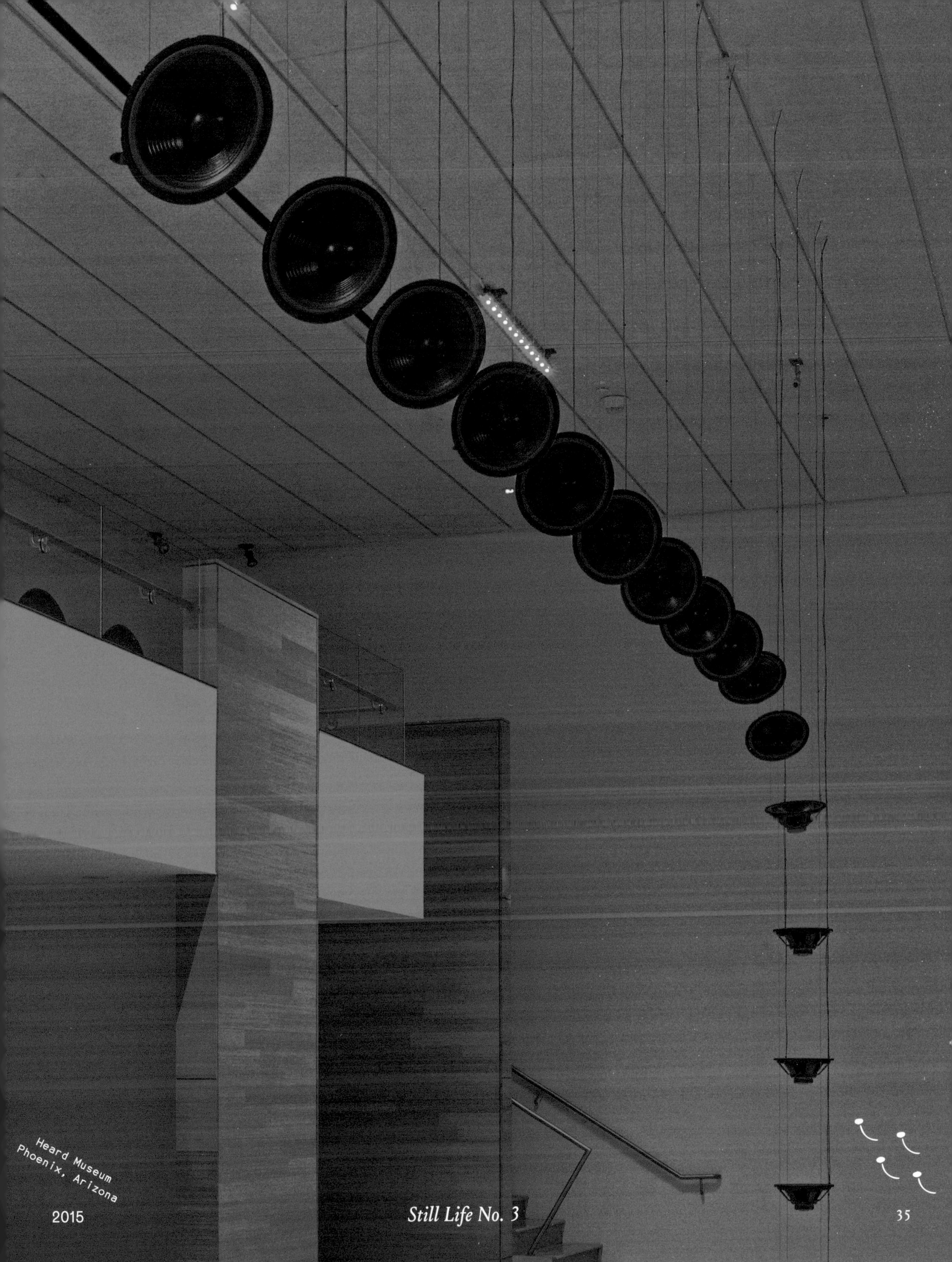

Heard Museum
Phoenix, Arizona

2015

Still Life No. 3

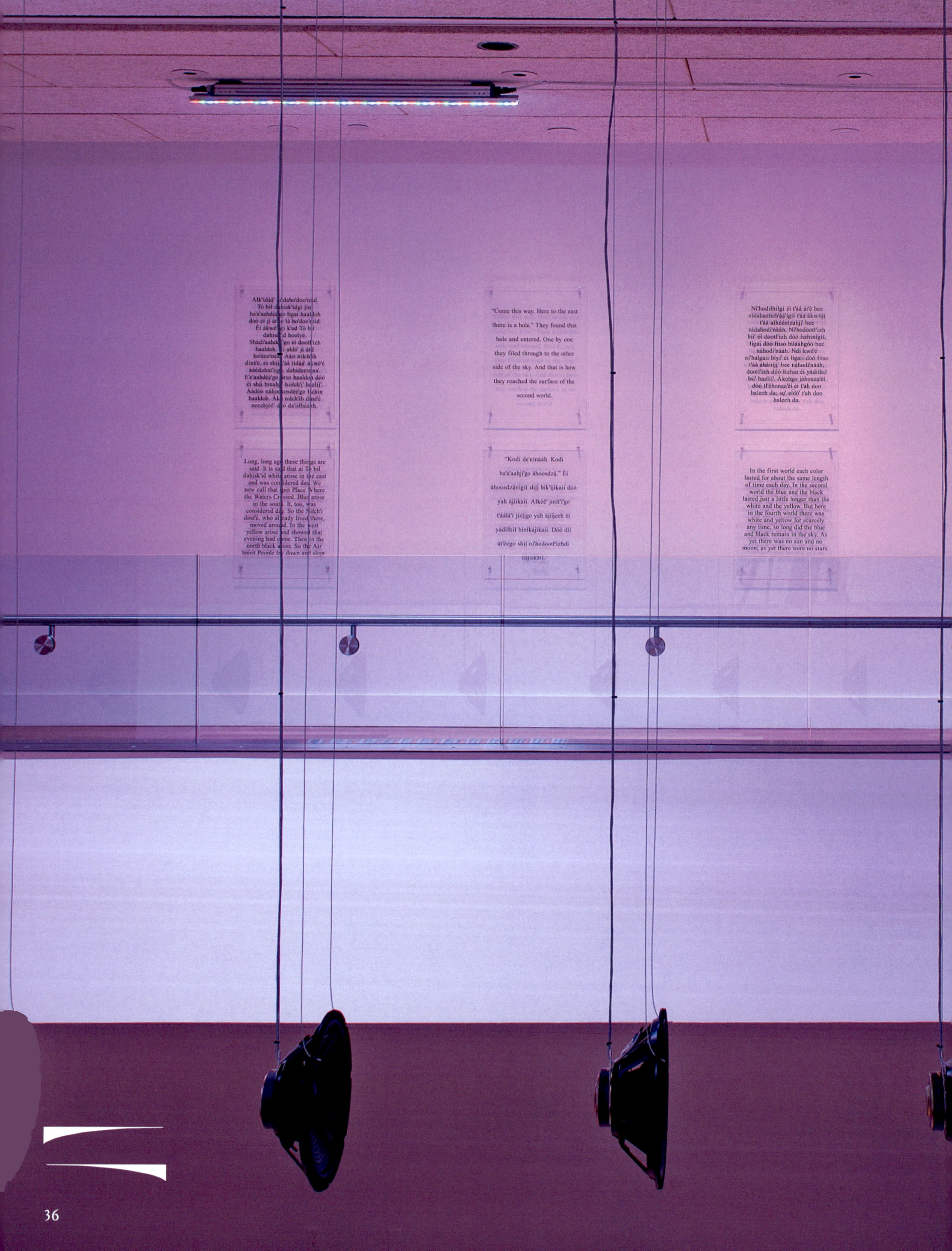
"Come this way. Here to the east there is a hole." They found that hole and entered. One by one they filed through to the other side of the sky. And that is how they reached the surface of the second world.
In the first world each color lasted for about the same length of time each day. In the second world the blue and the black lasted just a little longer than the white and the yellow. But here in the fourth world there was white and yellow for scarcely any time, so long did the blue and black remain in the sky. As yet there was no sun and no moon; as yet there were no stars.

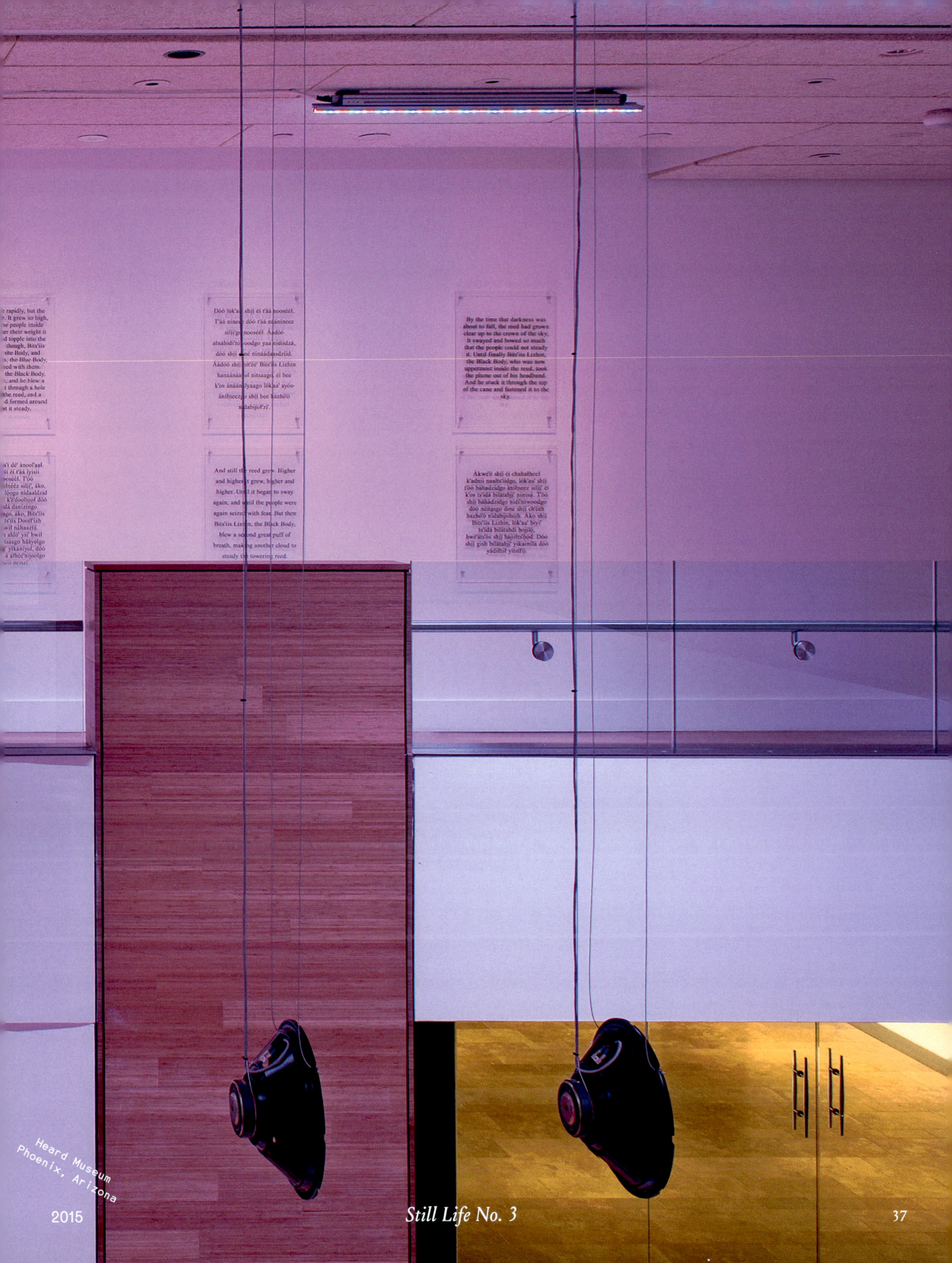

Heard Museum
Phoenix, Arizona

2015

Still Life No. 3

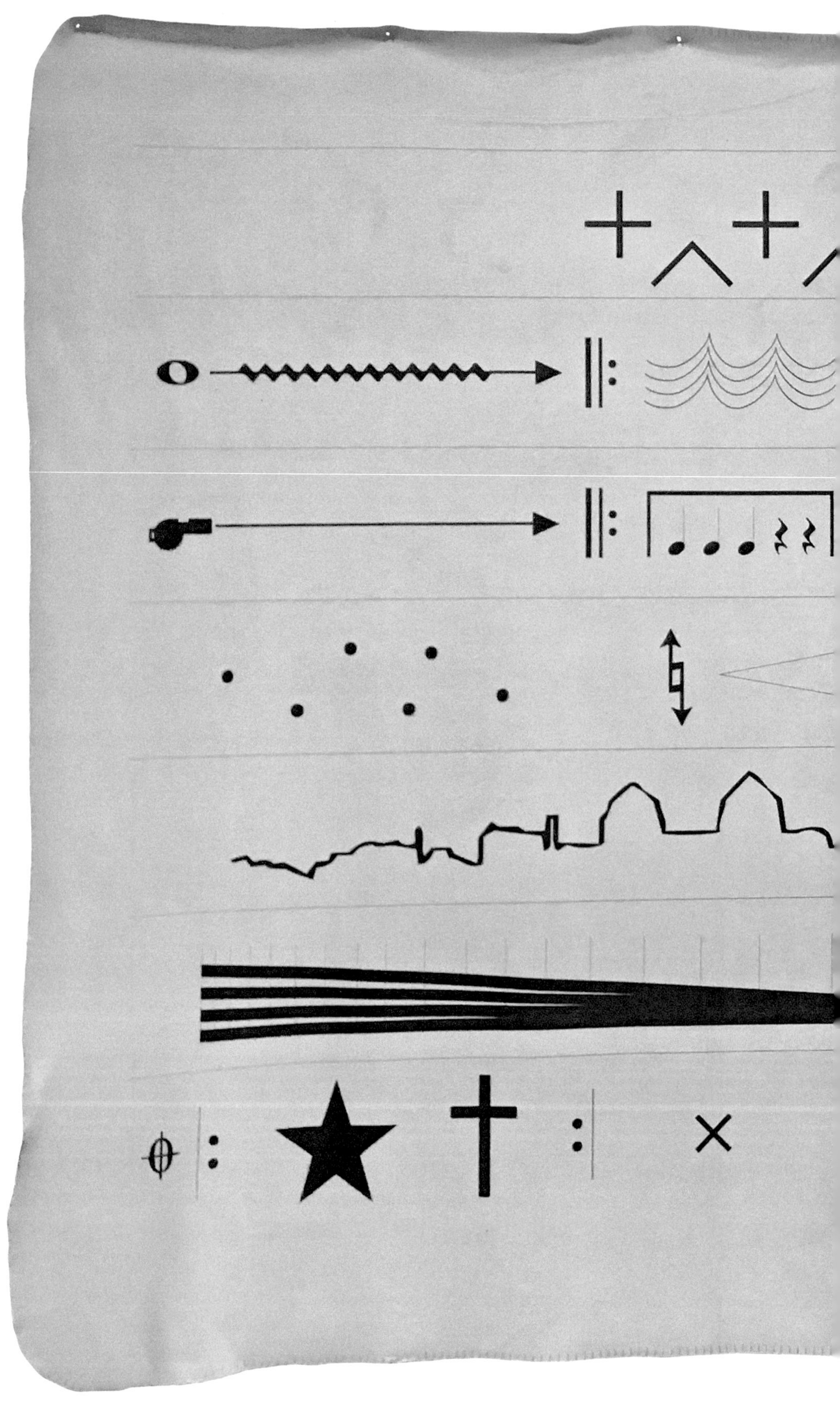

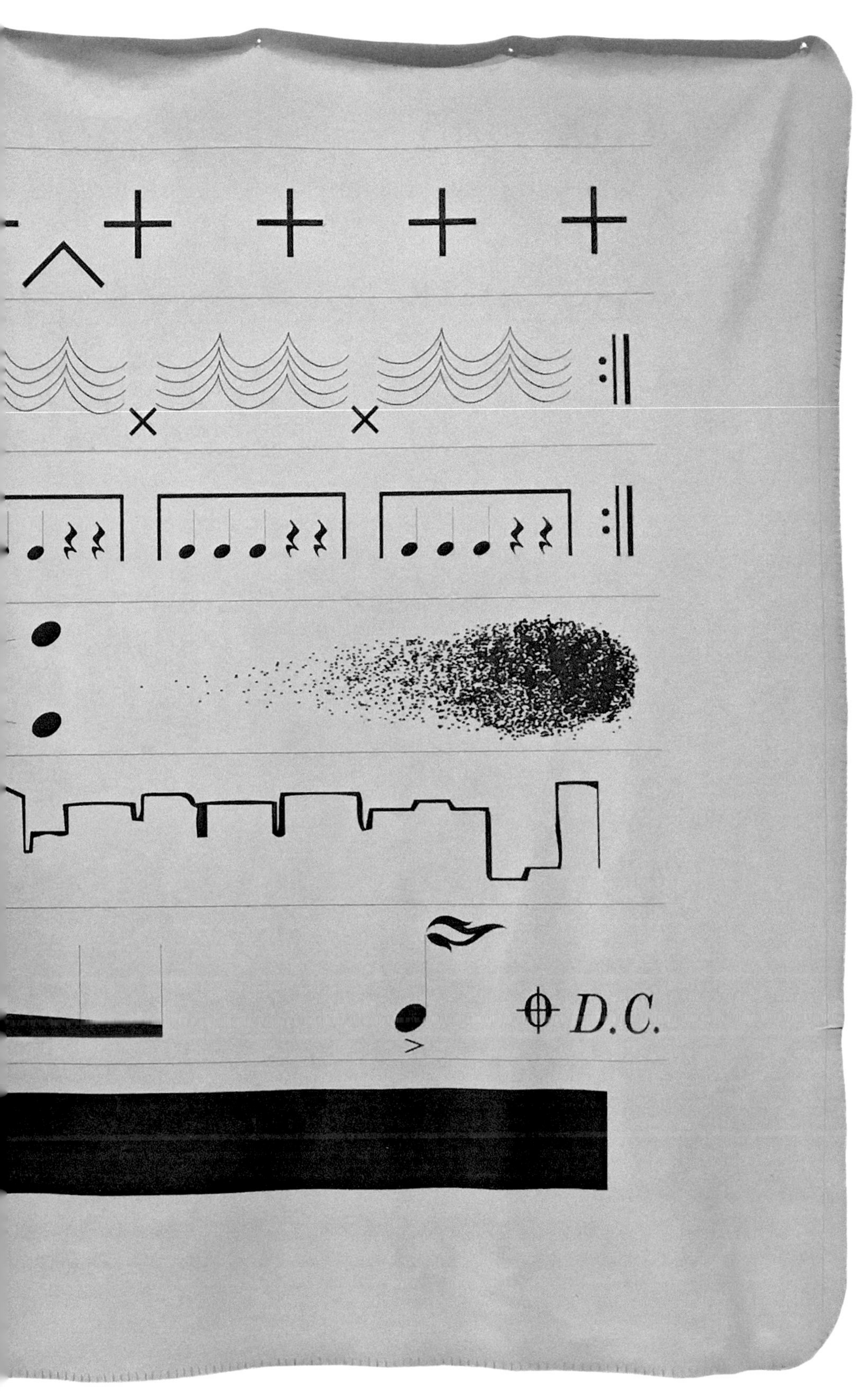
D.C.

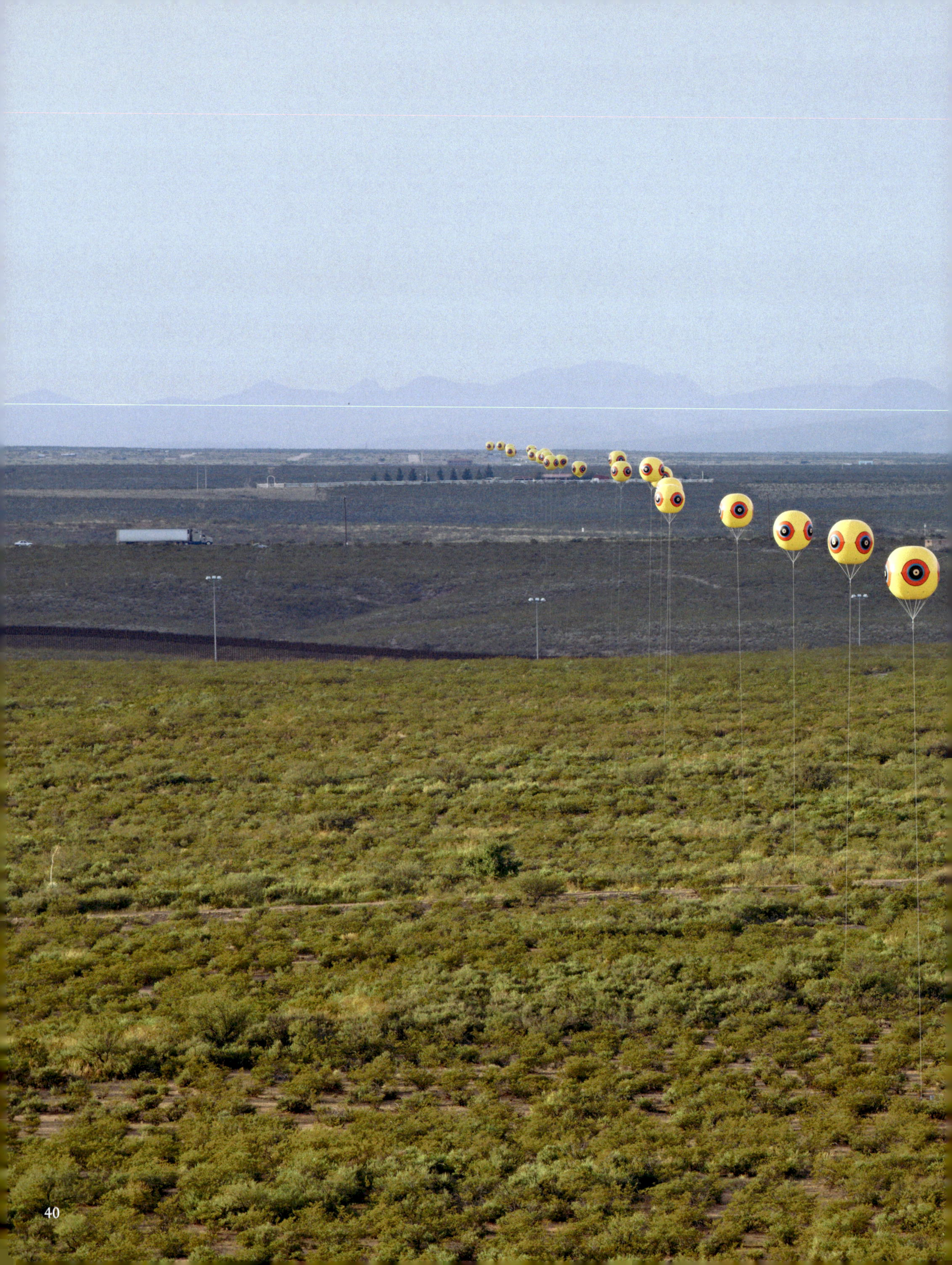

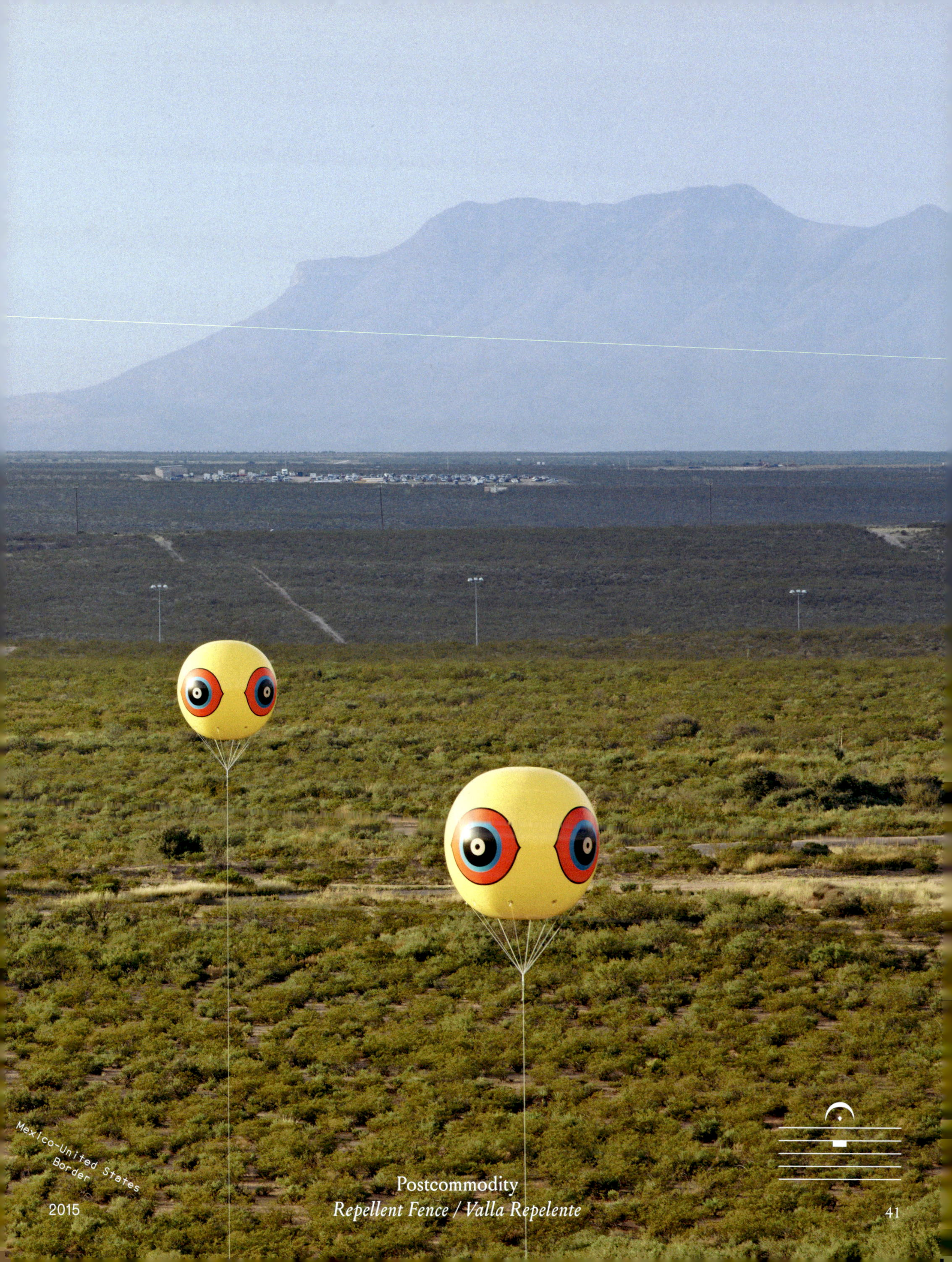

Mexico-United States Border

2015

Postcommodity
Repellent Fence / Valla Repelente

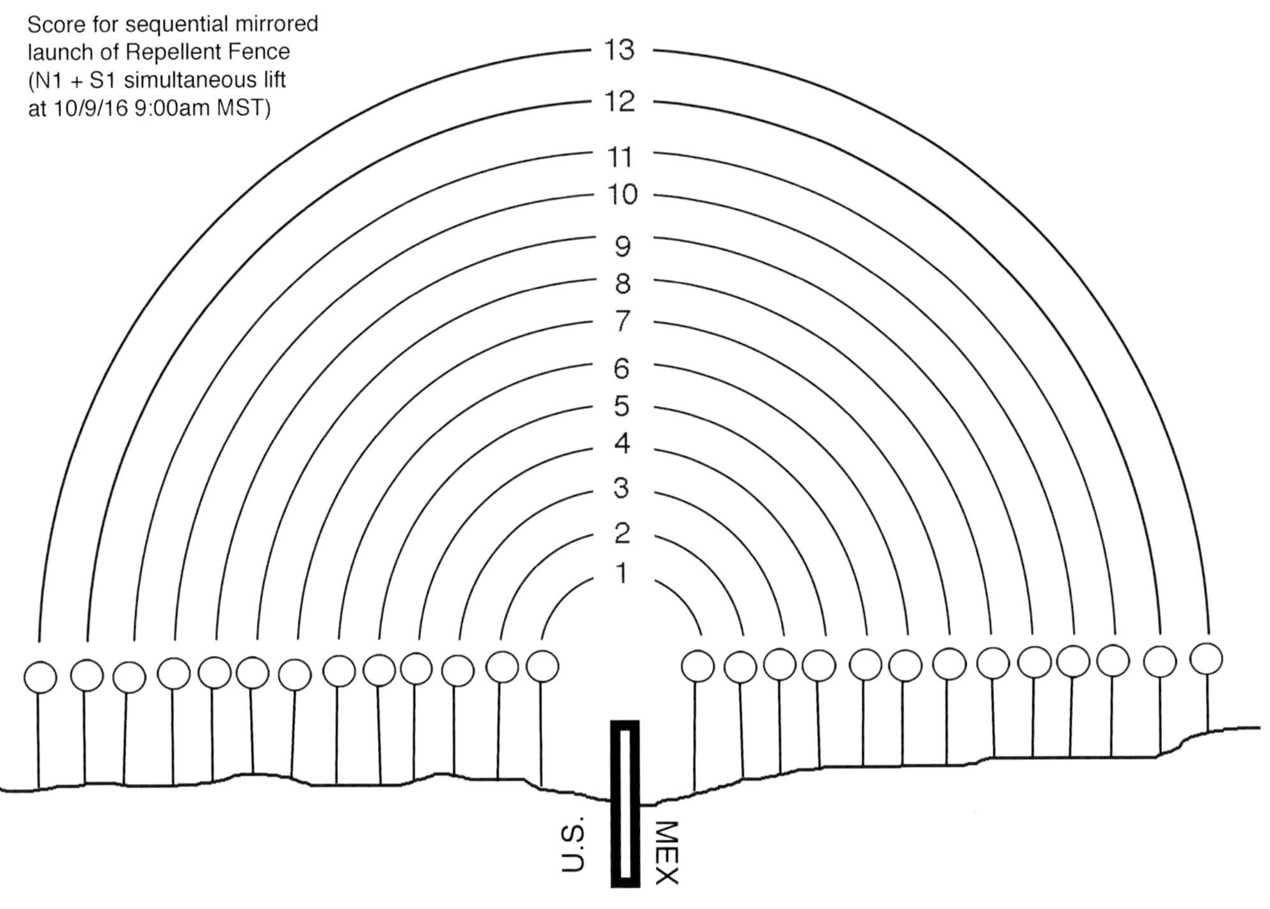

Chacon's score depicting the *Repellent Fence* installation 2014

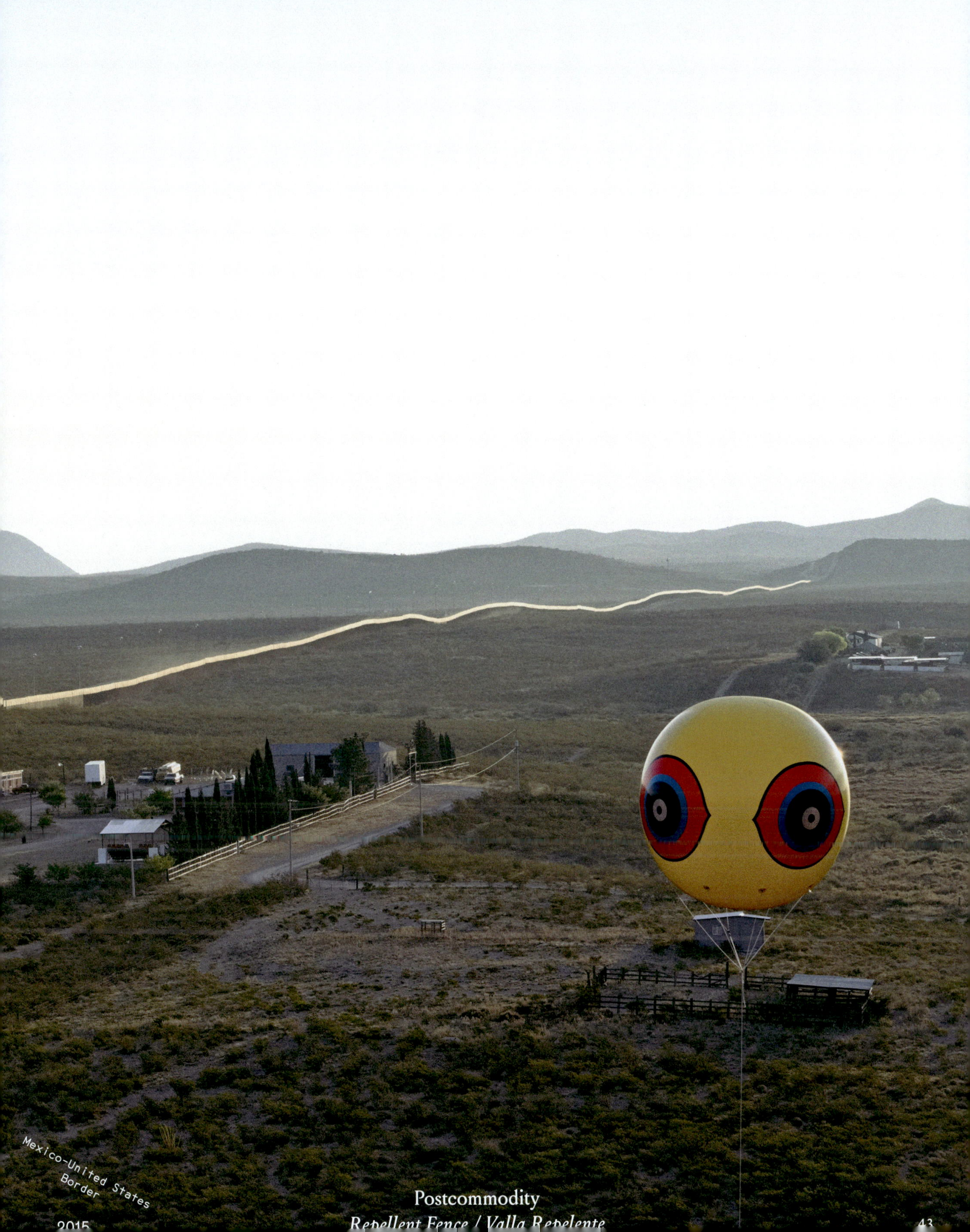

Mexico–United States Border

Postcommodity

Repellent Fence / Valla Repelente

2015

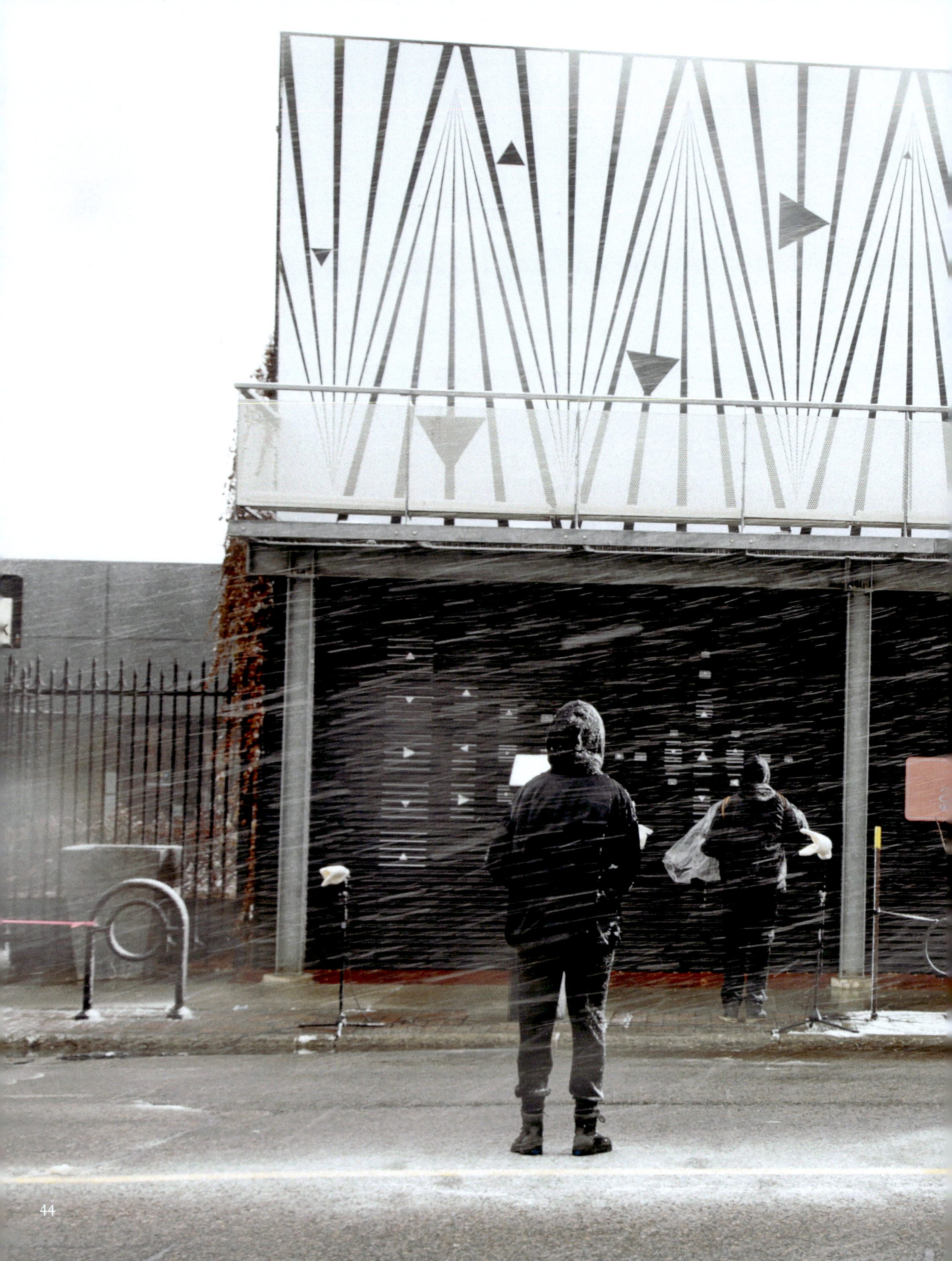

EXT. - DAY

AN AUNTIE

Remember, when you enter the room, it is important that you walk clockwise in a circle around the room and shake everyone's hand. This is the Old Way.

A TEENAGER

But my baby sister is in the room, and is lying on her back. She is staring at the ceiling, as if she is looking to some balloon in the sky. She is looking toward the stars, or maybe the moon.

Do I walk *her* clockwise or *my* clockwise?

AUNTIE

Don't argue with me!

TEENAGER

Sorry. Can I shake my baby sister's hand?

INT. - MOMENTS LATER

RAVEN

Of what this might mean, these relationships of knowledge, an ongoing synthesis of traditions, and how our ways might change through generations. I believe in the fluidity in the transfer of knowledge, that it may shift and change into a matured knowledge, because for better or worse, we have traveled to another world.

ANDE

Yeah. Yeah. It's very interesting because-- I think about the joik, that it comes from the earth, that the earth has sung that. And then I think that, well, every plant gets the strength from the earth. And if the earth speaks to me through my vertical neighbors, then I'm so fortunate because then I can-- speaks in my frequency, in my language so that I can make some sense of it. So my first strong encounter was when I was a 14-, 15-year-old boy who is in the boarding school, and it's springtime, and I really would like to go home, but I'm stuck there. And it's in May. So then the night start to come. So it doesn't become dark anymore.

So I'm there in my bed. And then I hear somebody who comes out from there. We had a corridor, and then we had a little room between two rooms. So I'm in this room here.

ÁNDE (CONT'D)

And then I hear this person come there. And I have sort of never been scared of ghosts and haunting because I have always thought that when something like what others call haunting, it's somebody wants to have contact. They want to speak, and they want to-- so then I'm with my back to the door. And I never turn my head, but I lay there, and this person is also there. And then he speaks to me. He says that, "Oh, you are one of the people we have been waiting for, for such a long time. It's so nice to see you here in this." And he told about the expectations and told about things that would come and so on.

I just was there and listened to what he had to say. So he said that, "You belong to the generation that-- you can never be tired because you belong to the generation who have to fight for our things."

(CONT'D)

And as he spoke-- and he spoke until he had told what he had to tell me. And then he just walked through the wall and went down there. And my inner eye saw him, that he had a white, old-ish gákti, and that is his Four Winds hat, was shaped a little bit different than the things that I do here. And he transferred to me knowledge, who I am. Transferred to me, where I come from, transferred to me what is important, transferred to me what is easy, what is hard.

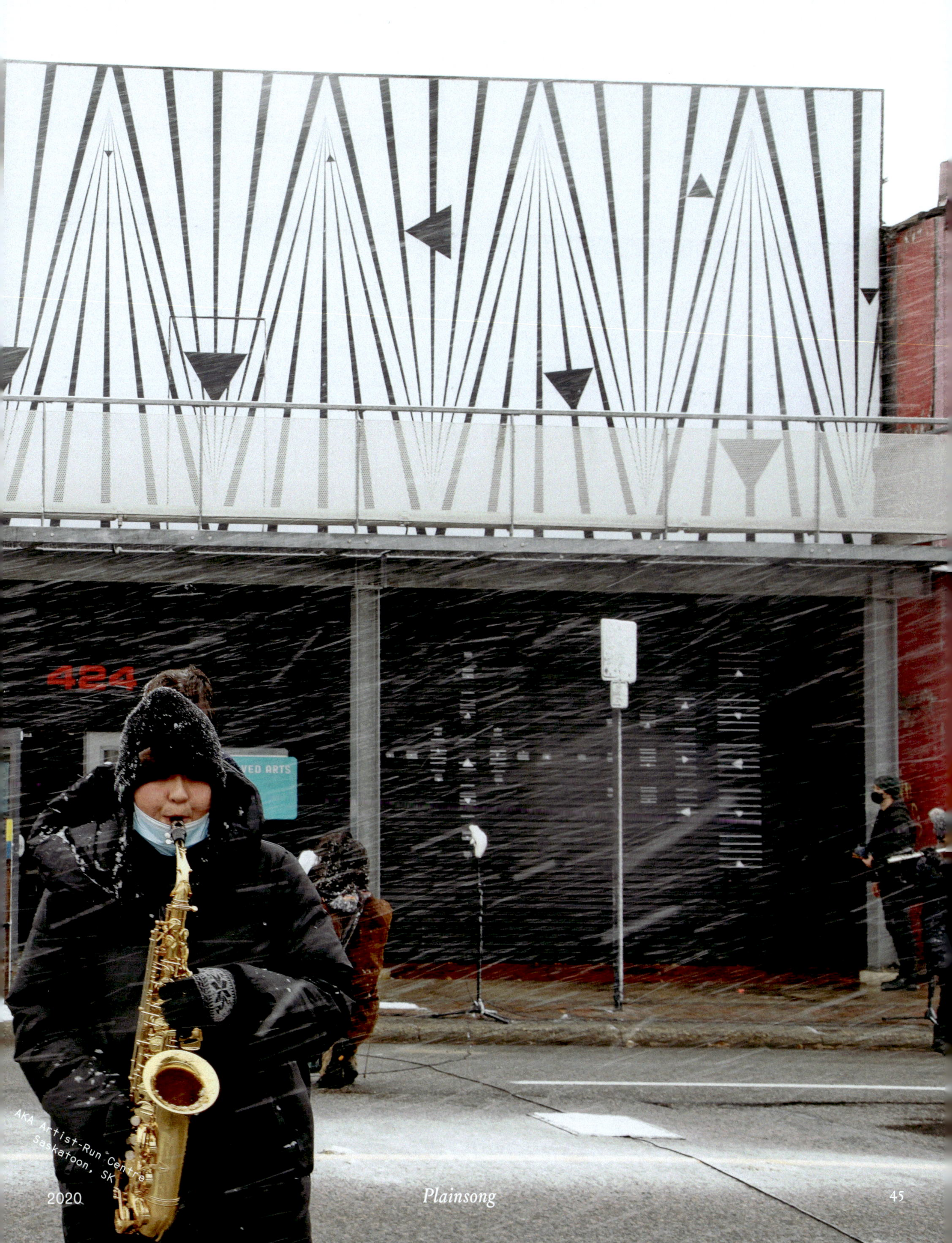

AKA Artist-Run Centre
Saskatoon, SK

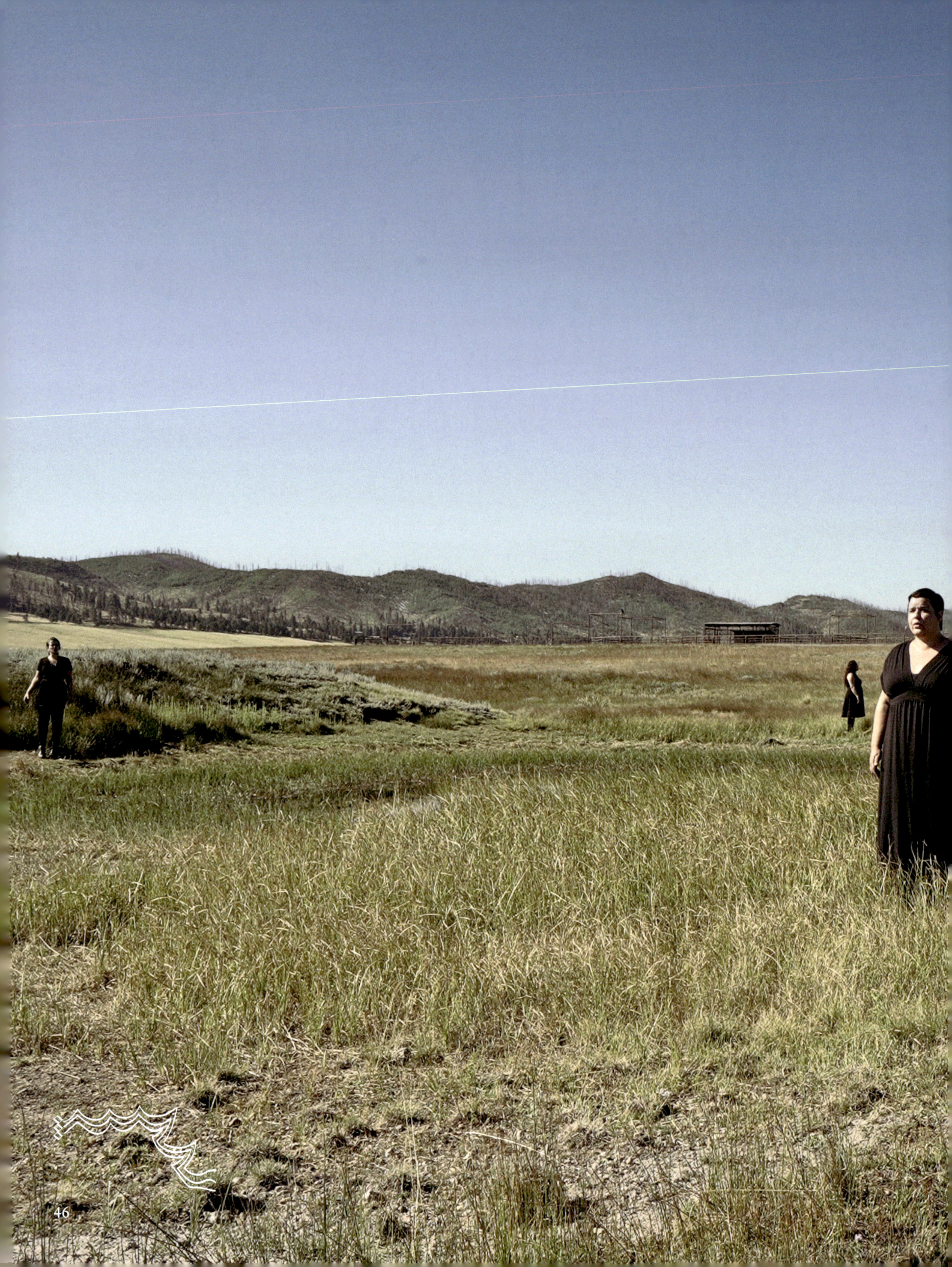

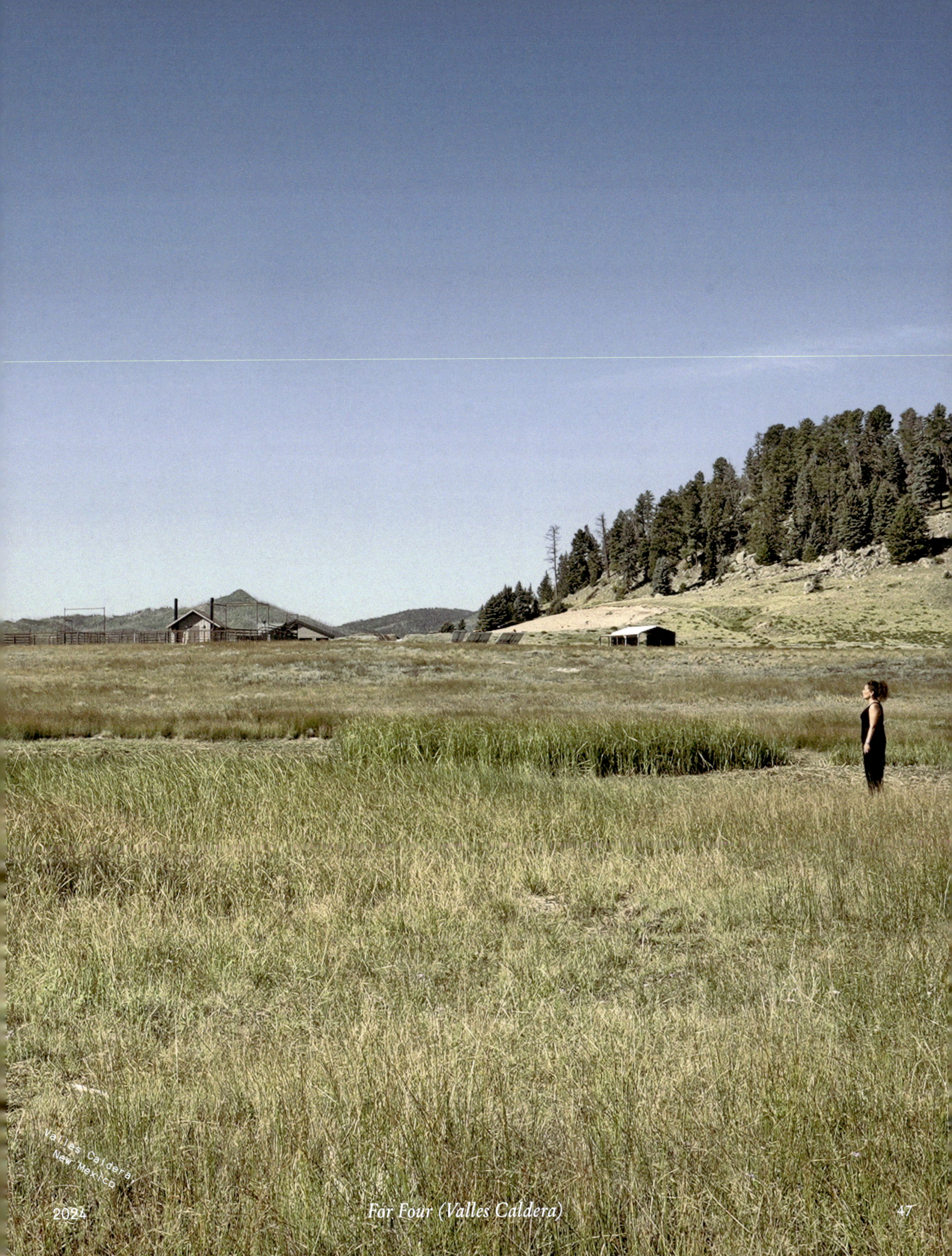
Valles Caldera,
New Mexico

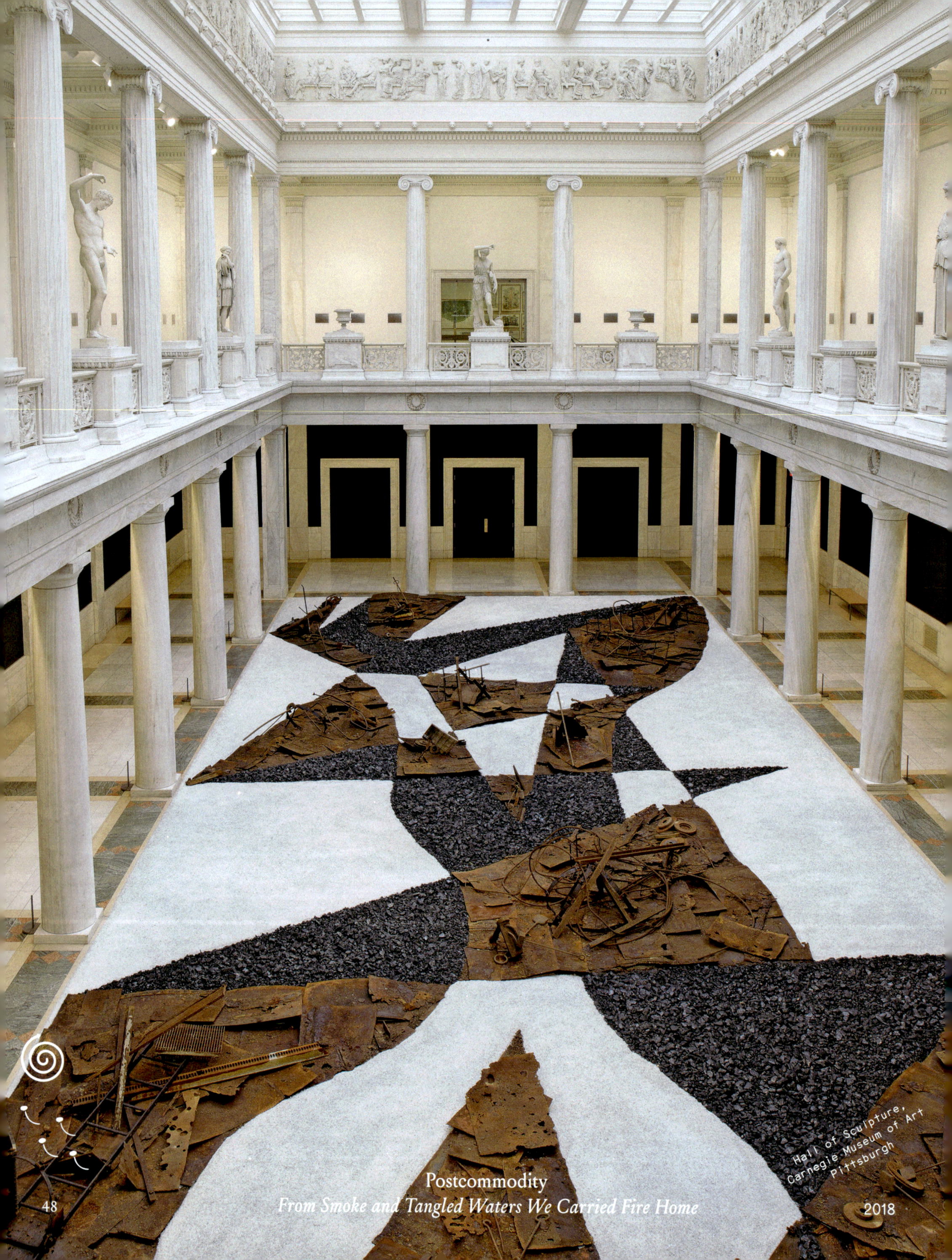

Postcommodity
From Smoke and Tangled Waters We Carried Fire Home
2018

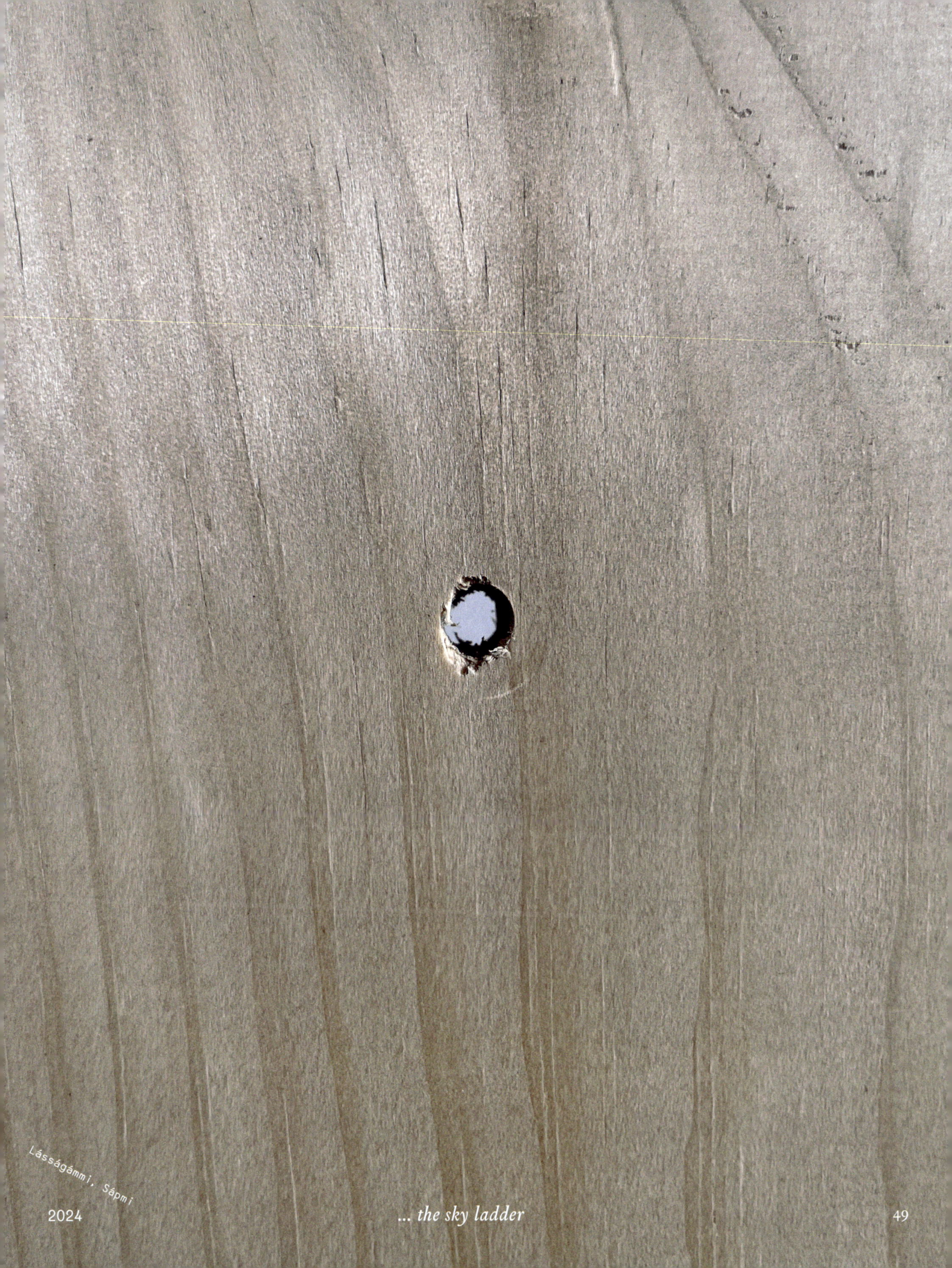
Lásságámmi, Sápmi

Eric-Paul Riege

H_'_'__H

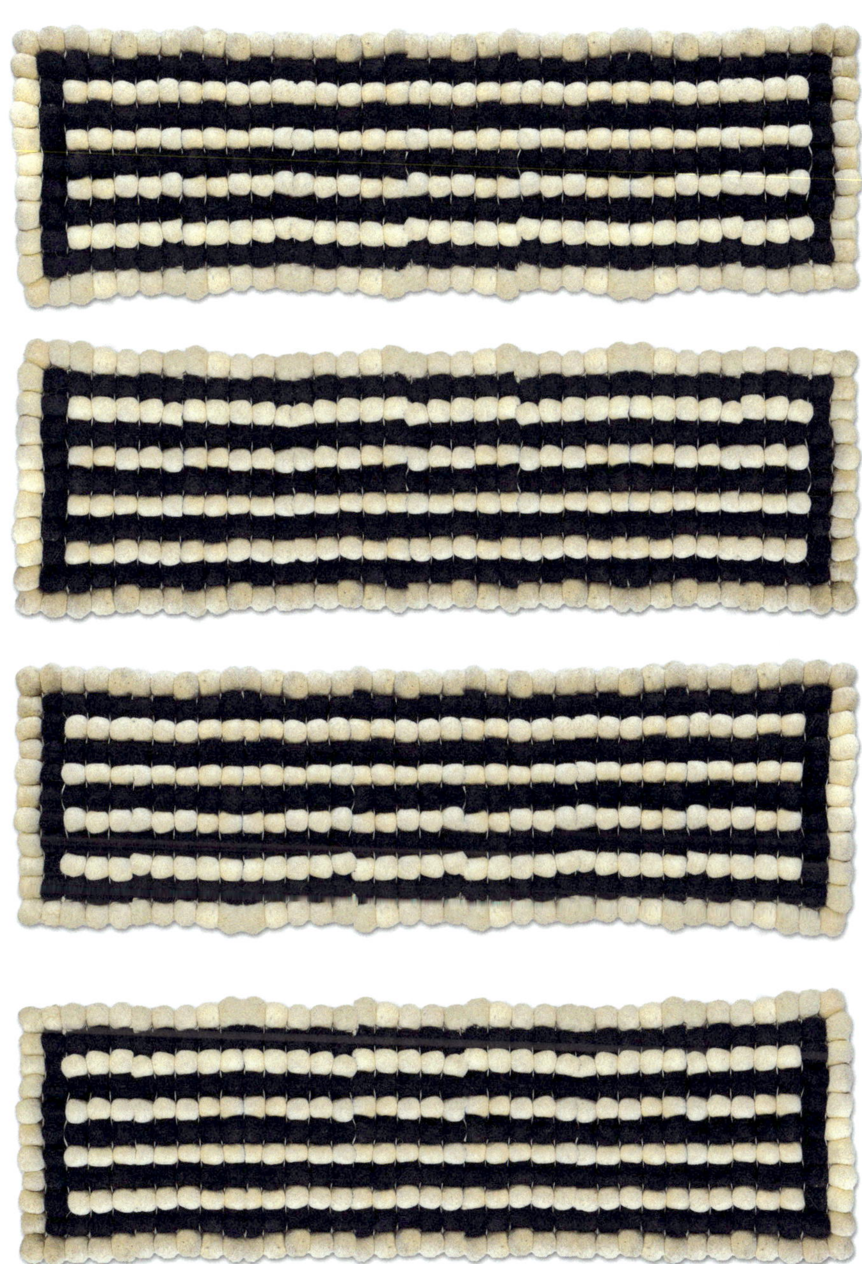

Eric-Paul Riege's loom/staff drawing made from felted wool and altered digitally, 2023

1 A story from Isabelle Deshchinny, Diné weaver, shared that at the loom u weave East so u can see the Sun through the warp in the morning.

2 Our homelands, DINÉTAH.

when U enter a hooghan in Diné Bikéyah [Diné- ("Navajo") [or da ppl (the people)] + bi- ("his/her/their/ its") + kéyah ("land, country")] u enter from the east [[HA'A'AAH]] turn left + go [gòò] clockwise.
Raven asked "is it clockwise for the bugs that enter from below and when they look up?"
Raven shared with me a story about his younger self asking this question about our vertical neighbors and the orientation of the hooghan or hogan or home or house and who lives there but also who is entering.

I wondered for those whose memories are now in the ground? We bury ancestors below and we bury them around and we bury them above.

burying up ! from the ground up it grows !
dahiistł'o [loom]—from the ground up it grows. I heard this interpretation of loom from one of my Diné bizaad [bi- ("his/her/their/its") + zaad ("language")] teachers, a climbing upon the warp yarns by the weft yarns.
pov:: ^.above.^ + v.below.v

we weave to the east.[1] IT [the place/our place][2] begins with HA'A'AAH;

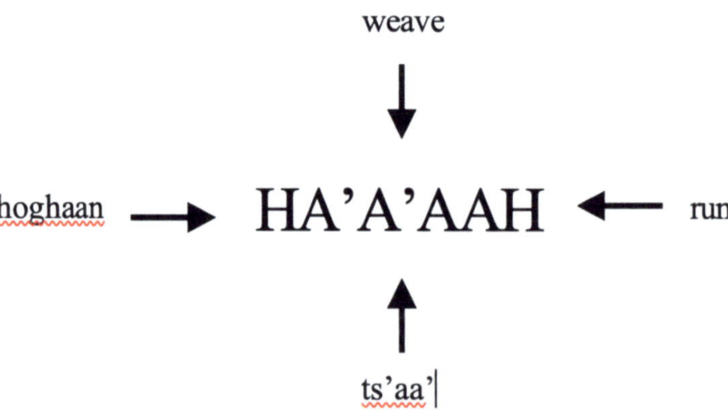

Being carried by our orientation to/too HA'A'AAH I think about the permanence + impermanence of a home. What lines define a home? Are lines of the music staff and the loom the home for the songs and stories we sing and weave? Do the lines of the staff and a loom act as a form of planning? When First Man + First Woman laid in the hooghan after EMERGENCE in the 4TH [łigai] world their thoughts mingled and they planned for what was to come. Planning as a form of goodness for the notes and weft to follow. Climbing along the axes of segmentations when do we jump from one platform to the other? Is that a syllable or letter of a word..a note of a song..a bead of a necklace? When we remove the staff off the loom I wonder what the notes of the weft become.

The LOOM as a map—creating a border and a line to travel on. To climb up the string or along the lines. The loom is a border between the inner and the outer. An object touching another object with a string thru it::

~~object object object object object object object object~~
~~yarn yarn yarn yarn yarn yarn yarn~~
~~note note note note note note note note~~
~~bead bead bead bead bead bead bead~~

I've been told as a weaver that "the tension between the strings [|||||||||||||||] of the warp should be equal." The integrity of the woven structure is determined by its veins. I'm wondering if now, looking at the staff of the score, does the note also remember where it's supposed to go if I'm looking at them kojígo [points with lips thus rotating orientation to where one is pointing]. I wanna ask a spider: is all matter in motion and a form of vibration? Is divination a means of artistic engineering? do We all create homes with the body like U?

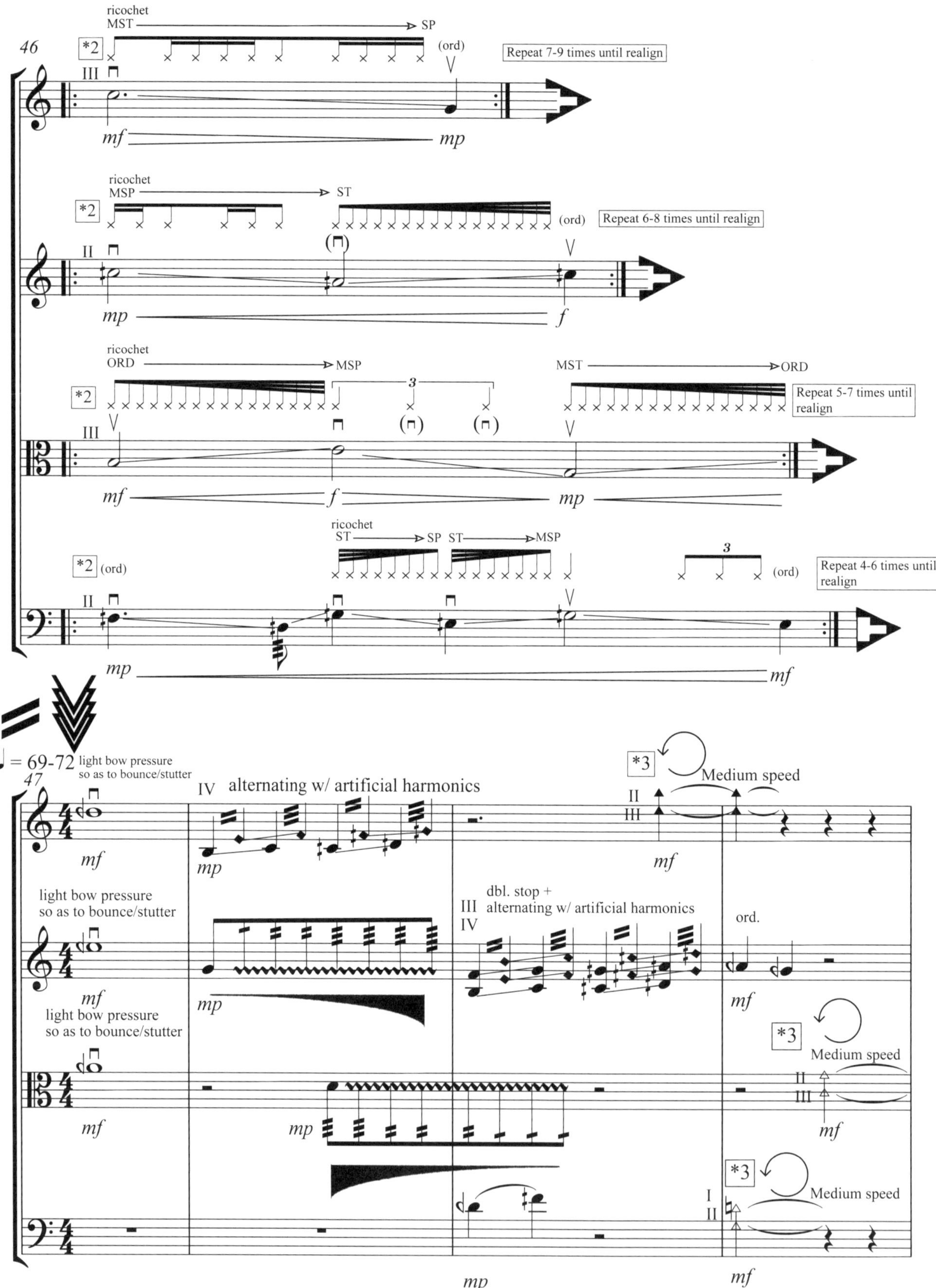
46
ricochet
MST → SP
*2
(ord)
Repeat 7-9 times until realign
III
mf
mp
ricochet
MSP → ST
*2
(ord)
Repeat 6-8 times until realign
II
mp
f
ricochet
ORD → MSP
MST → ORD
*2
3
Repeat 5-7 times until realign
III
mf
f
mp
ricochet
ST → SP ST → MSP
*2 (ord)
3
(ord)
Repeat 4-6 times until realign
II
mp
mf
♩ = 69-72 light bow pressure so as to bounce/stutter
47
IV alternating w/ artificial harmonics
*3
Medium speed
II
III
mf
mp
mf
light bow pressure so as to bounce/stutter
dbl. stop + alternating w/ artificial harmonics
III
IV
ord.
mf
mp
mf
light bow pressure so as to bounce/stutter
*3
Medium speed
II
III
mf
mp
mf
*3
Medium speed
I
II
mp
mf

— is a future creation story telling of a group of people traveling from west to east, across the written page, ↵

contrary to the movement of the sun, but involuntarily and unconsciously allegiant to the trappings of time. With their bows, these wanderers sought out others like them, knowing that they could survive by finding these other clans who resided in the east, others who shared their linear cosmologies. It is told that throughout the journey, in their own passage of time, this group became the very people they were seeking.

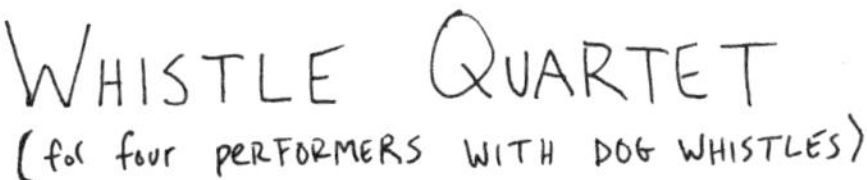

PERFORMER I.

REPEAT AS MANY TIMES AS DESIRED
NEEDED

PERFORMERS I + II

II ENTERS WHEN READY. REPEAT UNTIL THE END. IMPROVE WITH EACH REPEAT UNTIL YOU MATCH THE ABILITY OF THE LEADER.

PERFORMERS I + II + III + IV

III + IV ENTER TOGETHER WHEN READY. REPEAT UNTIL THE END. IMPROVE WITH EACH REPEAT UNTIL MATCH THE ABILITIES OF THE LEADER(S). LEADER I MAY TAKE A BREAK WHEN DESIRED
NEEDED

RAVEN CHACON (2001)

DURATION: ALL NIGHT

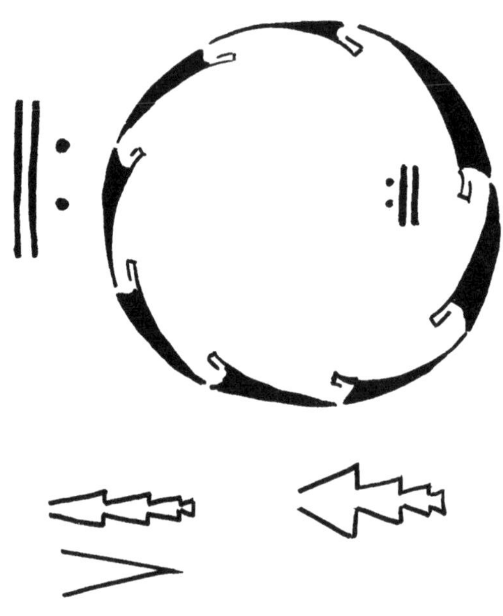

Score page from … *lahgo adil'i dine doo yeehosinilgii yidaaghi* 2004

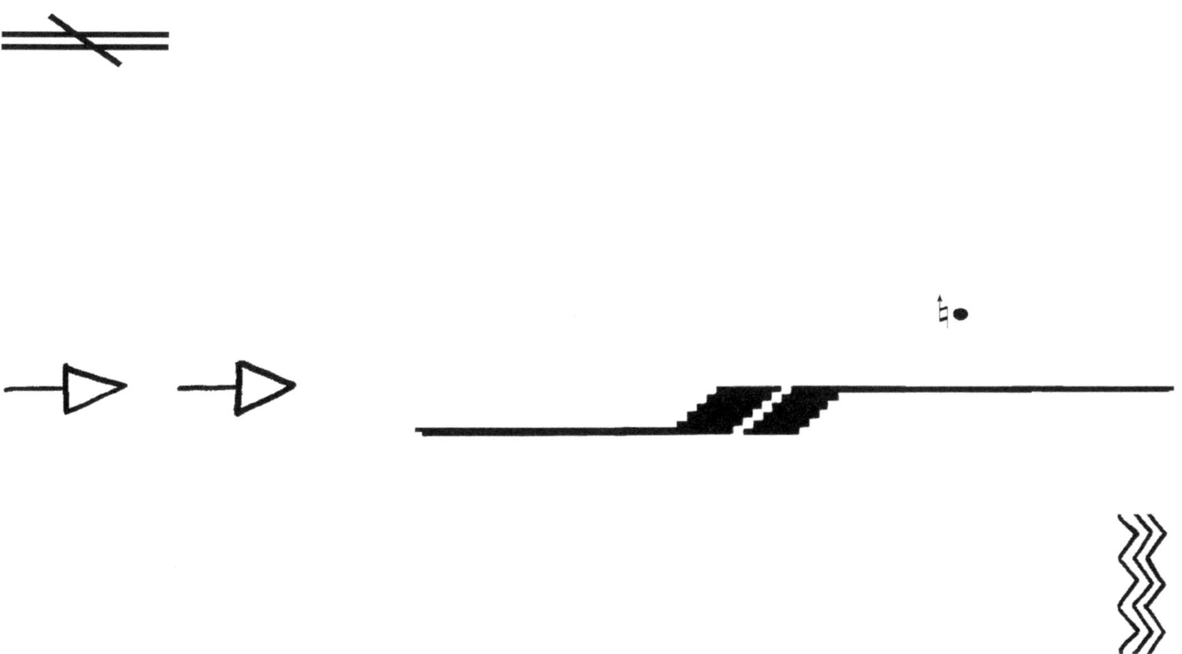

2004 Score page from ... *lahgo adil'i dine doo yeehosinilgii yidaaghi*

DISPATCH

written by

Candice Hopkins and Raven Chacon

J-CUT:

EXT. THE DESERT

A woman and a man are driving in a truck, speeding up and slowing down to cover their tracks.

The truck comes to a stop.

WOMAN

This rock is under threat. We need to gather here to protect it. Our actions begin and end at this place.

A large group of people have gathered in an encampment. They are:

HOSTS - People who live and have lived here for centuries.

SPIRITUAL LEADERS - Indigenous people from any tribe or nation.

FRONT LINE ACTIVISTS - (Native and non) ready and willing to engage directly with police, militia, or construction crews.

MILITANT INDIGENOUS PEOPLE - Group of their own. Willing to engage in direct action. Not necessarily in collaboration with front line activists or the hosts.

NARCS - (Native and non) undercover police. Any one participant can be a narc.

REPORTERS - Chronicle for those outside the grounds (as well as inside the grounds).

POLITICIANS - Bring attention. Appear to be listeners. Also there for face time.

COUNTER-SURVEILLERS - To surveille the police and encroachers.

HELPERS* - (Native and non) brings supplies, food, or a necessary skill. Stays out of the way. Take minimal space and resources.

WITNESSES* - Listen and observe.

ARTISTS - Engage in creativity, but also self-agenda/promotion. Has the potential to aid the camp in forming its identity. Their artwork can use up resources (water, heat, electricity).

GATEKEEPERS - Maintain the entrance to the camp. Vet those who enter. A host or trusted by the hosts.

TEMPORARY CAMPERS/SYMPATHIZERS - Bring attention to the cause, temporarily. Cannot or do not know how to belong to the camp.

OTHERS - Tourists, those without a home, others. *At a minimum, participants should join with the intent of taking the role of a WITNESS or HELPER.

WOMAN

Rocks have harmonics, resonant frequencies. They are also deities, lives begun millions of years ago, witnesses to the formation of the earth. They can pick up the tremors of extractive colonialism exposing wide caverns that lead to trails deep inside the ground, generating sludge and slurry, releasing poisons meant to stay undisturbed. The time is now to protect these rocks as though it is a last stand. Our gathering can open up the way to other worlds, those of our own making. These other worlds are not de-colonial ones, but non-colonial ones. Not bound by their frameworks, but by ours. Heeding this call is the first action. In this action we come together, in-person or at a distance, to open up a portal of shared experiences.

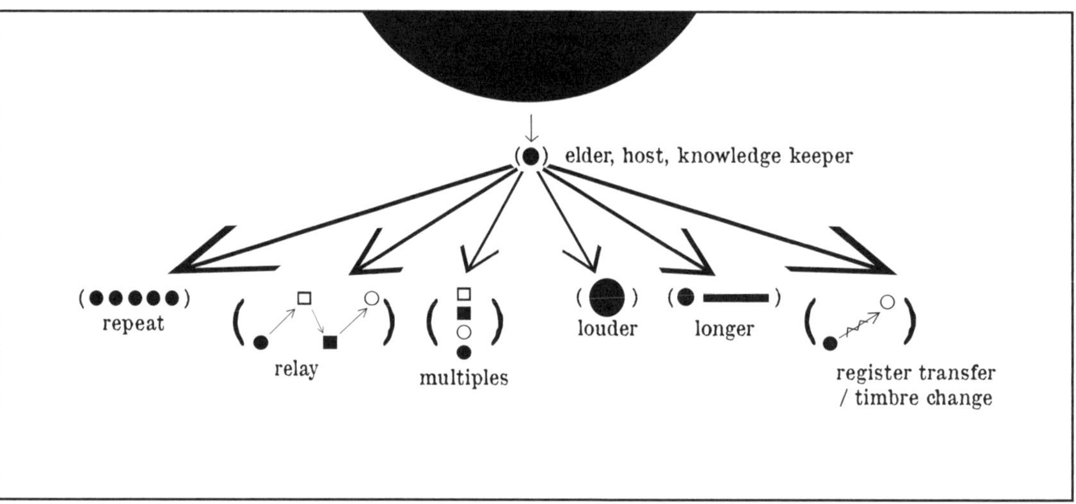

The WOMAN prompts the gatherers to act.

WOMAN AND MAN
Heed the call.

WOMAN
Hosts determine points of reference.

MAN
If you are not already there, arrive.

WOMAN
Gatekeepers welcome and relay protocols of place.

MAN
Or, if you want, you can do nothing. You can always do nothing. But always listen.

WOMAN
Listen beyond. To your immediate surroundings, to the land or water, to sounds outside your normal range.

MAN

Sustain yourself. Don't be in the way, don't encroach. At the same time, be useful, observe. Introduce yourself, unobtrusively. Deliver supplies.

WOMAN

Find your place, determine your role, humbly. Broadcast outward. Also determine what is not to be shared.

MAN

Create a small gathering for one activity. Do something: cook; pray; sing; teach a game. If necessary, initiate a larger gathering. Witness! Relay what you learned. Translate a broadcast for other listeners. Consider different languages, different tones.

WOMAN

In an increasingly fractured society, new paths and new formations are needed to refocus our attention in an attempt to find truth. Participating in this score may produce sonic or visual artifacts, these are as important as the actions.

DISSOLVE TO FUTURE:

WOMAN

What does the land need?
What do the hosts want?
Do you belong here?
Who do you look to for guidance?
What are your skills/strengths?
What are the threats?
Who do you trust?
What are you willing to risk? Who is in charge?
What is the model of leadership?
How do we maintain focus?

ALL
Establish the protocols necessary for the next defense

ALL
Amplify the call

ALL
Gather the players, new or existing and establish their roles

ALL
Determine the parameters of ally-ship with people and with the land

ALL
Move to another site needing protection but continue your actions here.

ALL
Together, define your actions. Maintaining the camp, defending the land and water and sky, and so on

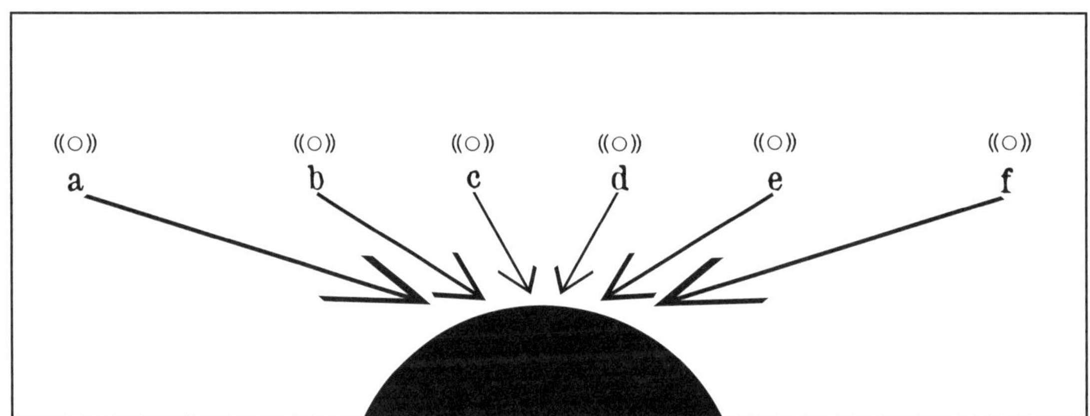

Everyone leaves in radiating lines, with purpose.

FADE OUT.

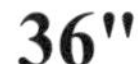
36"

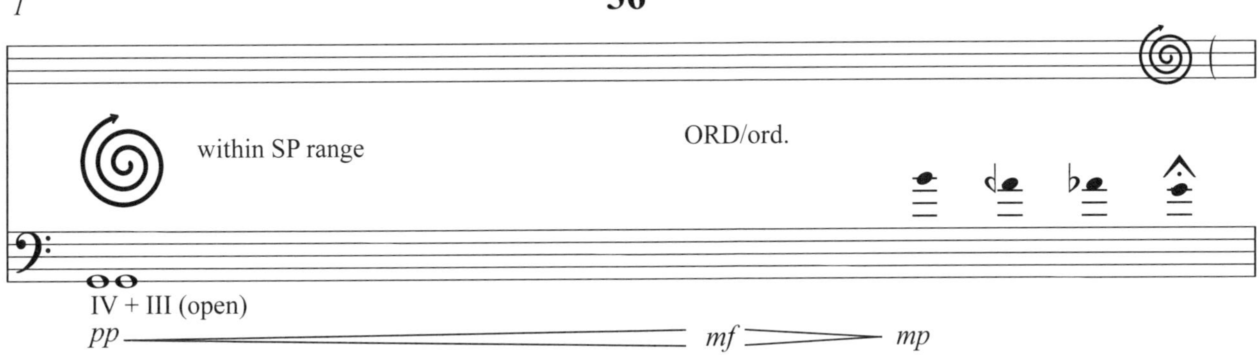
1
within SP range
ORD/ord.
IV + III (open)
pp
mf
mp

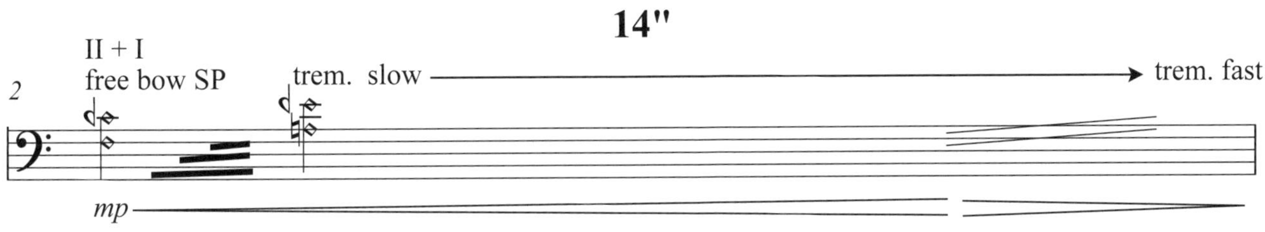
14"
II + I
free bow SP
trem. slow
trem. fast
2
mp

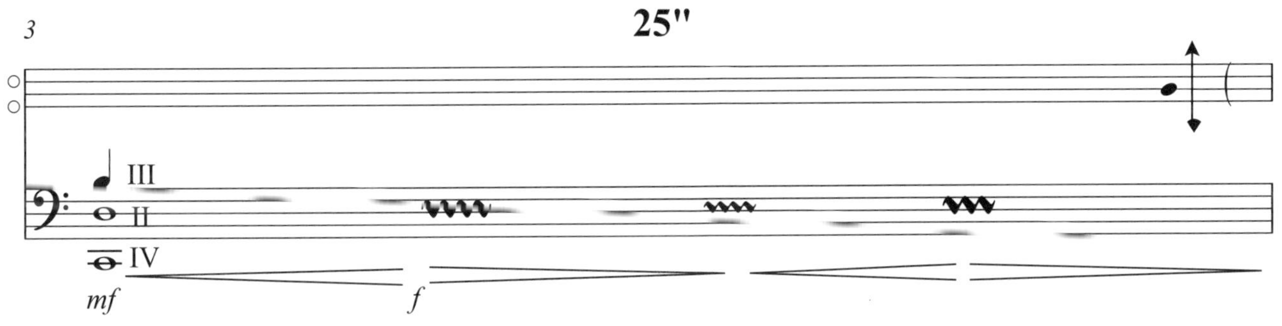
3
25"
III
II
IV
mf
f

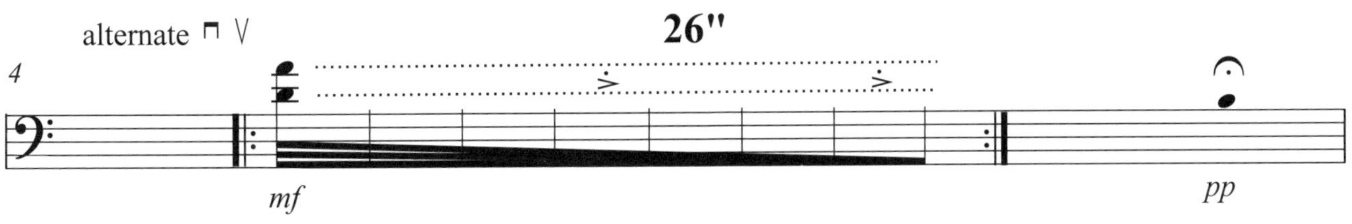
alternate
26"
4
mf
pp

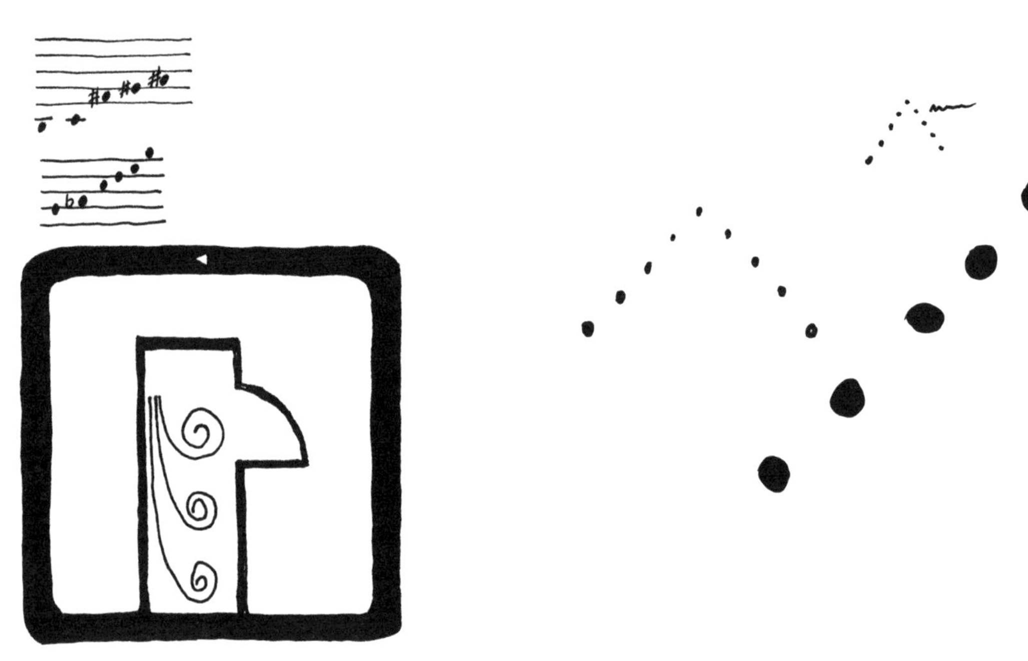

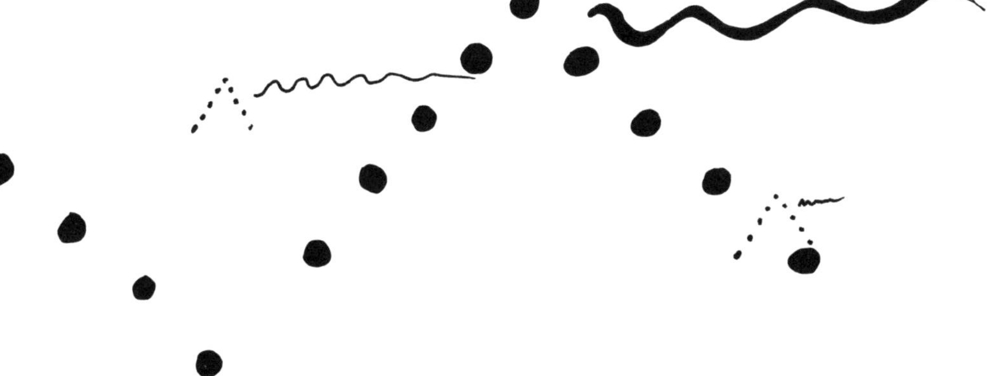

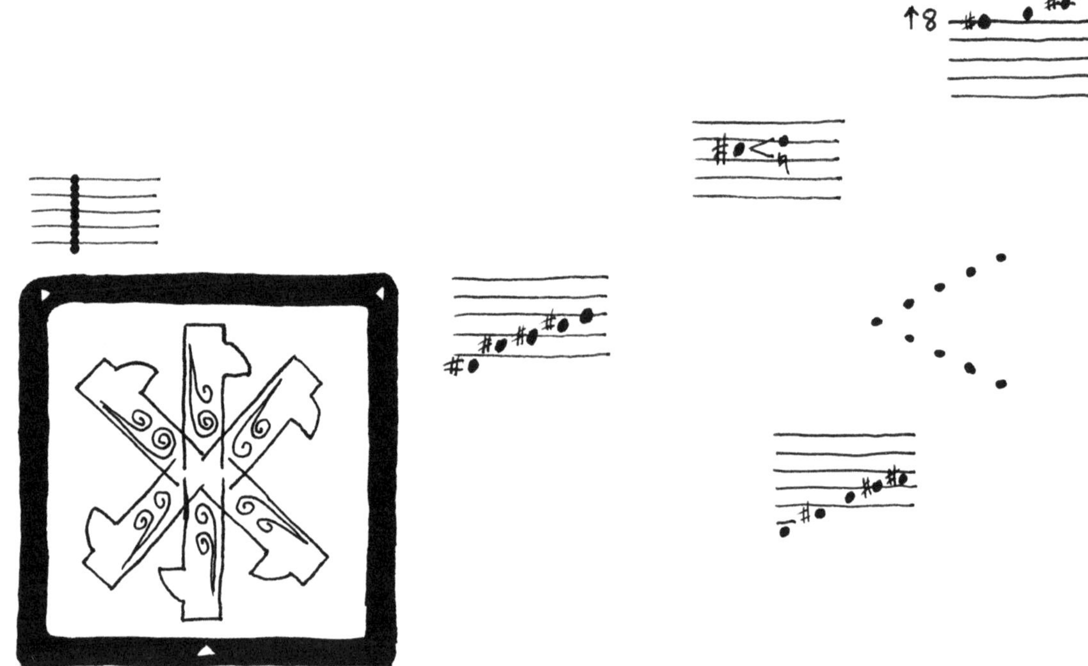
↑8

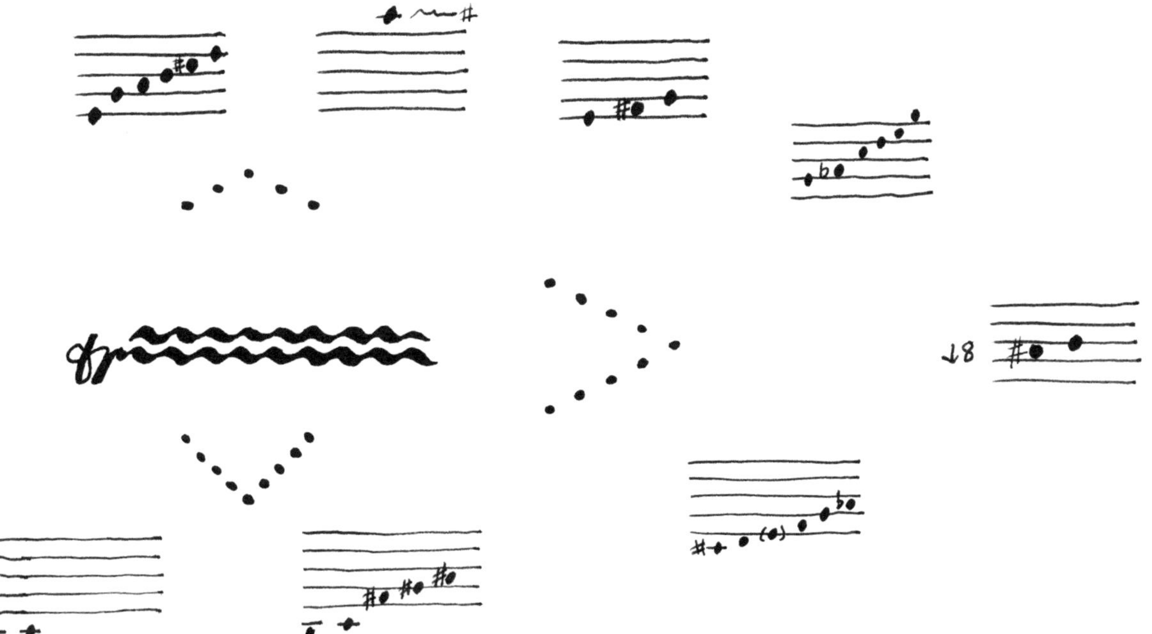
ff
↓8

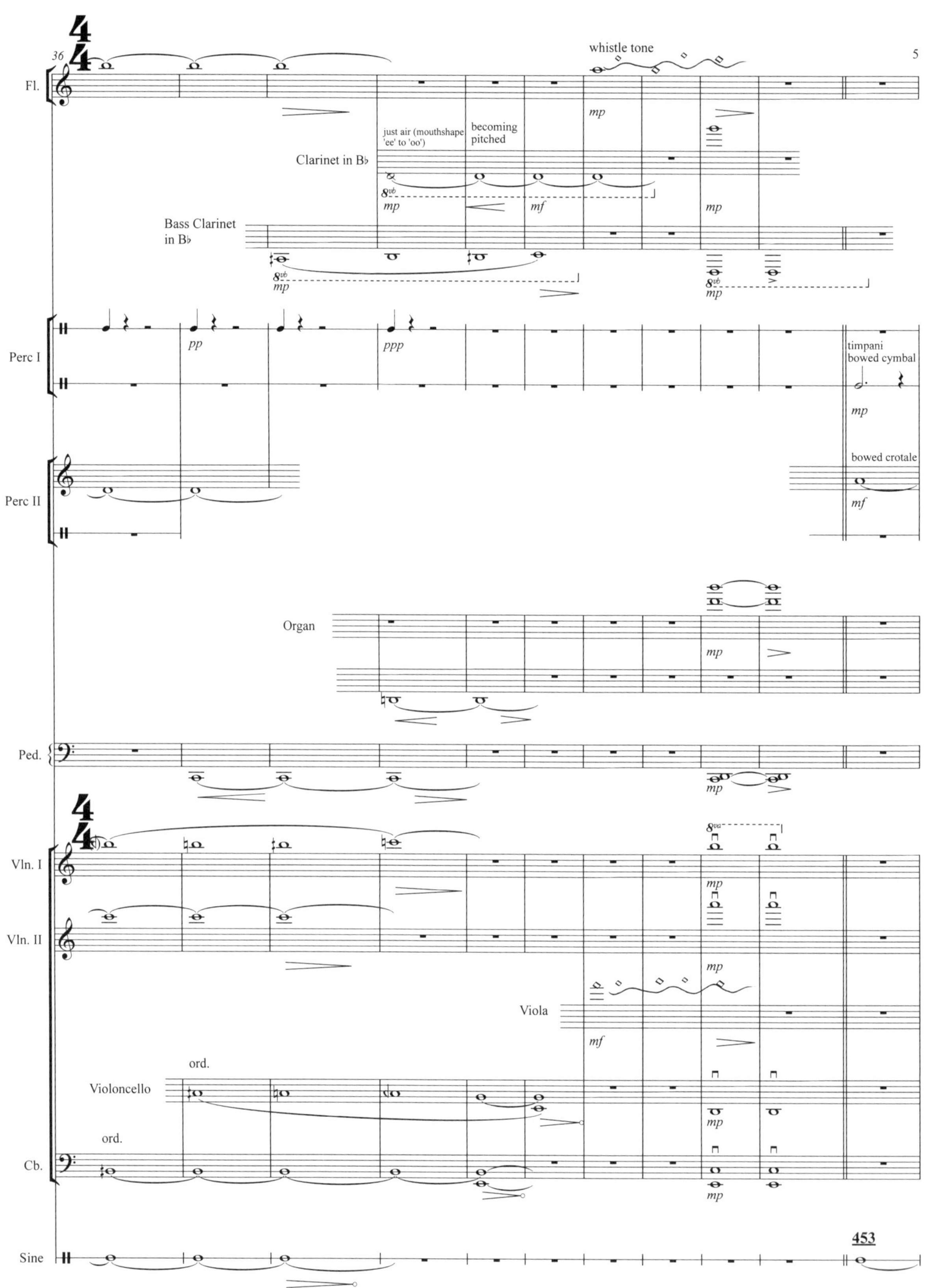

Score page from *Voiceless Mass*

2021

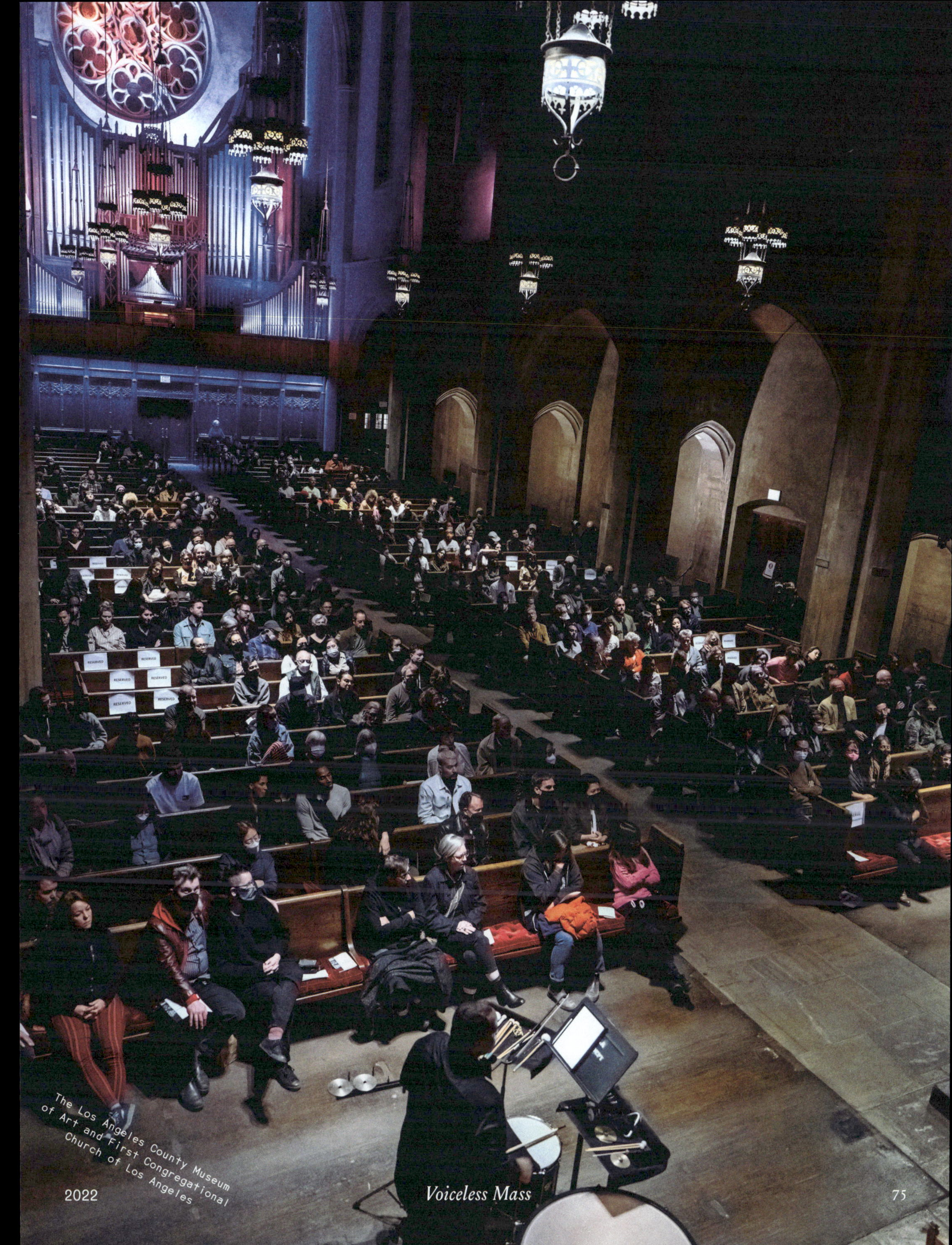

The Los Angeles County Museum of Art and First Congregational Church of Los Angeles

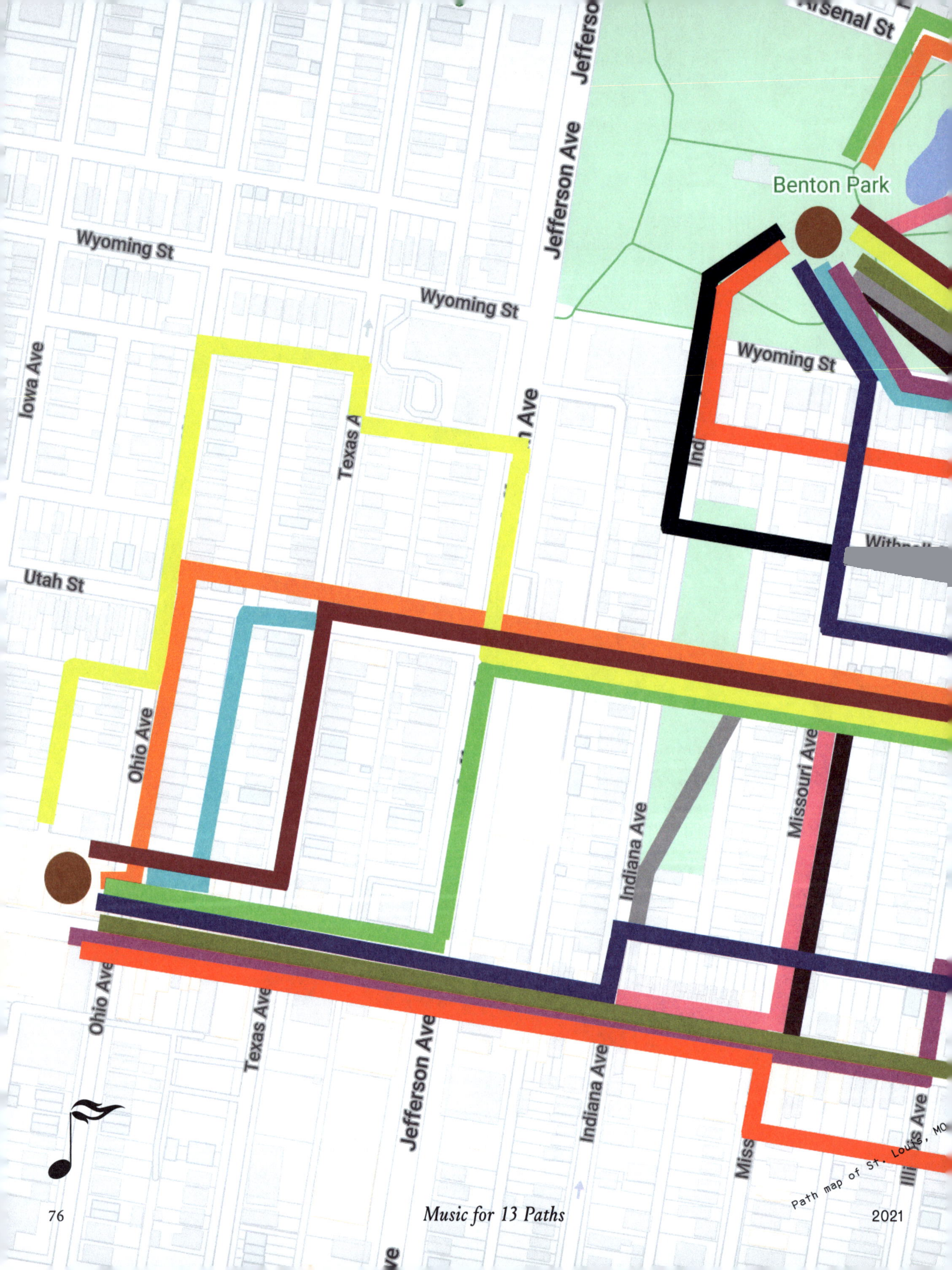
Arsenal St
Jefferson Ave
Benton Park
Wyoming St
Wyoming St
Wyoming St
Iowa Ave
Utah St
Ohio Ave
Ohio Ave
Texas Ave
Jefferson Ave
Indiana Ave
Indiana Ave
Missouri Ave
Illinois Ave
Path map of St. Louis, MO

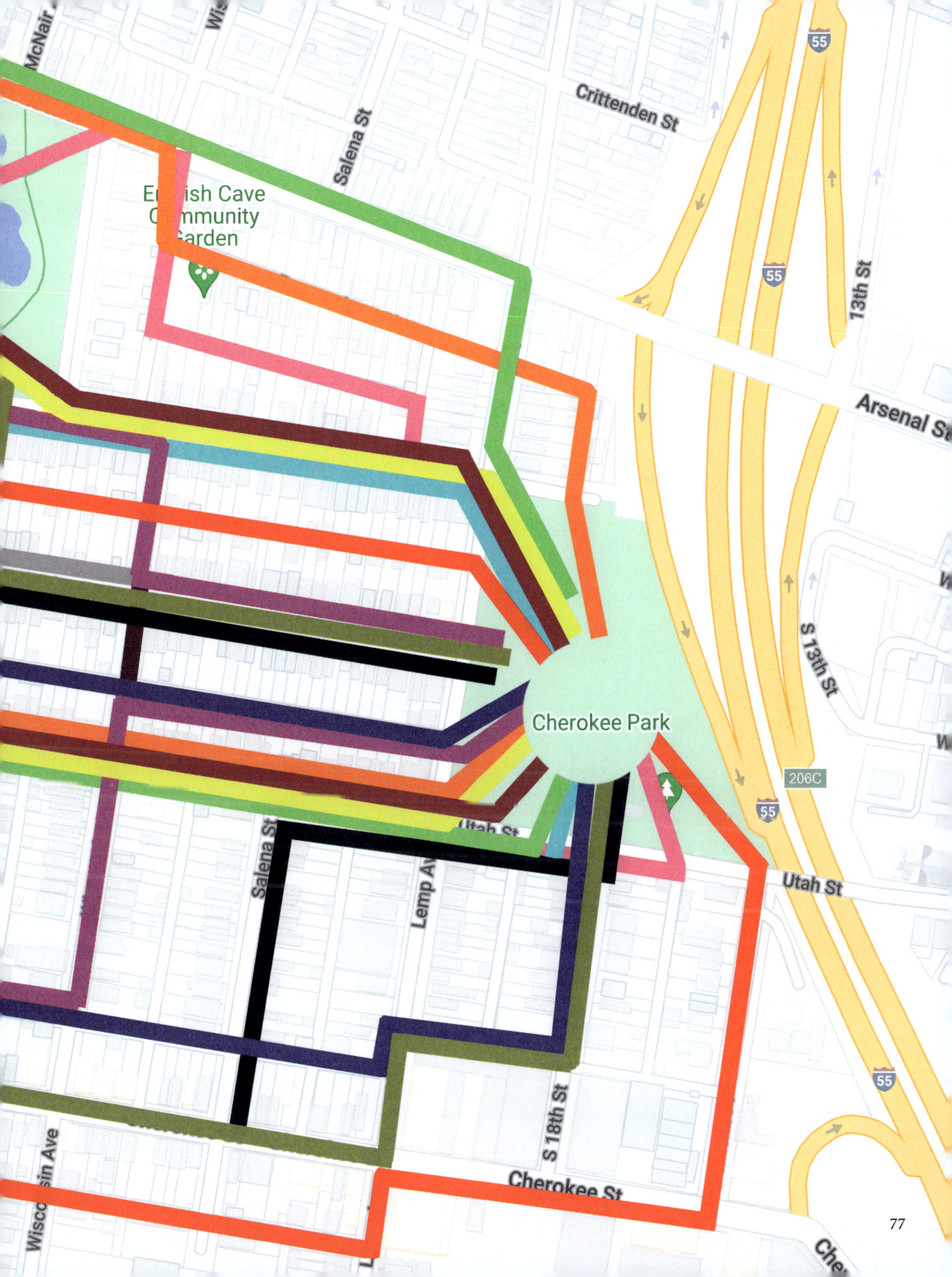

McNair
Crittenden St
Salena St
55
13th St
Arsenal St
S 13th St
Cherokee Park
206C
Utah St
Salena St
S 18th St
Cherokee St

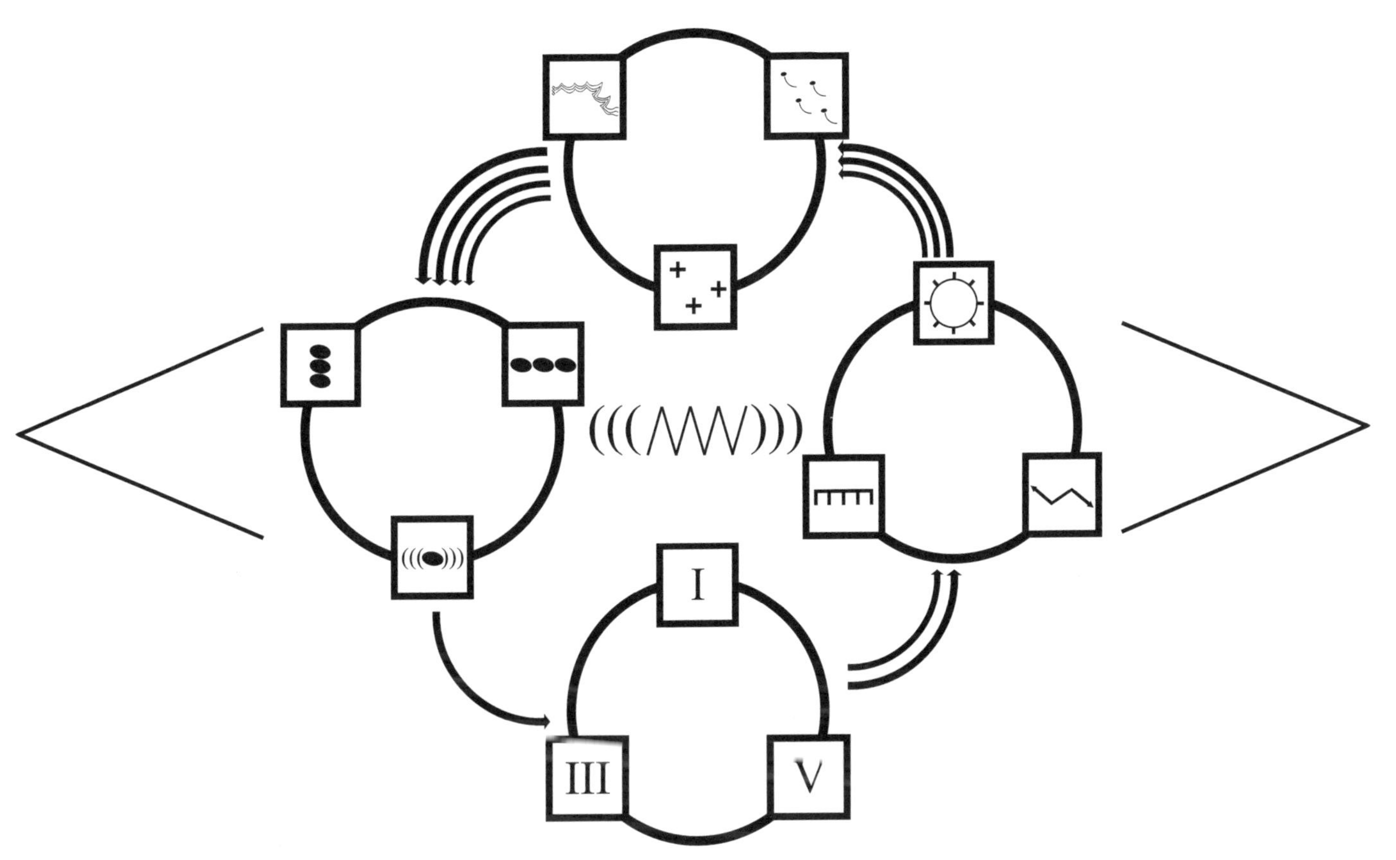

I
III
V

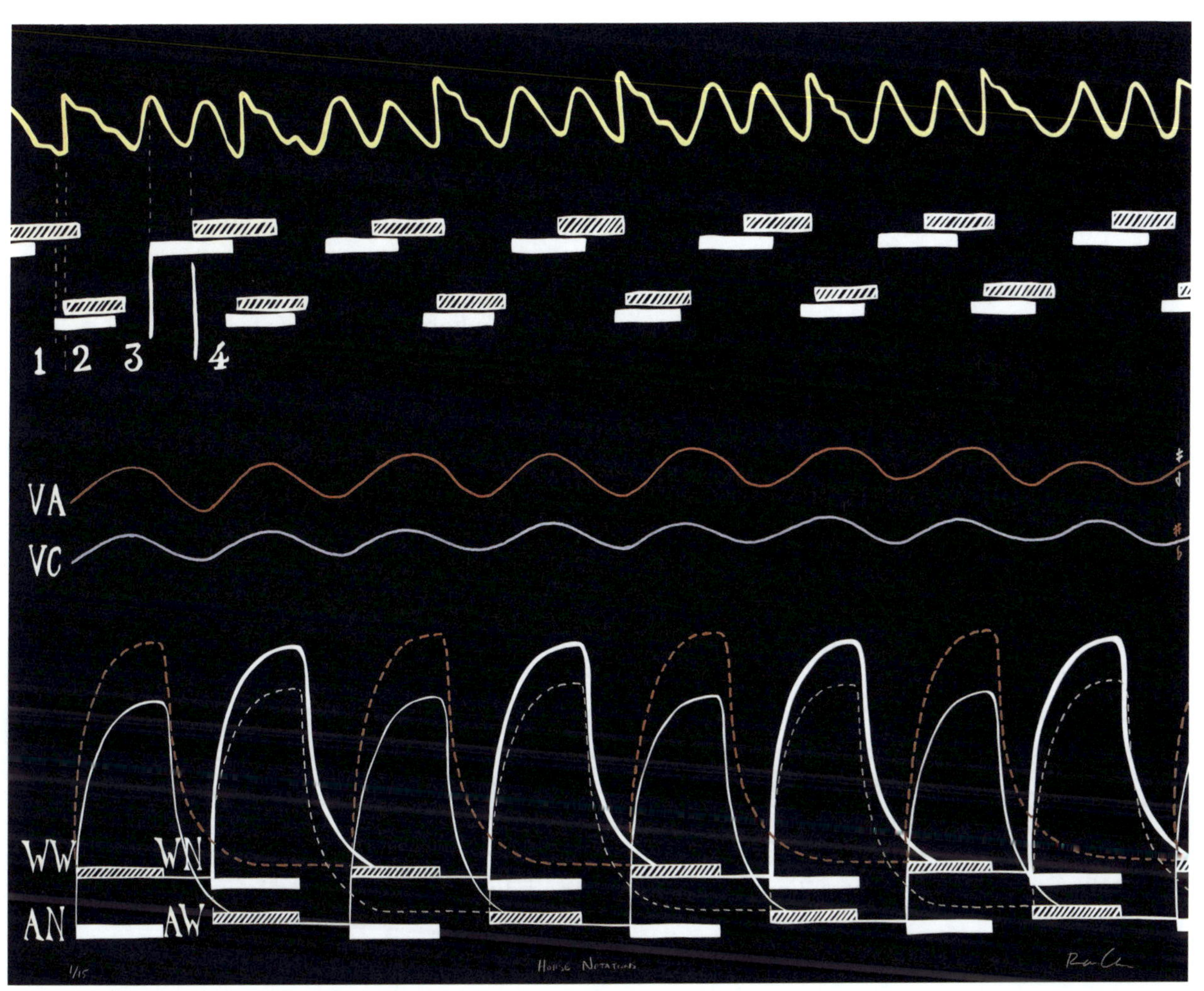
1 2 3 4
VA
VC
WW
WN
AN
AW

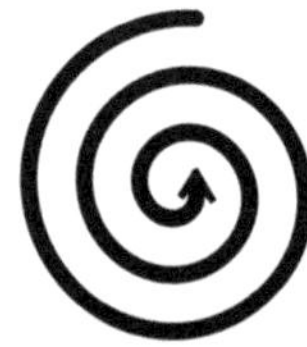

For several players surrounding a turntable

Setup:
- 5 – 10 performers
- each has an amplified (via piezo) sharpened wooden kebob skewer (effects optional)
- one turntable with one vinyl 12" LP
- group pre-determine a total duration

Procedure:
1.) All performers raise their skewers to the sky
2.) One performer activates the spinning of the record (push <play>, place tone-arm, etc) and all performers immediately stab at the spinning record until each finds a groove in which to position their skewer.
3.) At a group self-determined cue, the performers each perform a 30-second solo (effects preferred) on the spinning record, beginning with any pre-chosen performer, then rotating around the turntable clockwise, until each performer has completed a solo. The switching between performers can be quick cuts or overlapping transitions.
4.) After the final performer has completed their solo, all performers play as a group as they were in Procedure 2, until the determined duration has elapsed.

Duet

for two musicians
= 60
p mp mf
p mp
f ff
mf f ff
mf
mf
p mp mf f
p mp mf
ff f pp
f pp

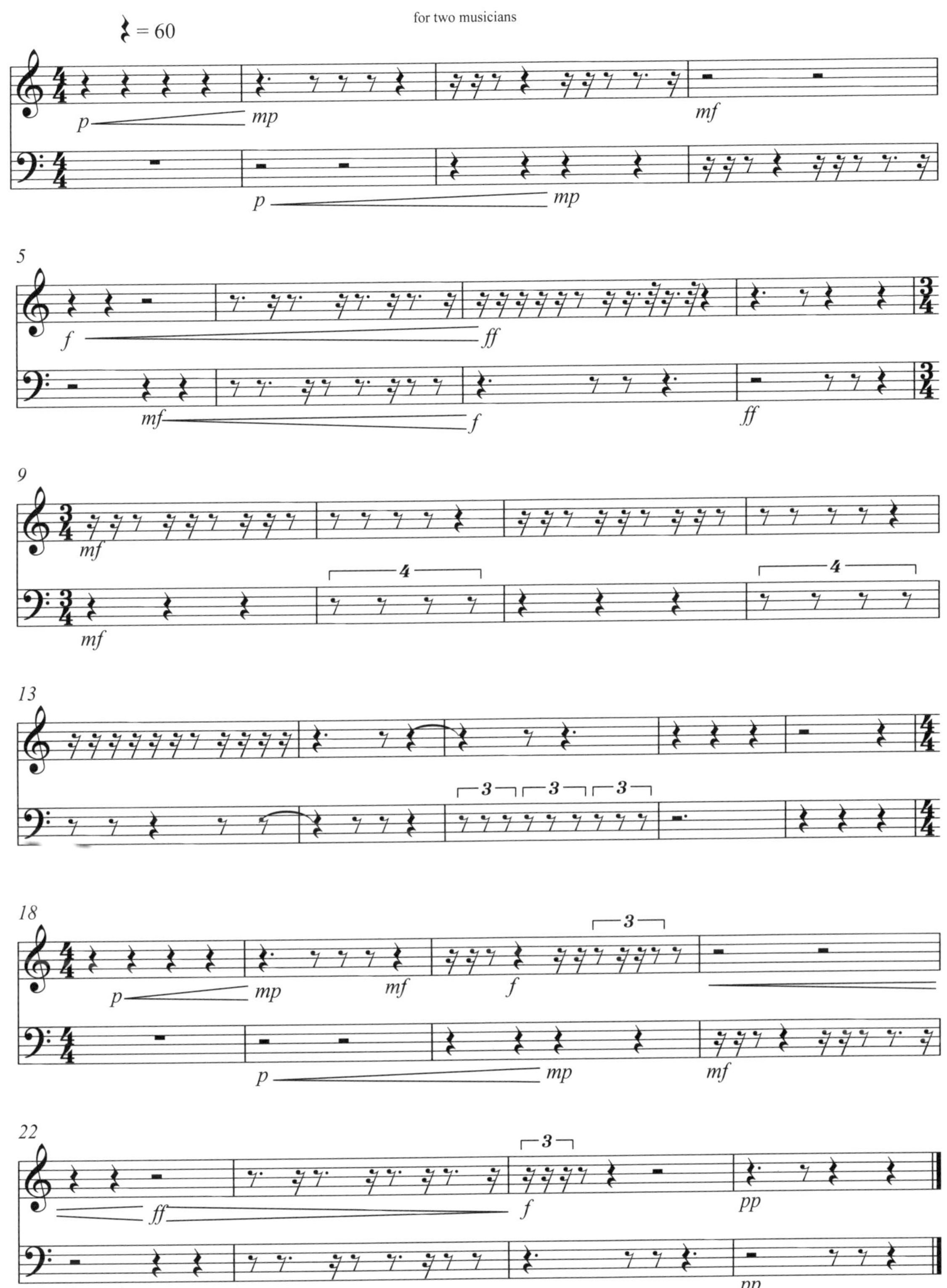

Dylan Robinson and
Patrick Nickleson

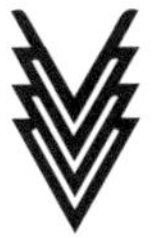

Notational Relations

One of the earliest memories I (Dylan) have of a conversation with Raven Chacon is about Western notation. I was talking with him about the Native American Composers Apprenticeship Project (NACAP), a project he joined in 2004 and where he has worked as a mentor for Native composers since. Knowing some of his graphic scores, I assumed that this was the primary foundation for his work with Native youth. I assumed that graphic notation allowed a form of expression untethered to the exclusivity of Western notation (among many other forms of Western theory and history) imposed upon many Indigenous musicians when they enter formal (Western) music training. Raven was quick to correct me, and note how the majority of what he teaches in NACAP is Western notation as a tool for Indigenous composers to express their ideas. As he has written elsewhere since that early conversation of ours, "I am a believer in the five-line staff, even though it is a Western tradition and it's something that most of the world doesn't follow or need for their music to exist. I do think it's still one of the best ways to relay to a musician what to play, as a visual marker for pitch and time. On the other end of that, there are a lot of things that standard notation can't do, and that's why one uses graphic notation or text."[1] That is, Western notation is a tool—one among many—that we as Indigenous people can adapt to suit our needs, that is not irredeemably oppressive, and does not need to limit the expression of our values as Indigenous people.

The false binary between Indigenous resurgence (privileging the specific Indigenous values held by our communities) and Western artistic practices and epistemologies has often reified commitments to mutual exclusivity. Mutual exclusion is, here, itself one of the most pernicious structures of settler colonialism that takes all of us out of relationship. To use Western music notation (or any other Western, Euro-American forms) does not need to mean adopting its practice or

1 Raven Chacon, "Contrary Motions: Raven Chacon in dialogue with Michael Nardone," *OEI*, no. 98–99: "Aural Poetics" (2023): 41.

associated value system wholesale; Indigenous people have always familiarized ourselves with and adapted Western tools in order to serve our purposes and aid our communities. Conversely, adapting Western notation to express Indigenous values, ideas, and histories is also not—in and of itself—subversive. Such adaptation can of course be used to put the normative ideological underpinnings of Western art music and its performance (mastery, invariance, genius ...) into contrapuntal relationship with other forms of relationality itself. In Chacon's scored work, much of the interest is in the clashing, noisy variance as a "Western" tool is used (maybe at least a little subversively) to animate a Navajo cosmology and ontology of music that is rarely if ever announced as such.

Whereas Dylan and Raven's first conversations centered upon forms of notation, I (Patrick) was keen to discuss with him his work as a noise performer, something I first heard live at a conference at Cornell University in 2018 organized by Benjamin Piekut and Jeremy Strachan. When I got the chance to ask Chacon about the relationship between his graphic scores and his noise music, I was struck by the description of his work as falling into several material practices. Alongside live performance (solo and with a number of collaborators) and running his record label, Sicksicksick Distro, Chacon told me that a key part of his practice is "making scores." Making scores is decidedly not, or not *just*, the normative Euro-American labor of "composing." The materiality of Chacon's scores—as we will show below, they are made objects or texts, and not transparent communiques—is key to how they serve their purpose as relational texts holding together new, novel, and generous interpersonal relationships. Dylan's invitation to co-write this essay was thus an opportunity to explore a variety of relationships: most immediately Chacon's relationship to scores, yes, but also Dylan and Patrick's ongoing collaborative writing practice, and our different and differently complex relationships with the institutions of Western art music.

On Relationship and Alignment

The Western art music score, like everything else, is founded on relationships, but it elides and refuses just as many as it might recognize. The normative relationships in play are sounding ones—harmonic, contrapuntal, and instrumental—that attempt, as much as possible, to obscure the social role of musicians in their production of music. For the performers in a professional orchestra, dressed in their "concert black," there is certainly a relationship between "Violin I" and "Oboe II." Any member would have an expansive vocabulary to describe that relationship through formal devices, harmonic syntax, timbral coloration, and textural interrelation. But everything about the orchestra—from its members' childhood training to the insti-

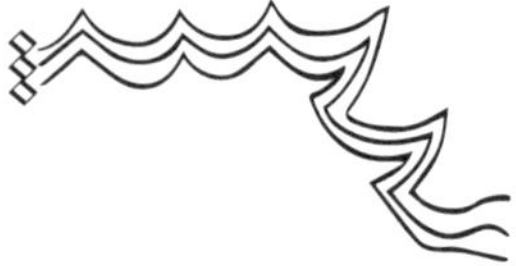

tution's centuries-old architecture—is designed to ensure that no one would ever describe their relationship as one of proximity, on a stage, in the same building, working together toward a shared goal.

In contrast to this, as Chacon has himself noted, "what I am fundamentally interested in are the dynamics of the musicians in a context: who they are, where they are geographically, the specific site in which they are performing, and the history of that site and its surrounding geography."[2] That is, Chacon is interested in that which Western art music performance typically seeks to disavow through the darkened concert hall, the de-particularization of musicians' individuality and positionality through uniformity of dress and placement, and the ways in which creative agency is restricted to a narrow range of musical choices.

As an example, in *Music for 13 Paths* (2021), thirteen chimes are "put into the **stewardship** of thirteen performers" (bolding in original throughout). The performers of thirteen chimes are asked to "self-organize themselves into a path." After various processions to different sites where performers are asked to become familiar with the pitch of their own chime "isolated as well as **in relation** to any other audible chime," they are asked to exchange their chime "with another performer at least once, and must accept an exchange if initiated by another performer." The performance concludes with the performers gathering and exchanging chimes until they find their original chime. When all "have become **reunited** with their chime" they must hold their chime high and ring them "as loud as possible as a **family**," as the "final stewardship" of the chimes.

If Chacon's choice of language for these performance instructions does not give us pause to consider the relationships between individuals and their "instruments," then the added emphasis of bolding should itself ring out with a kind of chime-like clarity. Musicians are not often explicitly asked to take on a stewardship relation to their instrument. While there is often a care and love (or at times "love/hate") relationship to one's instrument, "stewardship" here calls for a kind of responsibility paired with care that is also implicated with the way this term has come to index a much larger discourse of Indigenous relationships to land against the Western imperative of property ownership. Stewardship can also imply a nonpermanent and nonexclusive orientation toward care. What does it mean, Chacon asks, to take on the role of steward for an instrument—for a care toward its sounding and relations as part of or among "family"? Without wanting to overlay a false equivalency of human life onto these chimes, Chacon's score asks us to consider the intricacies of the overlapping relationship to our "own" and other sound, to the human stewards of those sounds, and to the places we traverse while sounding together. *Music for 13 Paths* is here an important example of what Chacon calls "aligning" in

2 Ibid.: 36.

3 Ibid.: 37.

4 Cf. ibid.: 35–36.

his compositional practice. Speaking about another piece (*Compass*, 2021), he notes his central concern with "reading the pulses and paces of the world around us ... we can read these things, we can be a part of them and then respond, and the alignment of the musician with the rest of the world is what creates the music."[3] "Aligning with the rest of the world" here includes other individuals, as well as recognizing points of disalignment (or what Chacon might also call "counterpoint").[4]

On the Mimicry Scores

Just this sort of (dis)alignment was a recurring feature of many of Chacon's early scores, particularly those that explore mimicry as a rote and rotational device to build up an extended form from extremely simple instructions. *Mirror Quintet* (2004), written for five violinists, provides a compelling example. The initiating Performer A "plays a note or a series of notes lasting 1–3 seconds." Performer B is directed not to listen to the first, but to *watch* "this (physical and musical) action" and recreate the sound "**exactly** as played." Performers C through E are asked to do the same, following not on from Performer A, but the performer prior to them. What might recall the children's game "broken telephone" is in fact more subtle when taking place in public. Rather than holding Performer A and Performer E in comparison and judging what level of fidelity was achieved in the transmission, the reproductions continue onward "for any duration." The piece requests and imagines the labor of reproducing not only the pitched, rhythmic, and timbral subtleties of another musician (something most professional musicians are well practiced in), but their physical carriage and gesture in doing so. Even describing the effort is exhausting. Still, as in all of Chacon's scores, we know that the slippages are the point—a prompt to develop a practiced empathy whereby the slight shifts and modulations produce interest. To be clear, Chacon's scores require a commitment to render what is on the page just as precisely as any score, but the social actions and relationality that result from this commitment are of equal importance to the sounds produced.

Other scores follow similar models musically, in using mimicry to create form, while differently narrating space and relationality; across these scores, Chacon has settled on a formal model but is exploring its potential in spatialized relationships. In *Echo Contest* (2005), two performers are "separated by a distance" that is ever expanding and contracting as a result of sharply contrasting directions. While both performers carry forward the ongoing, incomplete attempt to mimic the altered iterations of Performer A's original offering, a spatial dimension is added. Performer B attempts to move closer to Performer A each time they hear the call, while Performer A tries always to expand the distance while remaining audible.

The "Contest" of the title is well chosen. It's hard to imagine this working particularly well as a performance for an audience—a crowd following Performer A around would surely give away their position—but it serves as a powerful challenge to normative training in aural skills. Against the perfected, lab-like conditions passively imagined in listening curricula, *Echo Contest* imagines listening at a distance, while in motion, out in the world. Beyond the effort to reproduce and locate sounds, the performers are forced to move through space in pursuit and escape, producing a more relational, engaged, and productively distracted take on the normative soundwalk. Experienced from the outside, or from a bird's-eye view, the two performers would spiral around each other, locked together in a magnetic push and pull without a center or order.

The mimicry work seems to originate in the 2001 *Whistle Quartet*, for four performers with dog whistles. Each member is asked to "duet" with (or rather replicate in unison) Performer 1's melodic line. The work strikes, more than any other, as "early" Chacon: as a predecessor to the later openness to changing, mimetic reiteration, *Whistle Quartet* directs performers to "improve with each repeat until you match the ability of the leader." Unlike *Echo Contest* (but like broken telephone), *Whistle Quartet* thus implies something like an ideal fidelity, of performing in replicated identity with the leader who is, at least passively, implied to be in charge.

The piece also has a kind of punk rock conceptualist bent. Tucked into the bottom right corner of the page are three words: "DURATION: ALL NIGHT." The piece thus plays with the taboo, present in many parts of the world, including southwestern Native communities, on whistling at night.

The work blends a provocative flip on tradition with a conceptualist challenge directly out of a musico-philosophical provocation—does an inaudible dog whistle break the taboo in the same way that an audible whistle does? Whether this registers as a disembodied riddle or a clear breach of grounded community ethics certainly depends on one's positionality. Even as a riddle, this should not be heard as a Cagean provocation, as Chacon has repeatedly criticized two fundamental, underlying conceptions in experimental music: Cage's conception of silence, and what Chacon calls the privilege of deep listening as framed by Pauline Oliveros. In his early *Duet* (2000) for two silent musicians, Chacon insists that it is not about the Cagean attention to "the ambient sounds that compose a supposed silence," but rather "the interactions that are possible between two people." Similarly, two decades later, his *Silent Choir (Standing Rock)* (2016/2022) is "the sound of 600 people on a cold day, quiet and still, staring at the police." The tension of such a moment moves well beyond its location within a supposed silence/noise binary that exceeds or subsumes the Euro-American ideal of music. More importantly, it extends to some-

5 Ibid.: 37–38.

thing more expansive, grounded, and relational than the kind of tourism that allows one the privilege to arrive somewhere and listen "deeply" to an environment as if it's external to one's own personhood and mode of relationality. "You can hear the presence of all of those people as a confrontation. You can hear the weight of them being silent."[5]

Chacon's mimicry form finds its most comprehensive statement in *Drum Grid* (2010). In place of silent whistles or a mobile chase, "numerous drummers" are positioned on street corners throughout a neighborhood to create a square or rectangle. "Beginning with a single drum hit from one player," the sound is then imitated as it travels around the grid. The sharp crack of a snare drum in residential open air leads Chacon to designate, for the first time in writing rather than by implication, the possibility of "misinterpret[ed] cues" and thus the growth of "false echoes and polyphony" as the sound travels faster and faster. In this work, watching is given a central role—each drummer has a guide that they must be able to see, though they do not need to be seen by them, creating a constant relay that runs its way along the rigid, straight lines of a North American road grid.

Works like *Drum Grid* highlight many important facets of Chacon's work: the availability to amateur performers, the use of outdoor space, and collective listening in an environment likely to produce (generative) *mis*-hearing. Like much chamber music, the mimicry works rely on small group relationships and careful, interpersonal listening; in stark contrast to much chamber music, these relationships are named, physically embodied, watched, and centered. The scores—not the "works," but the physical scores—enable this work, creating a shared, legible reference point even across mishearings and as sounds and performers chase each other through public space. As Chacon writes of *Drum Grid*, in these works "a community has agency to change the landscape of their neighborhood, activating potential questions and new generative urgencies."

On Writing Family

Chacon's focus on relationships and family, neighborhoods and land, becomes ever clearer in the twelve scores that make up *For Zitkála-Šá* (2017–20). Each score is written in dedication and response to the practice of an Indigenous woman that Chacon knows personally, as a family member, friend, or collaborator. Aligning himself in writing with Cheryl L'Hirondelle, Suzanne Kite, and others cements long, ongoing relationships for those aware of Chacon's practice. Once again, the book of scores recalls a theme already present in an earlier work, *Scream Out of Each Window* (2005), which reads in full:

> For a family to perform,
> For as long as they want,

In a tall building,
On different levels, towards the same direction,
Scream out of each window.

As in many of his scores, the performing forces (a family) and the duration (as long as they want), are open enough to be broadly inclusive of any performance scenario, and yet specific enough to undermine normative convention in scored music, and thus feel singularly idiomatic to Chacon. The scream is a similarly recurring motif, particularly in Chacon's noise work, but the standout here is the location of performance: a tall building. Where so much of Chacon's work is explicitly grounded in its particular location and relationality, the tall building feels decidedly metaphorical—an institutional structure, whether a place of business, learning, or finance. A no-place rather than a particular place. As unique as the tall building is within Chacon's scored work, the act of screaming out of it with your (perhaps chosen) family provides compelling recognition of its place within Chacon's broader body of scored work.

And indeed, the *For Zitkála-Šá* scores address both chosen and born family. Among the many striking scores in the collection, the one that Chacon wrote for his sister Autumn stands out. The design resembles an orienting star carved out of graph paper, suggesting a surveyed and gridded landscape (as in *Drum Grid*). In the text, Chacon directs his sister, an artist who works with radio as a medium, to choose a territory and traverse it. Whenever she encounters a radio or a lamp, she is to turn it off if it's on, or on if it's off. Once she has crossed the territory and all of the radios and lamps are on or off, she is asked to sing a song about her travels.

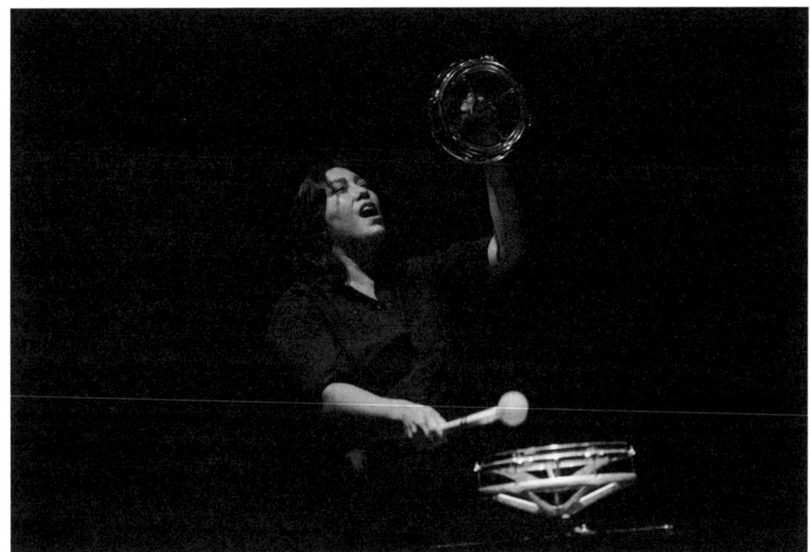

Ange Loft performs *For Ange Loft* from the series *For Zitkála-Šá* at the Whitney Biennial, Whitney Museum of American Art, New York, 2022

The score provides a powerful image—within the domain of scored music, music pedagogy, music institutions, musical performance—of a decolonial theory of change. One perspective on Autumn's labor might read it as tedious or net-zero, insufficiently radical or without enough emphasis on land and rematriation: all the radios and all the lamps being off or on hardly seems a drastic statement about turning the world upside down. Another perspective, though, would recognize that, as she sings her song, the chosen terrain would have been entirely remade: the same place and time, but newly vibrating and marked in every instance by Autumn's travels and inversions. Each and every thing remains in its place, though newly

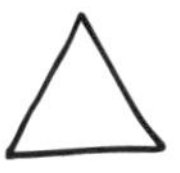

marked by a modality of interrelation and labor that generates major change, and even historicizes it in song, without extraction, theft, enclosure, or violence. Like Chacon's scores generally, "For Autumn Chacon" models the "undercommon" resources already available to us for producing change—we do not need to abandon "the score," but to reckon with how it has historically led us to foster relationships of exclusion, extraction, and hierarchy. Sedimenting these abusive relationships in a single genre of document and casting it out of our midst marks a failure to acknowledge and repair these historical (and ongoing) failures.

Chacon has asserted that many of his compositions have been written "primarily as an experience for the people who are performing them. They are all about creating relationships between the musicians." Indeed, often to the point that "the audience is sometimes understood as secondary to the process."[6] Commitment to performance is certainly of major consequence to the event originating in the score. But perhaps most importantly, the total event that results from the audience and performers committing to come together is of an interest equal to the "music itself."

For us, both working in university music studies departments still often oriented around the transparent score and its imperious "realization," Chacon's work relocates the score—holds onto an existing resource, flipping it toward productive new ends—by theorizing rather than disavowing the physical interrelationships that are inherently and obviously present from the outset. Perhaps most importantly, his name now encircles the fact that attacking *the* score as the enemy in an expanded, more inclusive music curriculum, is too simplistic. It is not the fault of notation, a tool, that Western art music's institutions have been remade, over and over, as white institutions of settler coloniality; it is the real, material relationships that we reproduce around scores over and over every day. We think here, in conclusion, of two model instances of Chacon precisely though indirectly staging the problem. In the score for *Journey of the Horizontal People* (2017), Chacon notes his preference that the string quartet that performs the work contain a female-identifying player who will serve as "the *guide* when all others are lost." He continues, "If there is not a female player in the quartet"—a very real possibility in many of the world's major string quartets—"the eldest man will guide, or the man who most identifies as a woman." Alongside this requirement, a few years later Chacon doubled down on his challenge to classical musicians to diversify their community. "Getting a lot of invitations to speak to music composition classes," Chacon tweeted on August 17, 2022, a few months after winning the Pulitzer Prize for his *Voiceless Mass*, "I can't participate unless your class is at least 50% women and 50% POC." Reaction was immediate and often quite negative from composition students and teachers (and whoever

6 Ibid.: 45.

else feels the need to engage in battles for equity that have nothing to do with them), noting that probably none of the composition classes in North America, if not the globe, would meet that demand. ("Guess I should've added a trigger warning to this," Chacon joked a few hours later.)

And indeed, the *Voiceless Mass* itself has been a cite of contrapuntal relation for Chacon and the institutions involved in promoting, recognizing, and hosting his music. The piece is meant to be performed in a church with a pipe organ, but its program notes are explicitly critical of the Catholic church's involvement in colonization and residential schools. Indeed, it is critical of the superficial efforts by institutions of settler coloniality to "give voice" without ceding power; Chacon writes that the piece "considers the futility of giving voice to the voiceless, when ceding space is never an option for those in power." Programming the work is thus no small demand on the churches who have hosted it or might host it in the future. But then again, we're in a changing climate for what, in our country of Canada, is officially called "reconciliation." Only two months after *Voiceless Mass* won the Pulitzer Prize in May 2022, the Pope's official apology to Residential School Survivors across Canada in July of that year actualized the piece's urgent form of staged self-critique. Even, still, when the Future Stops festival in Toronto gave *Voiceless Mass* its second performance on September 30, 2022, the presenters took the score's request that the work be performed on a church organ as an optional staging choice rather than a core element of the work's grounded critique. Perhaps because of the prestige value for the Toronto Symphony Orchestra, the piece was staged at its home venue, Roy Thomson Hall, while most of the festival's performances—by Kara-Lis Cloverdale, Sarah Davachi, Charlemagne Palestine, and others—took place on famed organs at the Cathedral of St. James or the Metropolitan United Church. The score itself is relatively conventional, at least by Chacon's standards; but in its concise critique the piece once again expands the plane on which the interpersonal dynamics of "Western art music" take place, this time to the level of patronage, presentation, and programming.

In Chacon's varied artistic practice, the score is multiply coded. It requests nonmusical action; it is a form of transcribing the world as it is and extending other possibilities; it is a matrix for reflection on existing relationships and calling forth new ones. Perhaps most importantly, Chacon's work highlights that we could alternately recognize all *scores* in their multiplicity as naming and drawing out complex interpersonal relationships. We only need to provide them the space and capacity to generate new relationships, rather than expecting them to reassert existing ones.

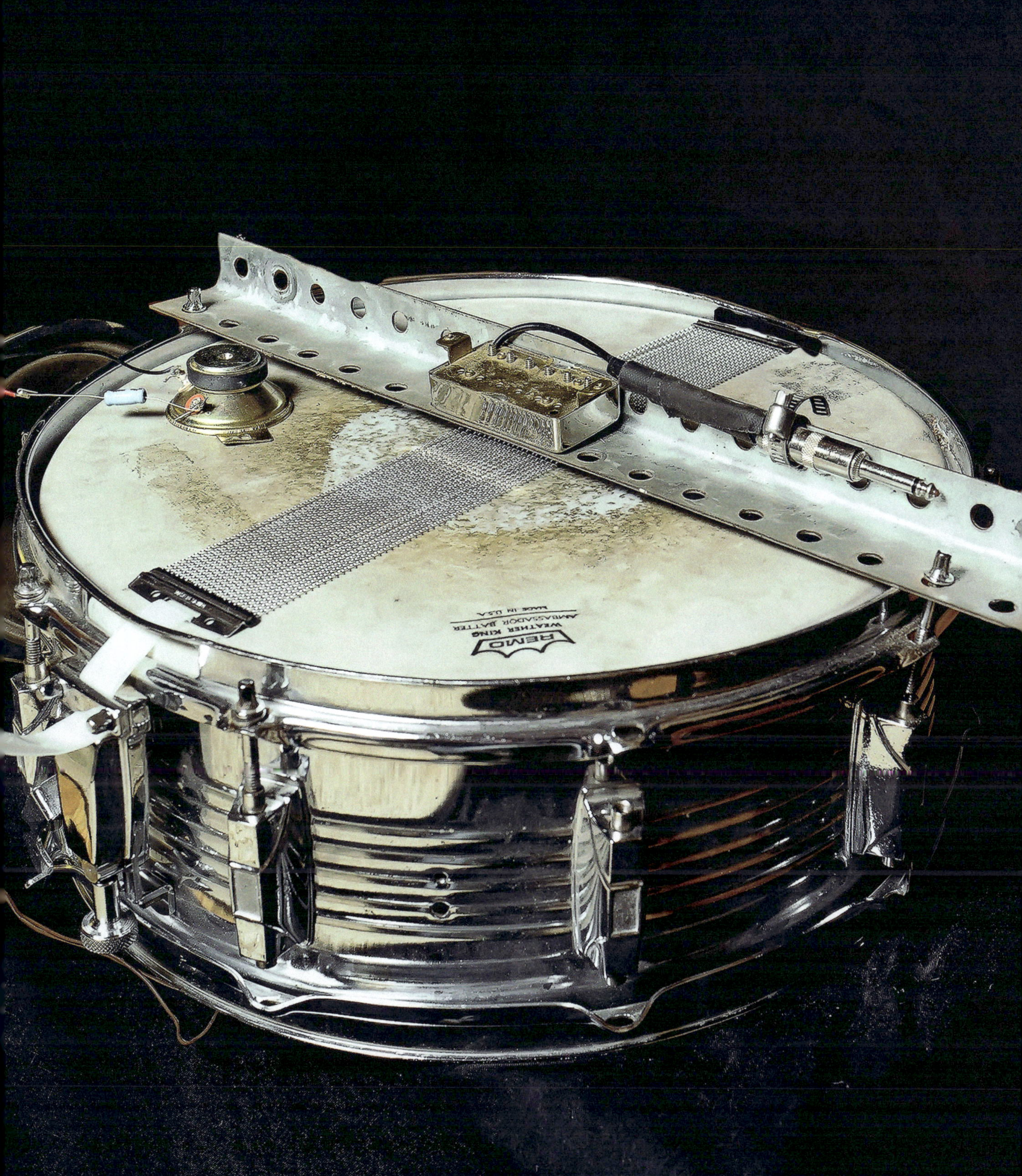

2002 *Feedback Drum*

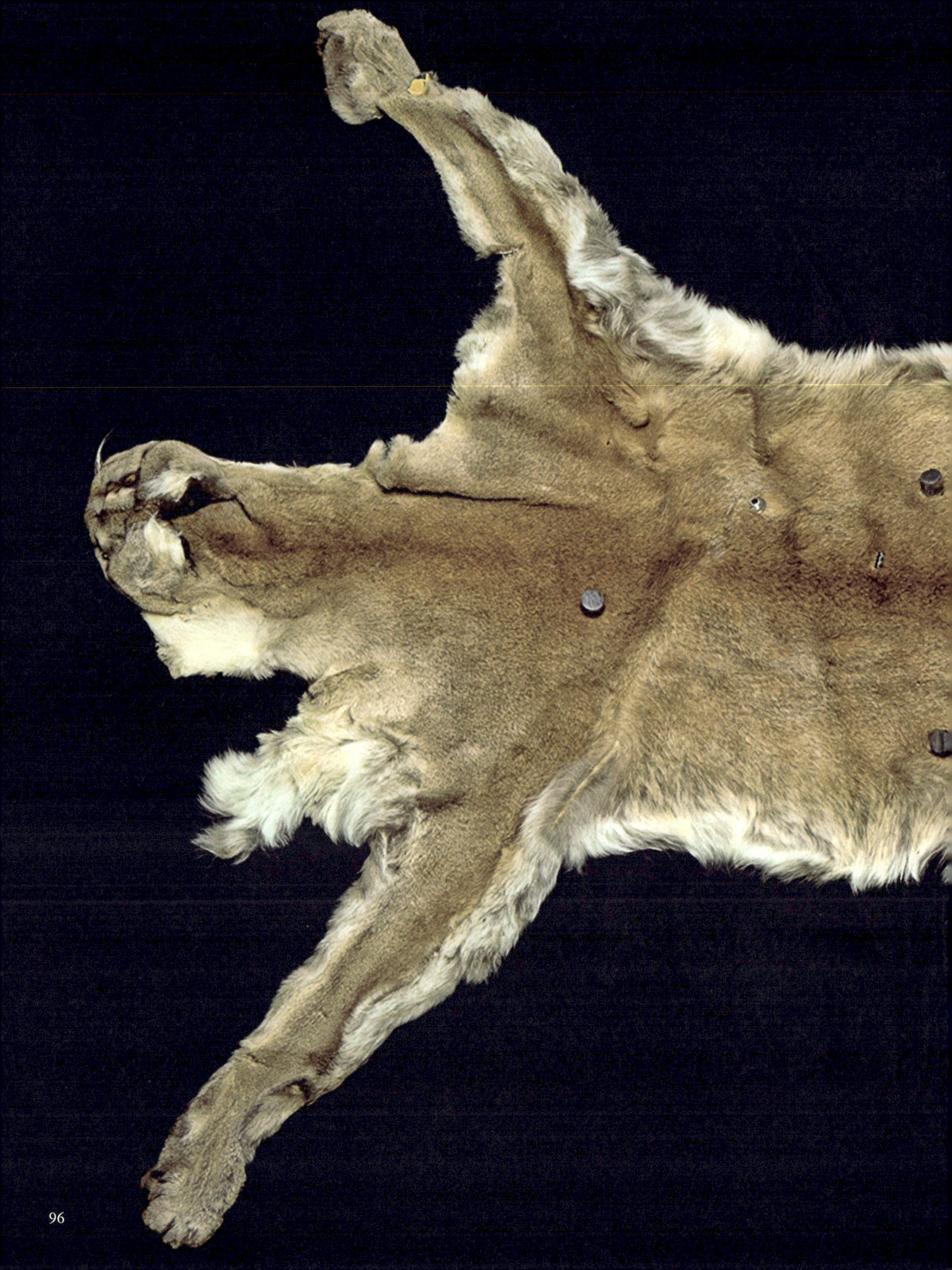

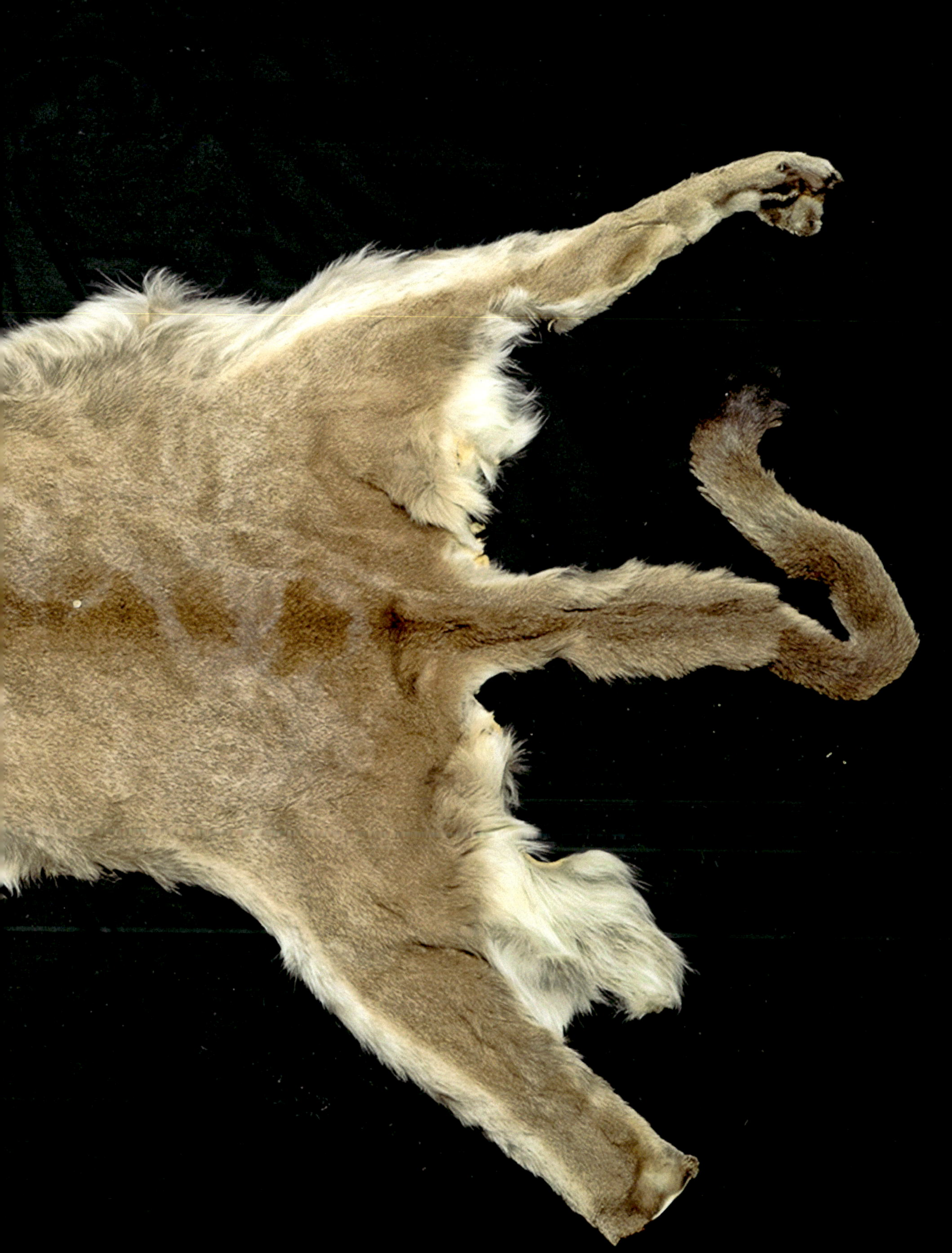

2011 *Cougar Pelt Synth* from Postcommodity's *Mother, Teacher, Destroyer*

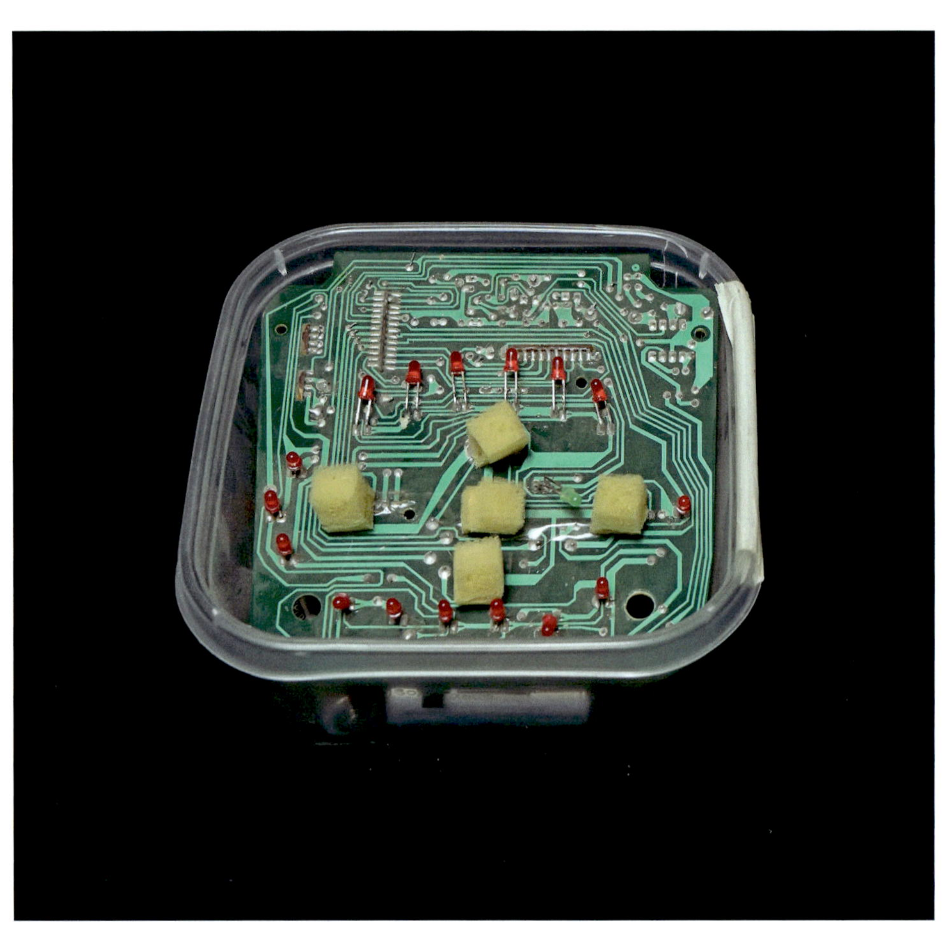

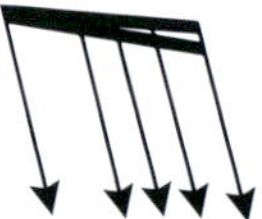

Untitled (circuit bent sleep machine)

2006

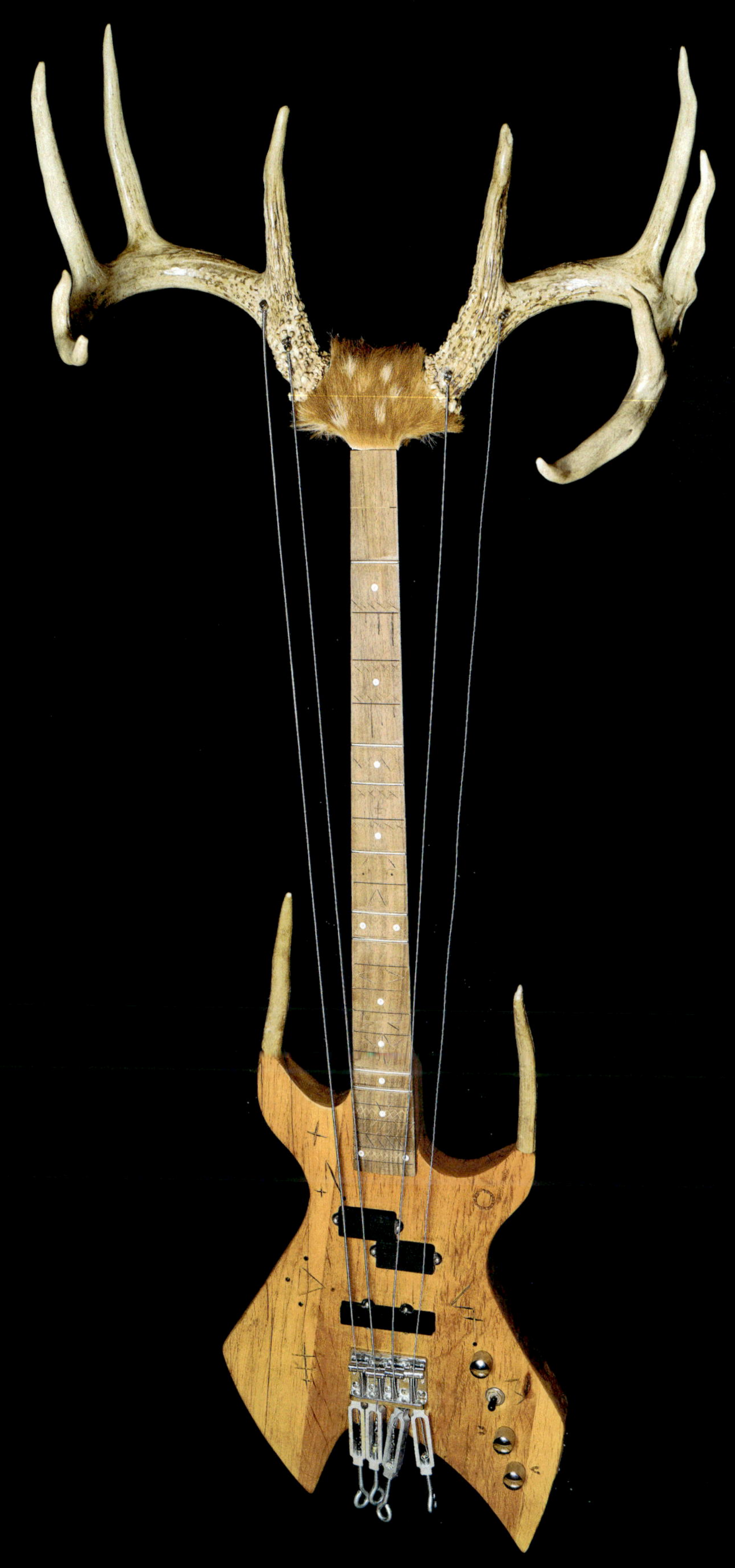

2011 *Antler Cello*, from Postcommodity's *Mother, Teacher, Destroyer*

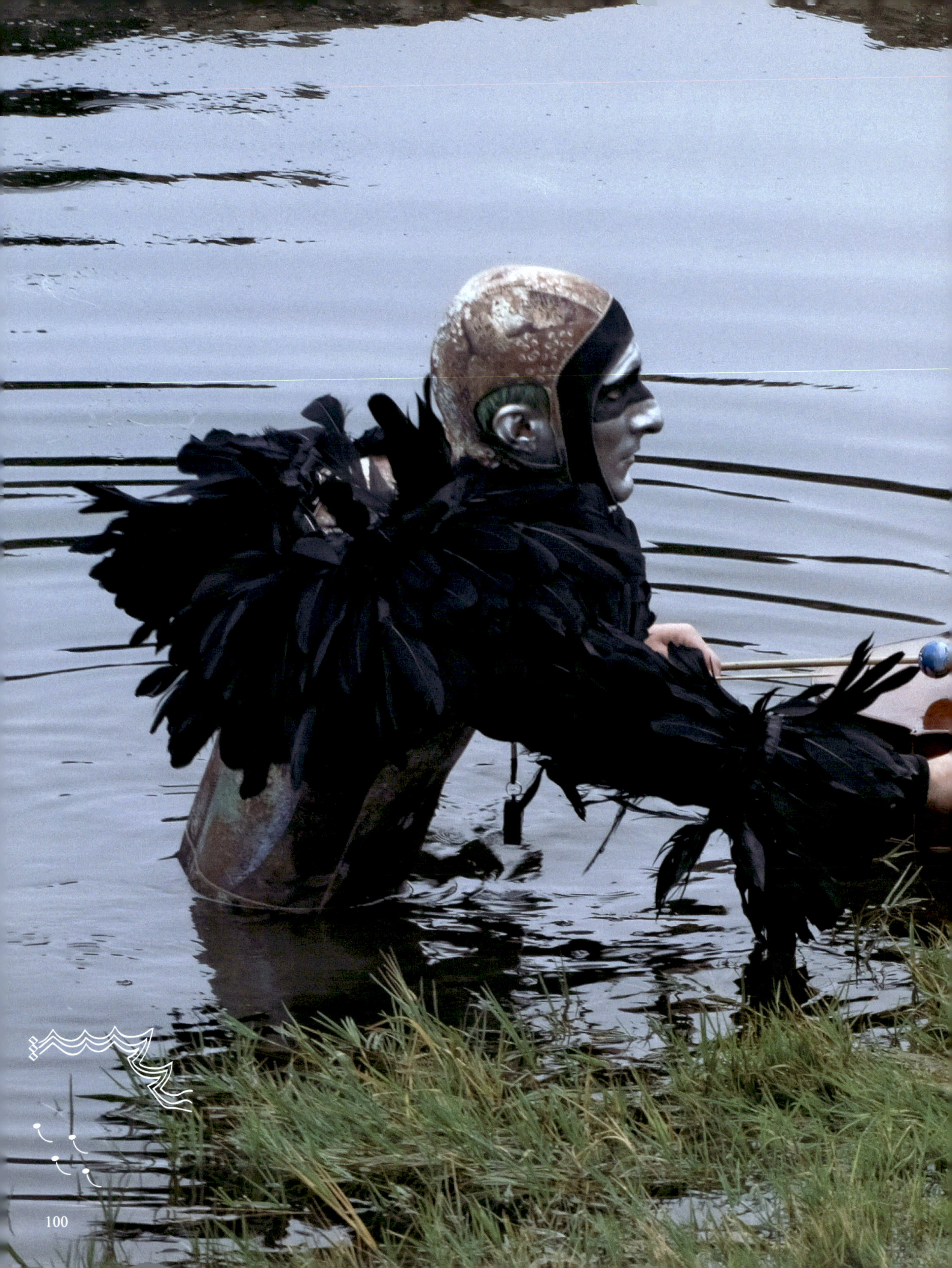

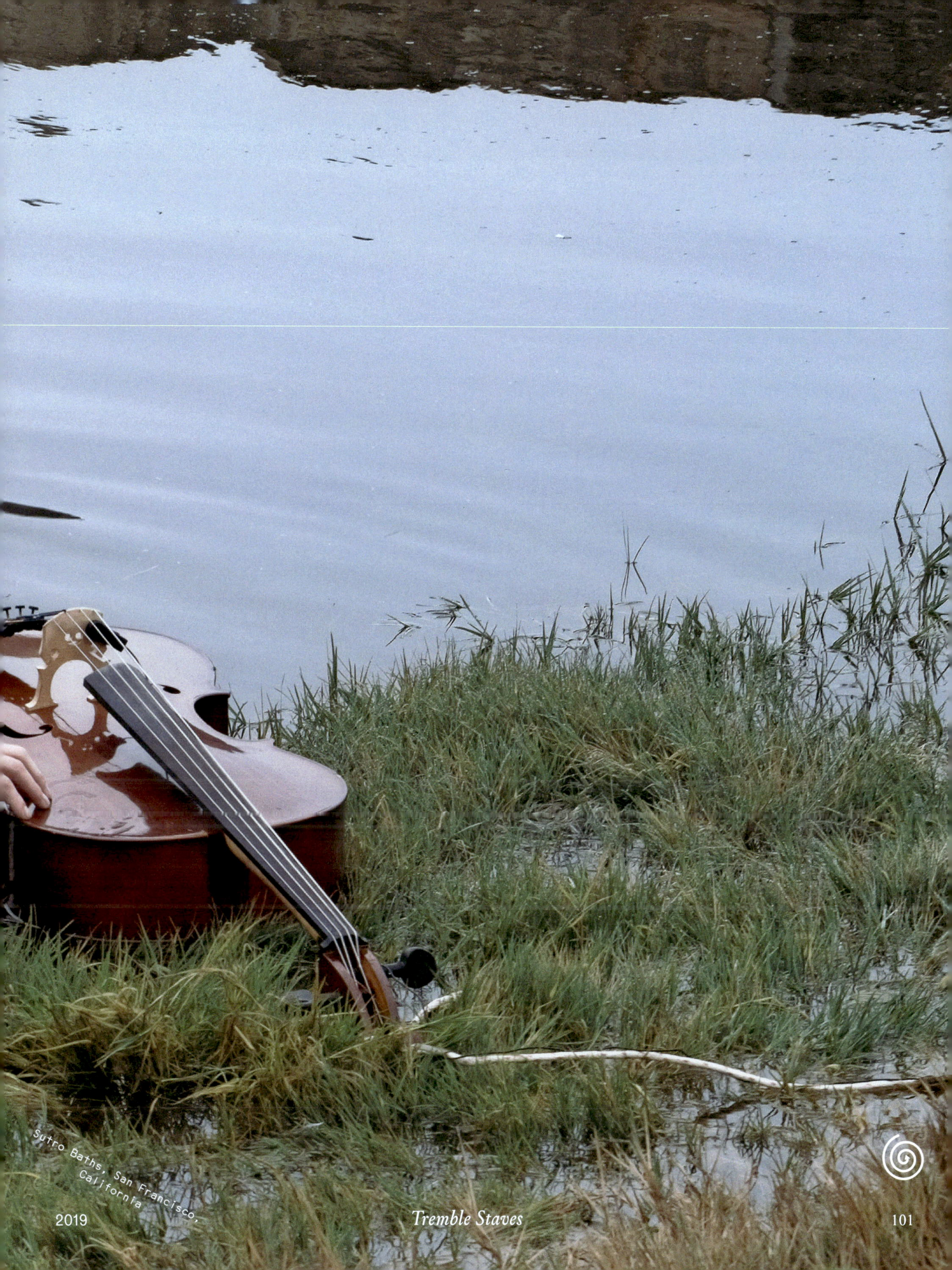

Sutro Baths, San Francisco, California

2019

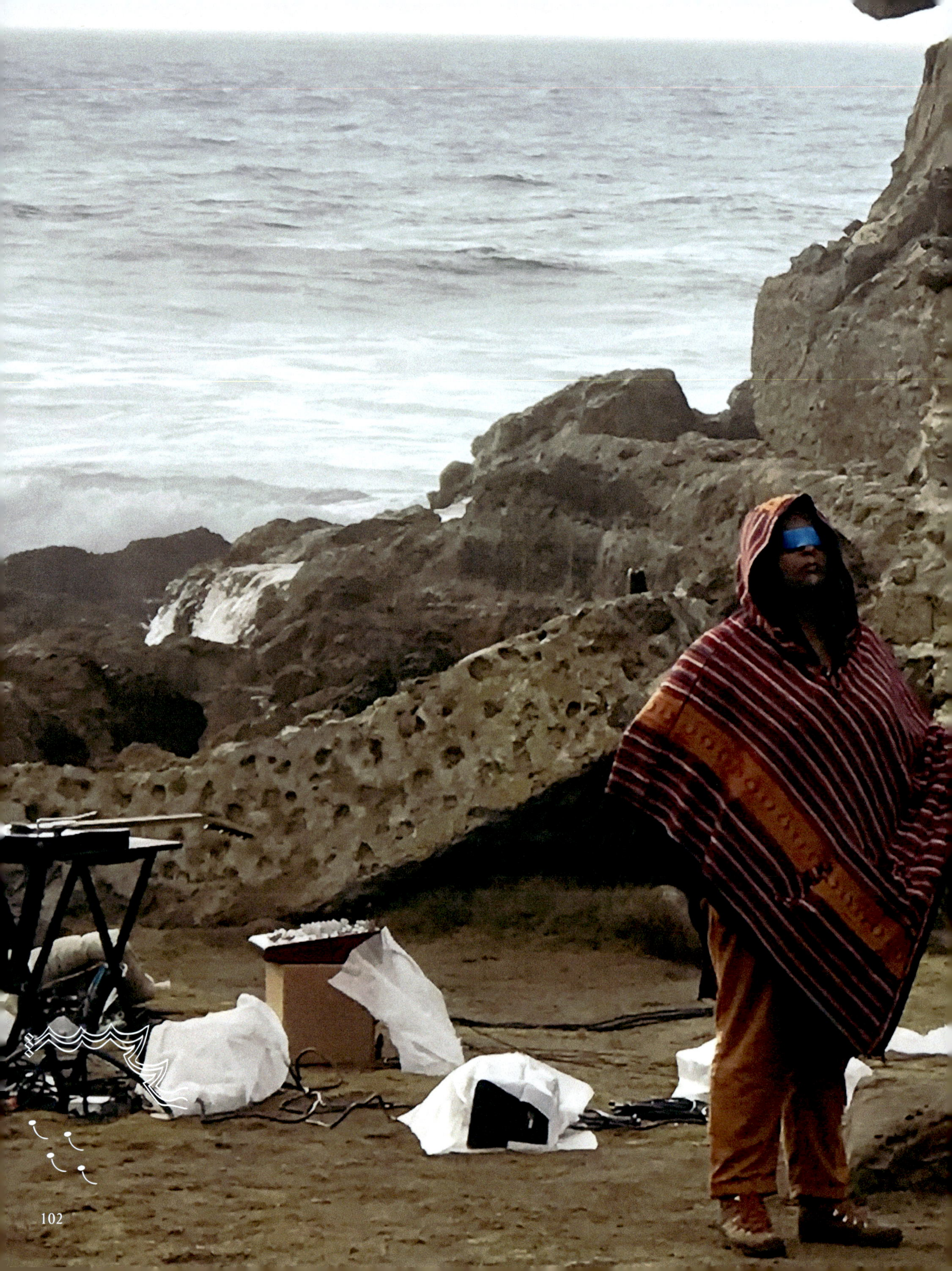

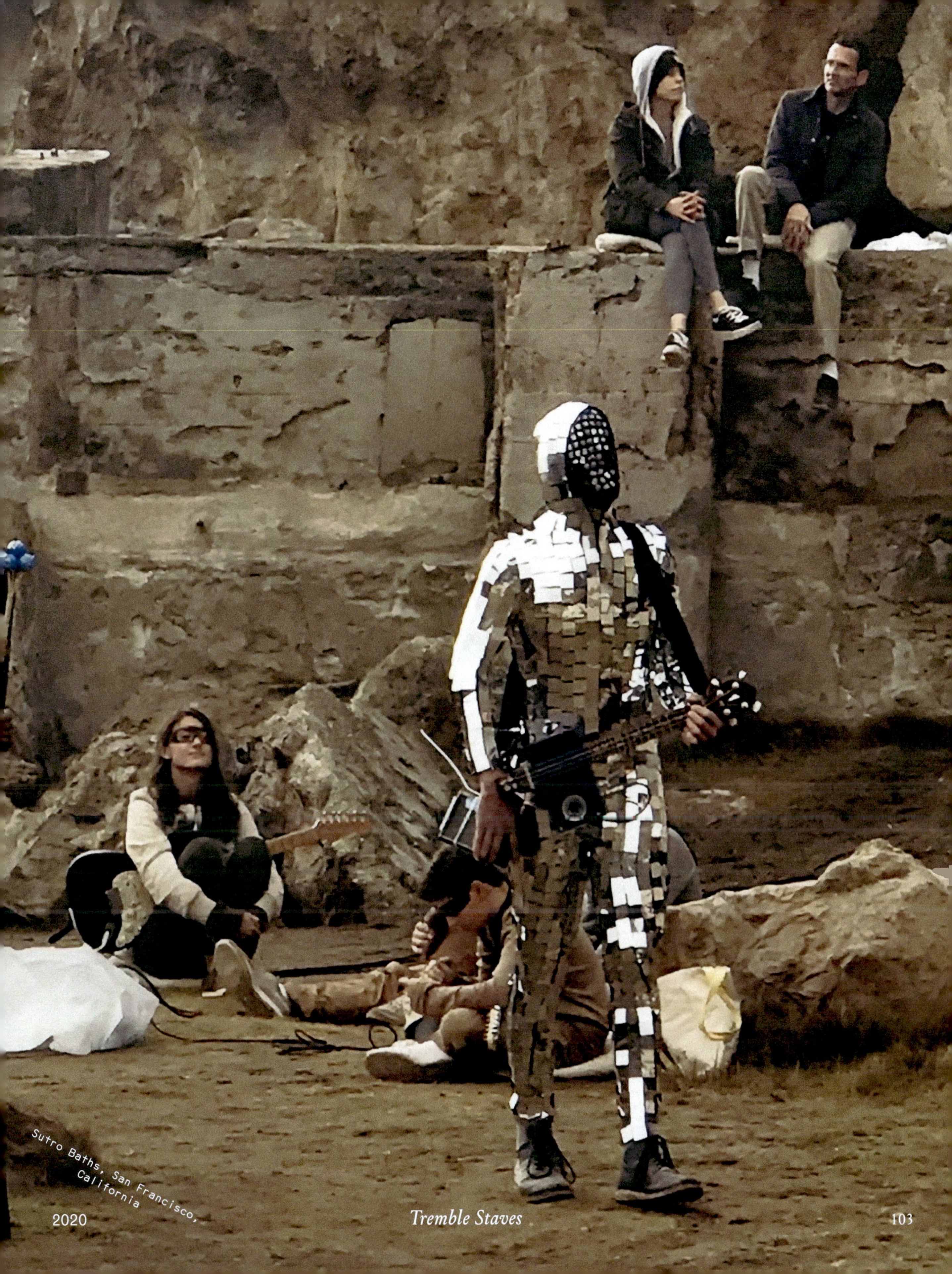

Sutro Baths, San Francisco, California

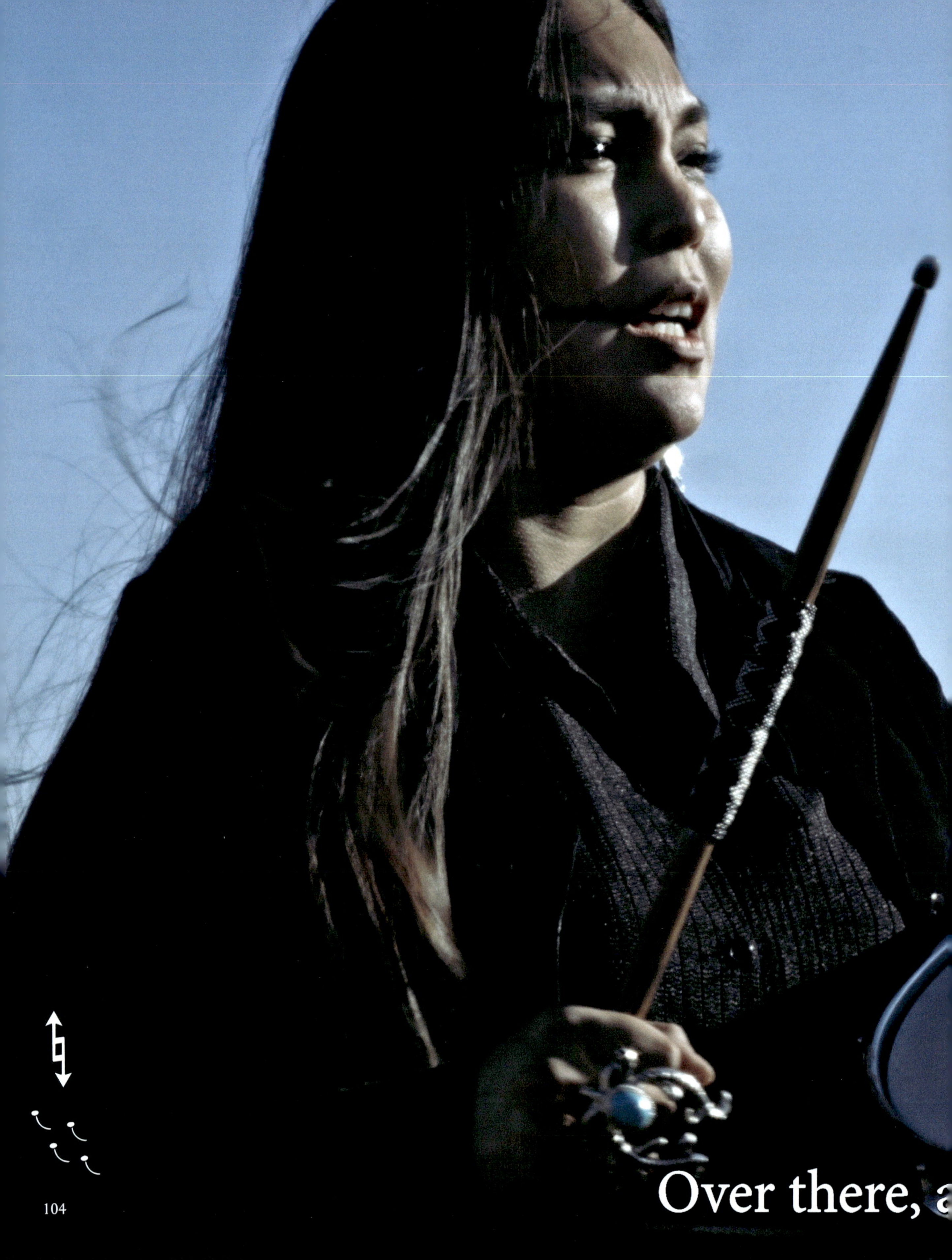

Over there, a

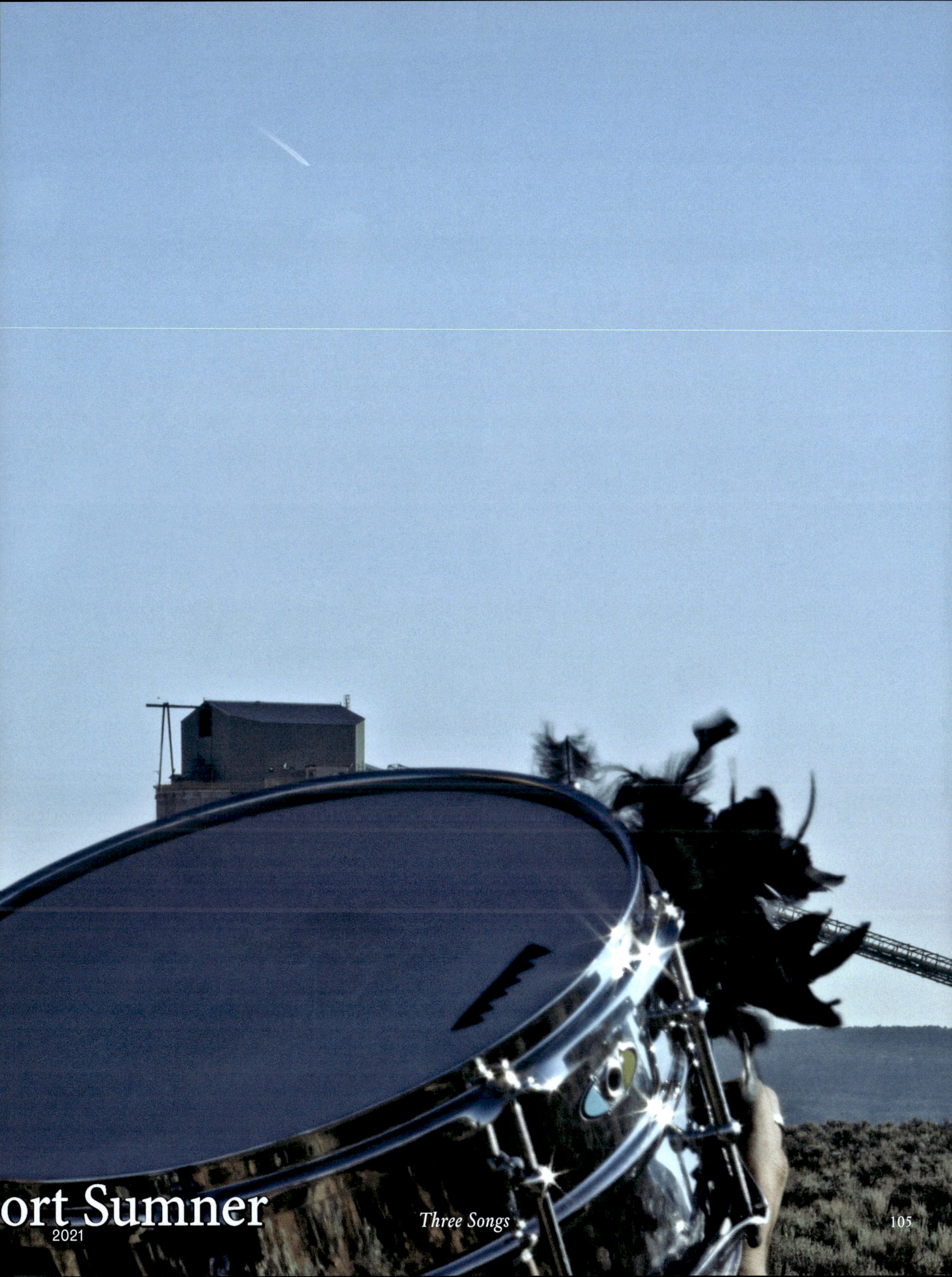

ort Sumner
2021

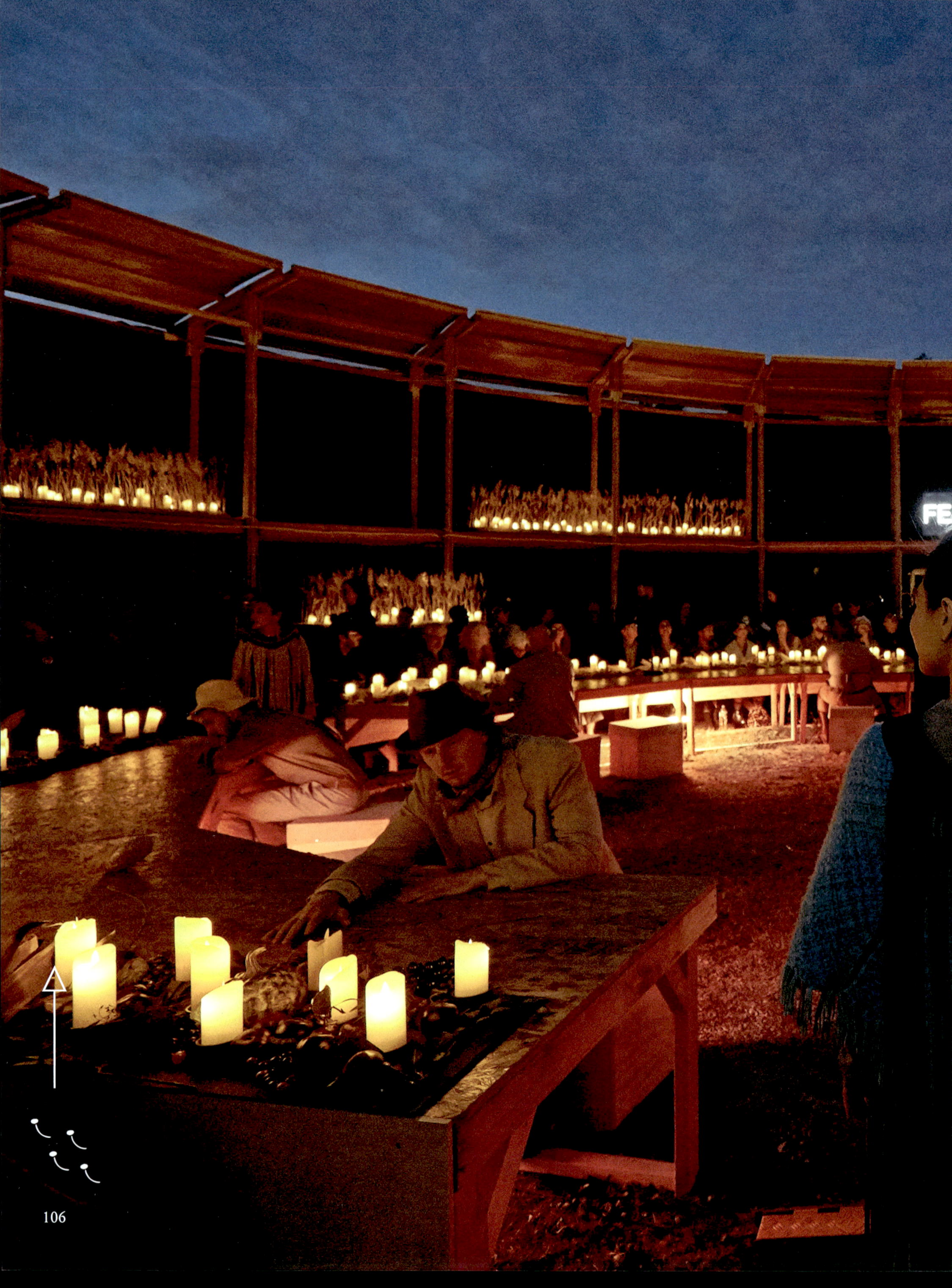

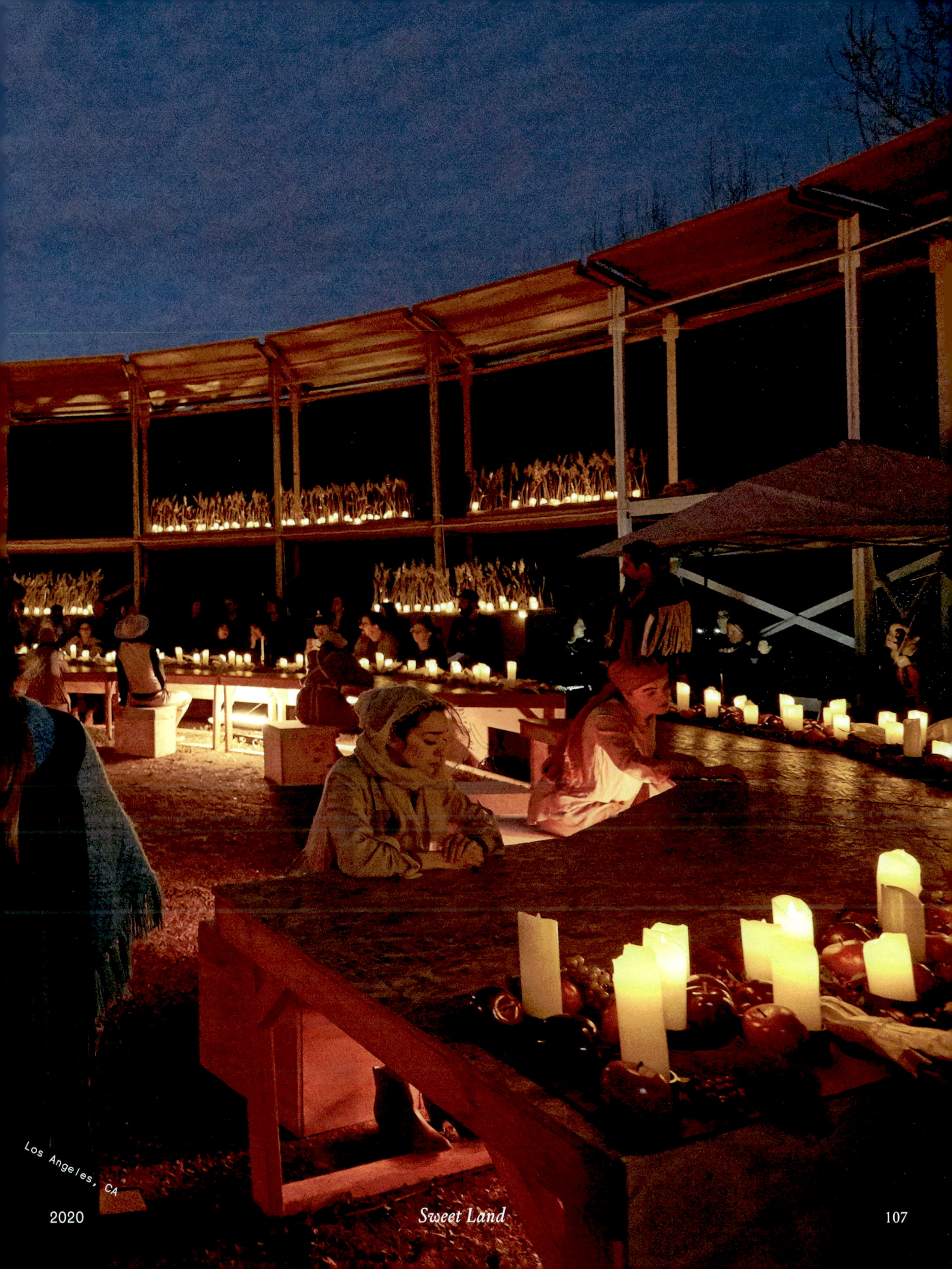
Los Angeles, CA

A lucky break
fro

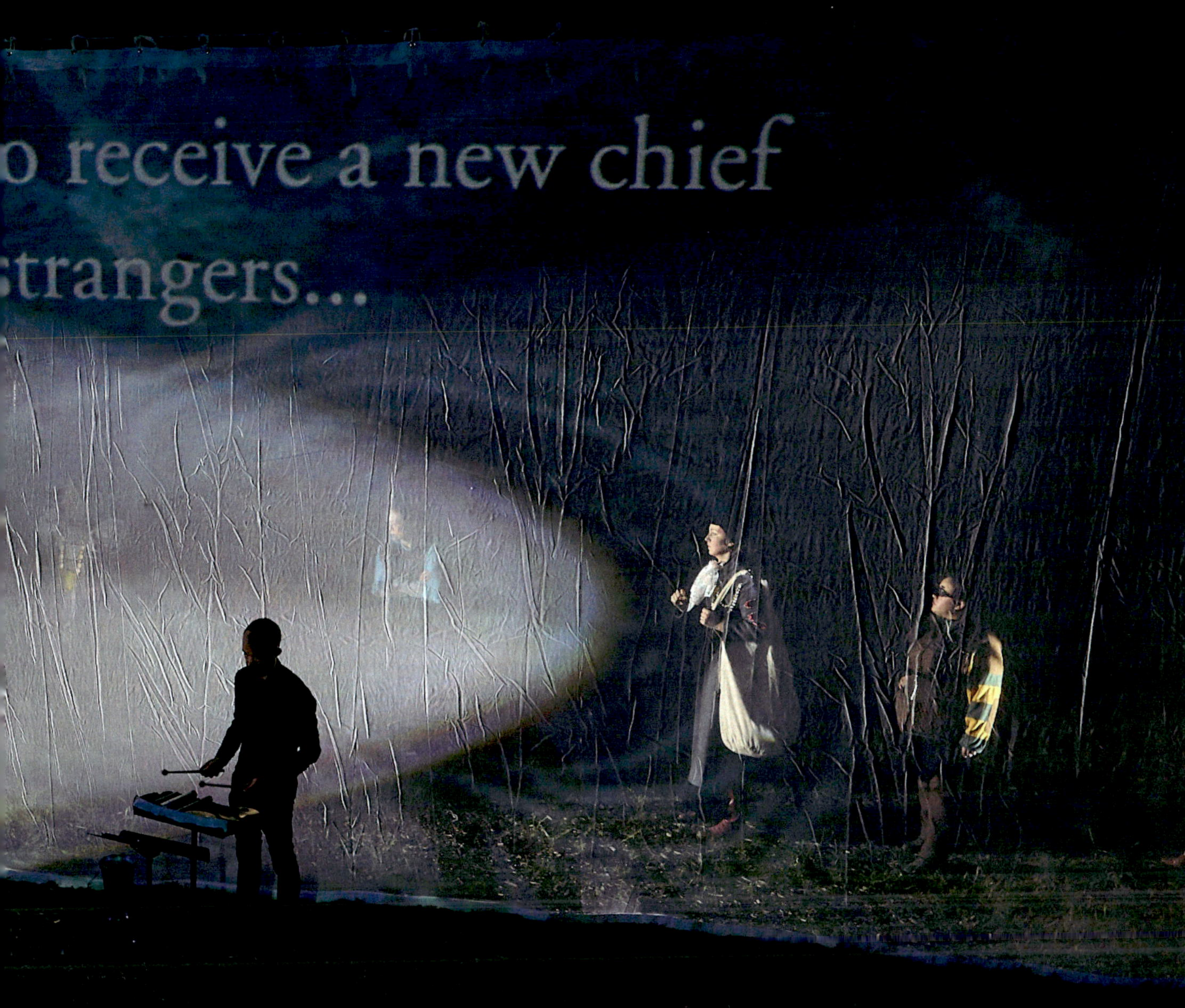

Los Angeles, CA

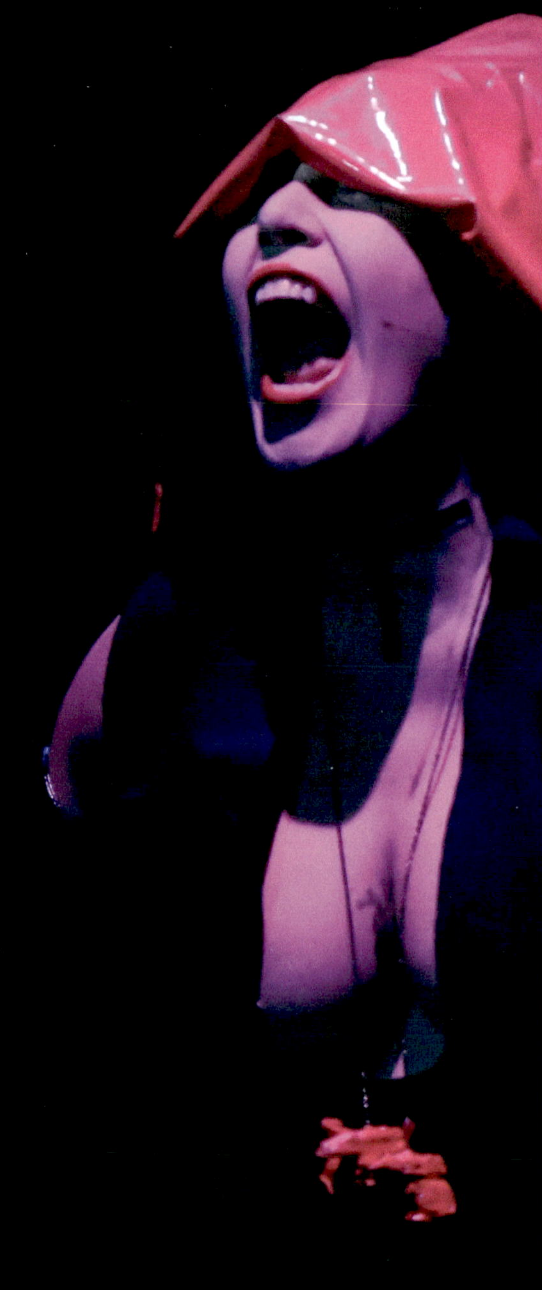

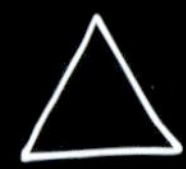

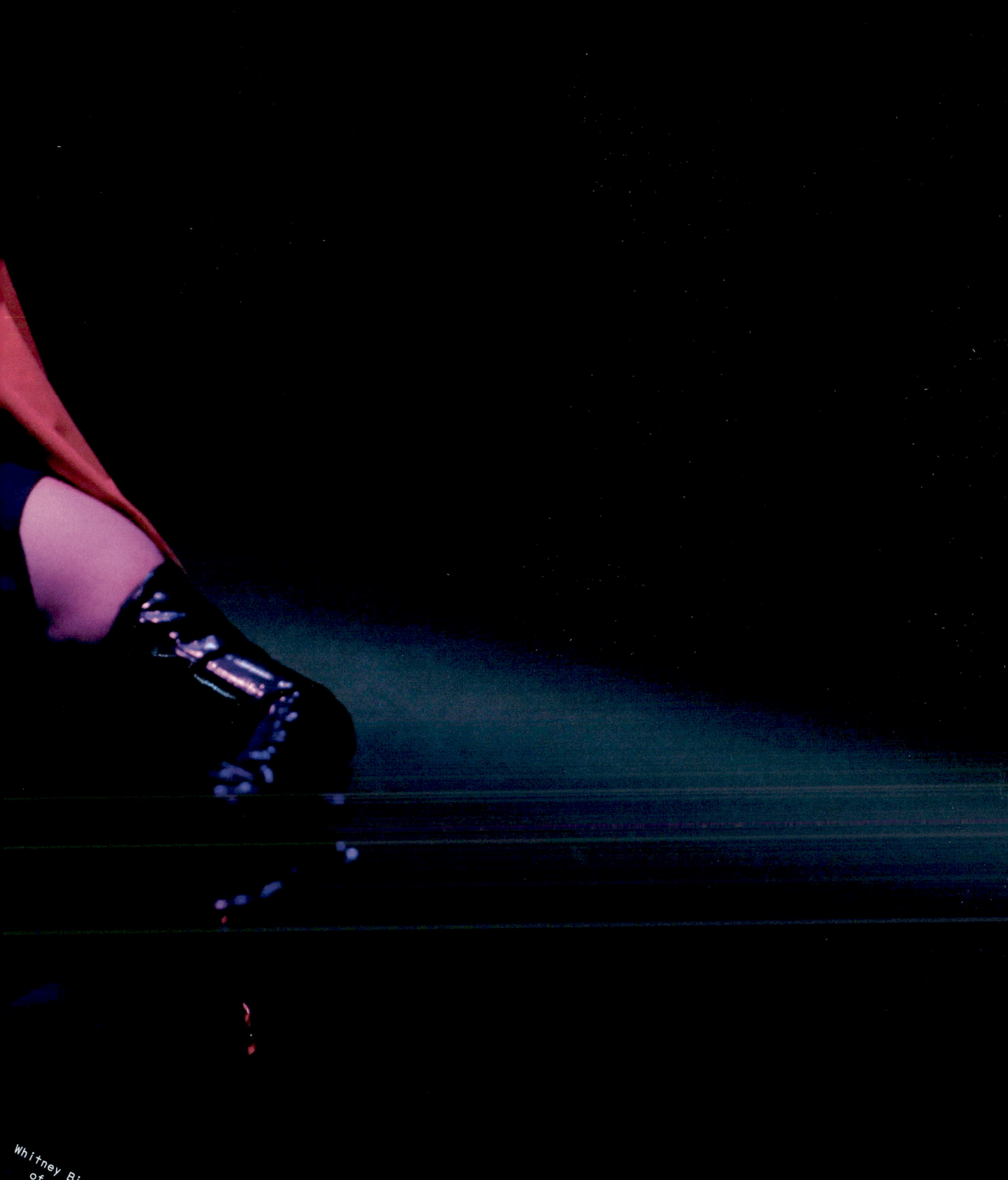

Whitney Biennial, Whitney Museum of American Art, New York

2022

Carmina Escobar performs *For Carmina Escobar* from the series *For Zitkála-Šá*

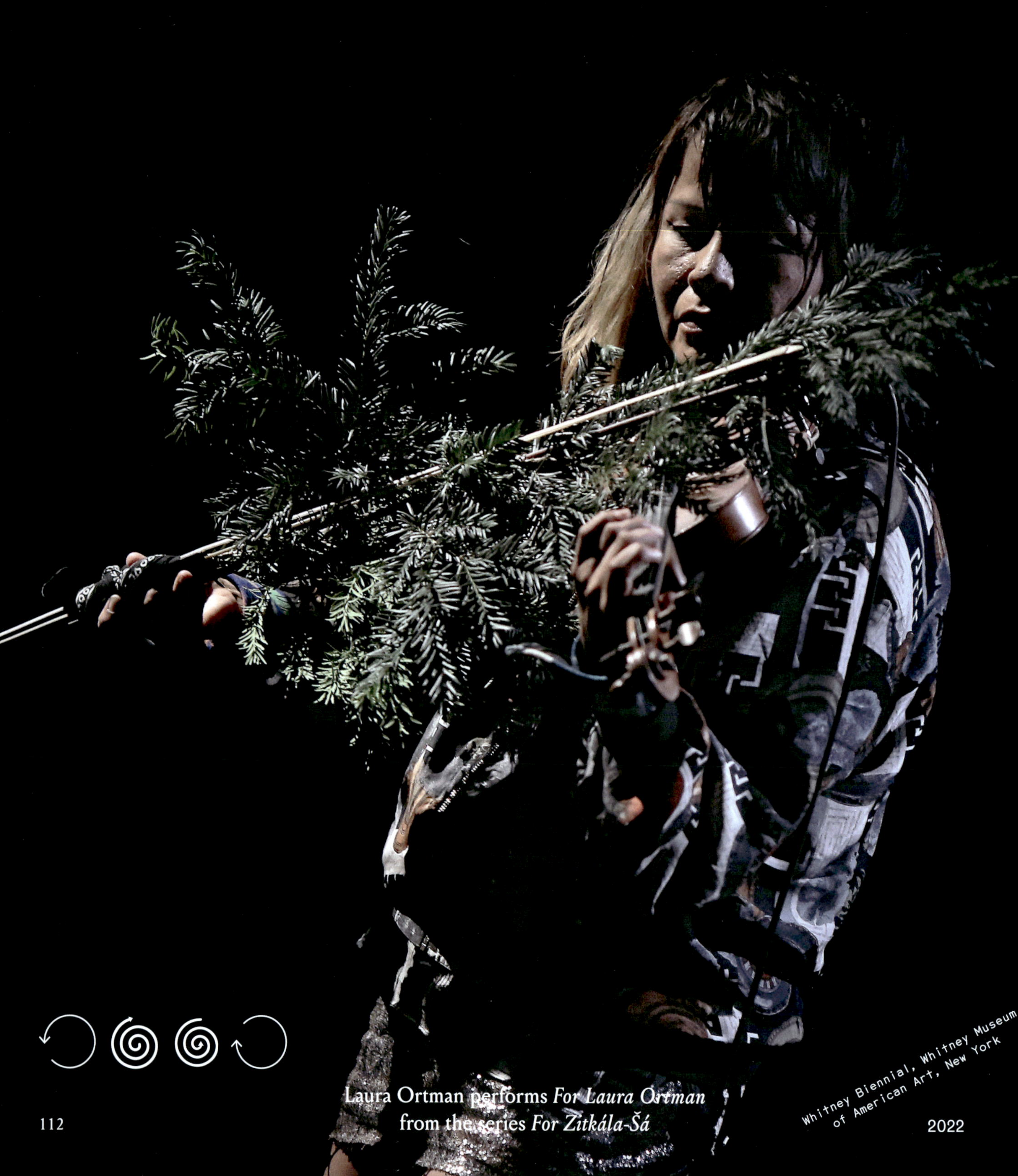

Laura Ortman performs *For Laura Ortman* from the series *For Zitkála-Šá*

Whitney Biennial, Whitney Museum of American Art, New York

2022

BACK TO SCENE

EXT. - NIGHT

ÁNDE

In a dark world, you need stars. So let people who have lost their way again can find home. You joik the Star Girl. You joik her with intensity. You joik her strength. You joik her with love. You joik her with compassion. In a gray world, you need colors so that people who have lost their joy again can find it. You joik the Star Girl. In the silenced world, you need tones. So let people who have forgotten their songs again can find them. We joik the Star Girl. So it's pretty melodic the way I'm singing.

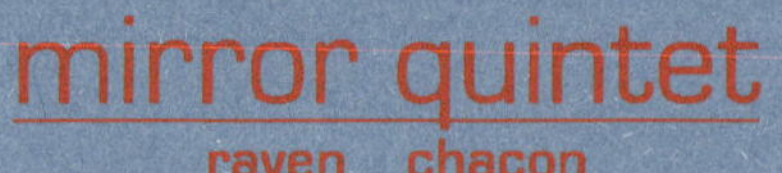

For 5 violins:
-Performer A plays a note or a series of notes lasting 1-3 seconds.
-Performer B watches this (physical and musical) action of Performer A and attempts to recreate the sound **exactly** as played. This reproduction must occur immediately following the sound being recreated.
-Performer C reproduces the sound and actions of Performer B.
-Performer D reproduces the sound and actions of Performer C.
-Performer E reproduces the sound and actions of Performer D.
-Performer A reproduces the sound and actions of Performer E.
-...and so on for any duration.

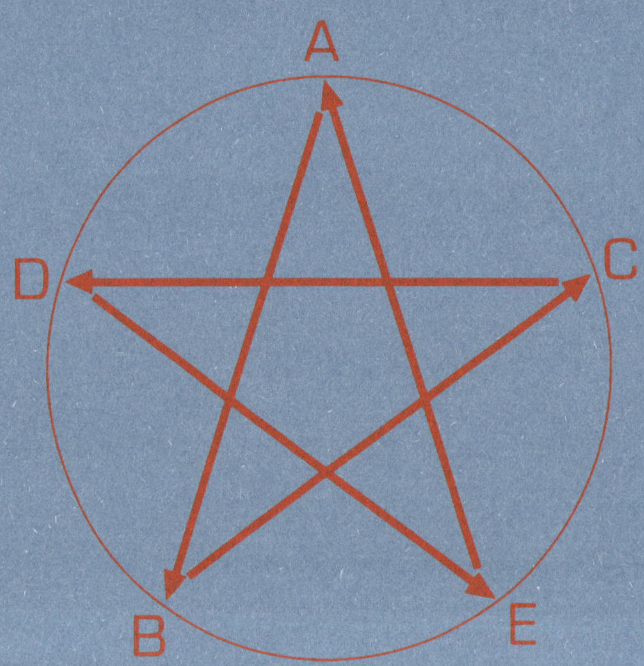

Variations:
-Other groups of like string instruments may be used (groups of violas, cellos, basses, or guitars).
-Audience can be situated circling around the outside of the circle.

Anthony Huberman

Next To and Nearby

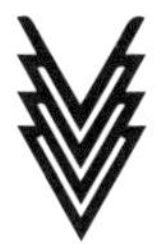

The late curator Okwui Enwezor liked to use a common Igbo proverb—*ife kwulu, ife akwuso ya*; where something stands, there is something else standing next to it. And while this phrase could be applied to a wide range of situations, it is perhaps most intriguing when read in its most metaphysical sense: whenever, wherever, whatever, or whoever you are, there is somewhere else, something else, and someone else standing right next to you.

The land we use and live on is always also someone else's land. It is used by our neighbors and fellow citizens, but also by those who lived on it for generations and centuries past. It is a home to countless animals, trees, plants, and other lifeforms. Wherever we might be standing, all of them are standing right next to us.

The sounds we make and the ones we hear are always accompanied by others, running right alongside them. Perhaps there are the notes of a melody or the scream of a newborn, but there are also the sounds of the heartbeat, of the city street, of a river flowing nearby, of the wind passing through leaves.

And even our own subjectivity and sense of self is always in proximity to the many other people who have made us who we are—parents, friends, siblings, children, teachers, students, enemies, and the countless others who leave their marks on our path. Wherever something stands, there is something else standing next to it. *Ife kwulu, ife akwuso ya.*

The proverb also clearly applies to the contexts of art and music. Not only is a paint color meant to have another next to it, but it also has countless other colors mixed into it, making it what it is. If a sculpture looks like it is made of steel, it is also made of gravity, operating right alongside it and determining the sculpture's shape just as much as the steel is. In any band, orchestra, or ensemble, a musician always stands next to another musician, and as soon as we hear one note, we lose track of it and hear another.

Music is an activity that always has "a nearby"—it is made for, and often with, *someone else*. People make music with others and play music to others, and a musical score, by definition, is *for* others. And while a beat can be something an individual creates, with a goal or an expressive intention in mind, a beat can also be something that is always there, happening nearby, like a "celestial heartbeat" that waits for people to tune into and make their own. In the context of West African percussive polyrhythms, for example, the drummers don't pay attention to the skill or technique of any of the individual performers, but they work together to locate a rhythm that best expresses the shared ancestry of a community. As such, they embody a social and political ethos of reciprocity, whereby anyone is also someone else, beating alongside another beat, allowing one rhythm to occupy, undo, redo, and intensify another one nearby. Echoing the theorist and filmmaker Trinh T. Minh-ha, the work of representation is not to speak about, not to speak for, but to speak nearby.

The Rwandan philosopher Isaïe Nzeyimana describes life (and politics) in musical terms—to live, in his view, is to inhabit a rhythm of giving-and-then-receiving-and-then-giving-again-and-then-receiving-again and so on. This back-and-forth movement between two contrasting points, like any rhythm, generates a sense of coherence and binds disparate parts to each other, like glue. The word he uses to describe that rhythm is *injyana*, where *kujya* means "to go, to walk, to move, to put into motion," and *–na* means "with." Because rhythm is not just about movement, but about movement alongside others. To move is to move with. To live is to live with. To form a society is to coordinate the gestures of others and to find the *injyana*, the sociopolitical groove that puts people in motion alongside other people.

People, but not just people. Yes, there are those other musicians in the ensemble who are working on making music together, or those other members of a community who are working on making a society together. And yet there is also the presence of ancestors and spirits, the presence of animals and rivers and mountains—all of whom are also standing nearby, all of whom make up another part of the *injyana*, even if their voices are often not taken into account. *Ife kwulu, ife akwuso ya.*

The larger implication of this simple proverb is that each of us remains *incomplete*. It means that any one beat is always subject to the ensemble—that orchestra of other people, spirits, ancestors, rocks, and everything else that is inevitably standing nearby. To paraphrase the poet and theorist Fred Moten, each of us is not an individual; we are attached, we are a part, we are next to, we are incomplete. Just like that polyrhythmic percussion ensemble, it means that we could reject a society that puts separate individuals in relation to each other, where any one person will always work to compete with and dominate another, and instead imagine a society that is not based on the individual at all, but rooted in a shared sense of being nearby and being incomplete. *Ife kwulu, ife akwuso ya.*

*

The artist and composer Raven Chacon is interested in all that stands nearby. Central to his work is an acknowledgment of the work of others—young, old, alive, dead, close by, faraway. These people are sometimes his collaborators, but not always. They could be students he is teaching, friends he is hosting, or musicians whose work he admires and wants to promote. To appreciate the work of Raven Chacon, it is important to understand some of what is standing right next to it.

Chacon teaches chamber music to high school students on Native American reservations near his hometown of Albuquerque, New Mexico—the Navajo Reservation, the Hopi Reservation, the Salt River Pima community. In 2000 the Grand Canyon Music Festival founded the Native American Composers Apprentice Project (NACAP). Chacon joined NACAP in 2004 and began reaching out to high schools all over the reservations to see if he could teach students there. It was harder than he expected, because most of the schools didn't offer music and didn't have a music teacher. Chacon figured out that the schools that *did* have a music teacher were the ones that had a sports team, because each game needed to begin with a school anthem played by the school band. The music teacher would select a few students—all between fifteen and eighteen years old—to work with Chacon.

Over the course of a week, Chacon would teach the students how to read music and help them write a score for a three-minute string quartet. Many of the students played guitar, but Chacon taught them how to apply their knowledge to other string instruments. He also taught them that there are countless *other* ways to play their instruments: *here's how to play the strings of a violin*, he might say, *but you could also tap the hollow body of the violin with your hand, you could pluck the strings, as if it were a guitar, you could place it flat on a table and drop things on it from above. What else? In what other ways do you want to use this instrument?* Without privileging any specific historical canon or style over any other, Chacon guided his students as they

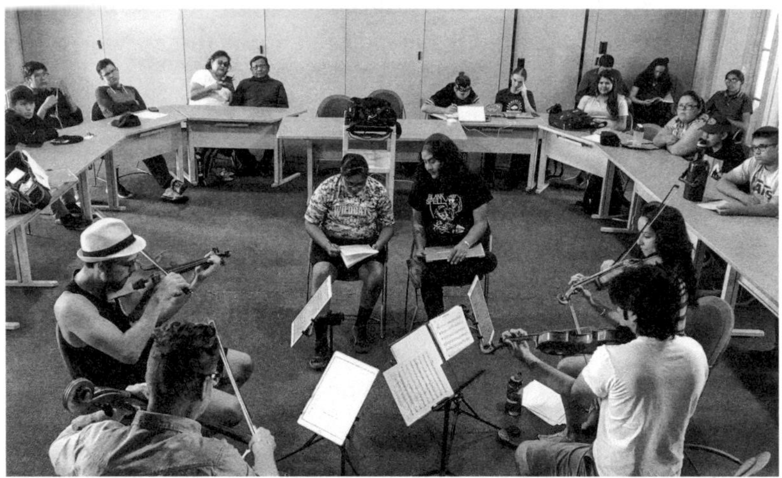

Raven Chacon, working with Native students on musical composition. Since 2004, Chacon has served as composer-in-residence for the Native American Composer Apprentice Project (NACAP), mentoring over 300 high school Native composers in the writing of new string quartets. Photograph by Clare Hoffman

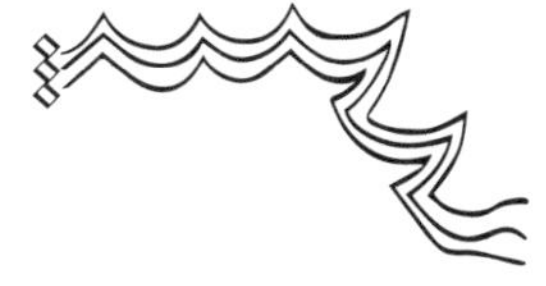

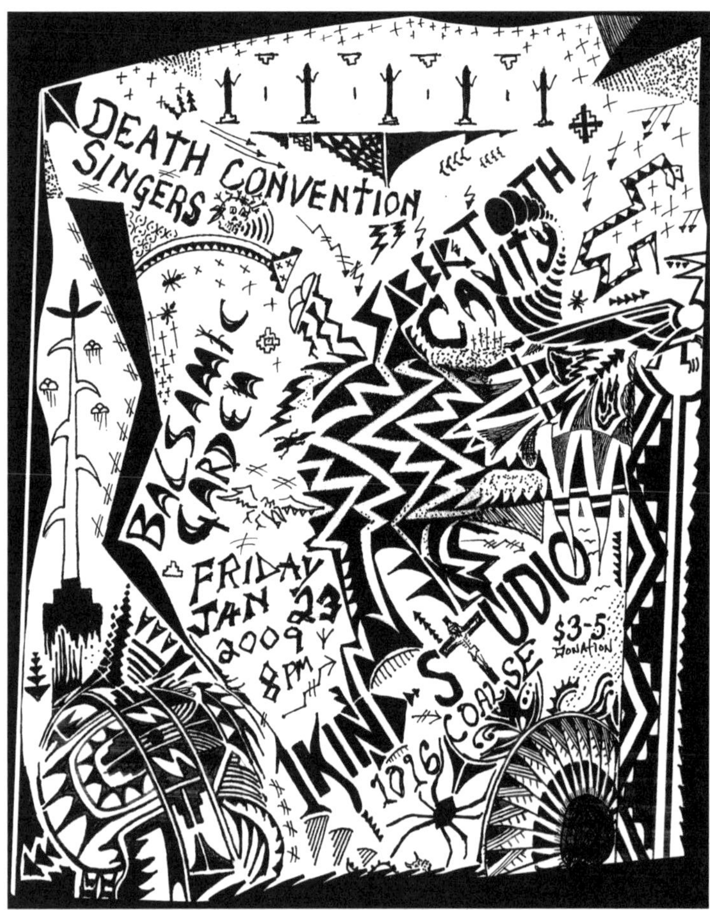

Hand-drawn flyer by Raven Chacon for a concert at a venue he cofounded in Albuquerque, New Mexico. The space changed names over its one year of existence: 1Kind / Unkind / Rio Grande Satanical Gardens

worked to locate and articulate their own musical vocabularies and techniques. His hope was not that they learn a skill imposed onto them from elsewhere but that they learn to trust their own stories and to use them to make music that was their own—a lesson that relates to pedagogy just as much as it does to politics.

Chacon himself had learned to listen to the music of others and find ways to make it his own: he had listened to the stories contained within the songs his grandfather used to sing, he had mixed them with the heavy metal he heard on the radio at the Navajo reservation in Arizona where he grew up, and he had become a maker of noise music, a composer of chamber music, and an artist with a keen awareness of what ties specific sounds to specific sites.

His students brought their compositions to the Grand Canyon Music Festival, where they were performed by a professional string quartet, and recorded by Chacon. He has approximately 300 recordings of his students' compositions. For Chacon, the act of recording is just that—*recording.* It is less about doing anything with the recording than it is about the act of recording itself: these kids are here, these performances took place, these stories were told, and they have inscribed their presence into the surface of the canyons nearby. *Ife kwulu, ife akwuso ya.*

A few years earlier, in 2001, Chacon started his own record label, Sicksicksick Distro. He chose to limit it to music from the Southwest of the United States—the music that was nearby, that he felt he knew or could access, but that lacked distribution elsewhere, "Loud Music from the Southwest U.S." The story of the label is the story of the ebb and flow of friendships, and follows the currents of how musical communities form, dissolve, reform, and endlessly evolve. In the beginning, Chacon would record the (very) small group of people living in Albuquerque who shared his obsession with New Music. Later, he recorded people who crashed on his couch while they were on tour. In his circle of noise and metal musicians, this was how it worked: you go on tour, you play a show, and at the end of the show you ask around if someone has a couch you could sleep on. Someone always did. You slept on the couch, you woke up, drove to the next town, and did it all over again. And when you weren't on tour, you would return the favor to any musician who was passing through, letting them sleep on your couch after their show.

The first six or seven releases on Sicksicksick Distro were Chacon's own music, all published using different aliases like Los Subliminados, The Kleptones, or Modernativensemble. After that came seventy-three records, cassette tapes, CDs, and thumb drives by bands such as Occasional Detroit, Bigawatt, Sabertooth Cavity, and Death Convention Singers. While some grew to become close friends and even collaborators, others were simply passing through town, and Chacon recognized each of them as being part of his own journey and his own process of understanding what connects specific sounds to specific places. For over twenty years, Sicksicksick Distro has distributed music from the Southwest to listeners all around the country. *Ife kwulu, ife akwuso ya.*

Albuquerque means a great deal to Chacon. Even if he and his long-time collaborator and life partner, curator Candice Hopkins, now live in upstate New York, they maintain a home in Albuquerque and often remind friends that they are free to use it if they ever pass through town. From 2004 to 2015, Chacon also ran galleries and project spaces there, where he and his collaborators would stage exhibitions and present concerts. Small Engine was a gallery he started in 2012 with Mateo and Malinda Galindo, Lucas Hussack, and Scott Daniel Williams. The artist collective of which Chacon was a member, Postcommodity, had a space it used as a shared studio, and Chacon also used it to run Spirit Abuse, a project space for exhibiting video art and hosting experimental music concerts. Artists and friends from across the country would send their videos via online servers, and a community would gather at Spirit Abuse to watch them. All was peer-to-peer.

Teaching others, distributing the work of others, presenting the work of others, collaborating with others, honoring the memory of others—Chacon is deeply aware that others are always nearby, standing next to him. And he recognizes—intellectually, politically, and/or intuitively—that he is incomplete without others and can only mature as a musician if accompanied by this chorus of other voices, no matter how cacophonous it may get. He finds ways to always keep them nearby. *Ife kwulu, ife akwuso ya.*

In early 2021, in the midst of the COVID-19 pandemic, Chacon began a residency at the Wattis Institute for Contemporary Arts in San Francisco. The pandemic put our need for standing next to others—as nearby as possible, even—in dramatic and often traumatic relief. Since the Wattis galleries were closed, taking any possibility for a public performance off the table, Chacon turned to a tool that has long been able to help people listen to and feel connected to each other, even across vast distances—radio. Produced with Wattis assistant curator Diego Villalobos, Radio Coyote launched in the spring of 2021 as a short-range FM station, broadcast to 88.1 FM for anyone within a few blocks from the Wattis Institute, as well as an online streaming channel, with a custom-designed website at www.radiocoyote.org.

It is worth clarifying that what Chacon did was not produce a radio show or a handful of podcasts, but create an entire radio *station*, running 24/7, with shows produced by friends and past collaborators, and recordings from his personal collection, along with the entire back catalogue from Sicksicksick Distro. And while Radio Coyote was meant for everyone who tuned in, its initial purpose was to give Chacon and his collaborators a mechanism to keep talking with each other while all were sheltering in place in different parts of the country. Chacon himself was in San Francisco, a few blocks from the Wattis, spending his residency in a four-bedroom apartment inside of a university dormitory building that was, except for him, completely empty. Ginger Dunnill was in New Mexico, and produced a series of interviews with Indigenous, activist, queer, female-identifying, BIPOC, and lost/stolen heritage artists. Michael Begay, also from New Mexico, shared his collection of Indigenous metal music, including the voices of young Navajo and Hopi students from NACAP, where he also teaches. From Oakland, Zachary James Watkins crafted a sonic journey with field recordings, harmony tunings, and saturated sonic environments. Poet Ashley Smiley produced a show about Black/BIPOC artists in the Bay Area. From upstate New York, Mark Trecka used the chat function of Radio Coyote's website to involve listeners in a collaborative process of sharing popular and avant-garde music, archival recordings, interviews, and original work. The hope, as Chacon said in an interview, was "to find the least accessible music that's out there—things that have gone out of print, things that are no longer available. Things that were released on analog formats and never digitized."

As Chacon prepared to leave the Bay, with his residency coming to an end, he worked to find a new host for Radio Coyote, so that it could continue beyond the limited duration of its run with Wattis. His friends from Atomic Culture, in Tulsa, Oklahoma, were able to set up a short-range local FM signal at 90.1 FM, take over the administration of radiocoyote.org, and keep expanding the programming to include Warren Realrider's program of poets reading their work at locations specific to their life experiences and cultural background, Akin Deckard's show of Brazilian electronic music, and Kara Lynch's *Blues U*, a queer/feminist, Black, and Indigenous platform for a twenty-first-century Blues University syllabus, among many others. *Ife kwulu, ife akwuso ya.*

If the Bay Area has struck a chord with Chacon, it could be because of the presence of ancestors standing nearby. The infamous nineteen-month occupation of the abandoned federal prison on Alcatraz Island, in 1969–71, by the Indians of All Tribes, a group of Native American activists, drew national attention. John Trudell, a member of the Sioux People, set up Radio Free Alcatraz and made daily broadcasts directly from the occupied island. In late 2022, in response to an invitation to contribute to Julio Morales's exhibition *Undoing Time: Art and Histories of Incarceration* at the Berkeley Art Museum, Chacon listened to each of those broadcasts and layered excerpts of them in a live sound performance staged in what had once been the hospital wing of the former prison. Many found themselves standing nearby each other: the ghostly bodies of sick prisoners, the sounds of Native American activists, and the presence of a live audience, who were tasked with tuning into what, and who, still resonates with the present day. *Ife kwulu, ife akwuso ya.*

The Bay is also the protagonist in *Tremble Staves* (2017–19), Chacon's outdoor opera. The score calls for the performance to take place nearby moving and stationary bodies of water, and its premiere, in 2019, was set within the ruins of the Sutro Baths, just north of San Francisco's Ocean Beach. The reason for this is not only because the work is a meditation on water—"the scarcity of it," as Chacon notes, "especially in the desert where I am from, and of course its sacredness: we are water"—but also because it makes use of the water as a percussion instrument. While the musicians performing the piece hit their drums, there are waves crashing into rocks or objects falling into the calm surface of a pond or basin. Those drums are always there, nearby, waiting for the performers to hear and tune into them. *Ife kwulu, ife akwuso ya.*

Whenever music is being played, it is never possible to separate it from all that is happening next to the music. There is the technology behind the instruments, the social norms and rituals that govern how people listen to and assemble around music, the aesthetic standards that determine how the music is culturally valued, the histories haunting the site where the music is played. The musicians are those who weave these proximities together and find the *injyana* that attaches them to each other, even for just the length of a song.

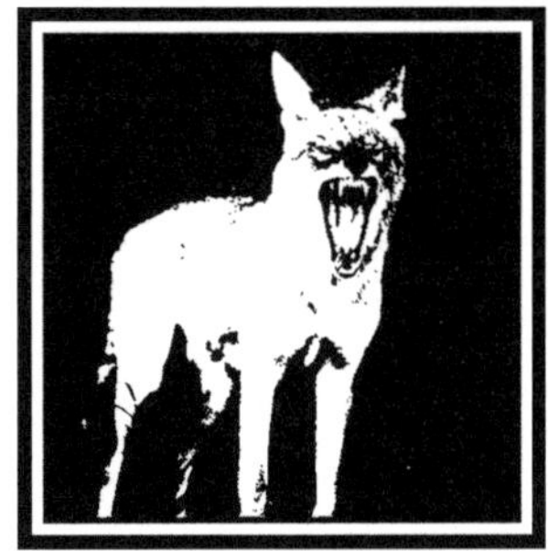

Radio Coyote logo

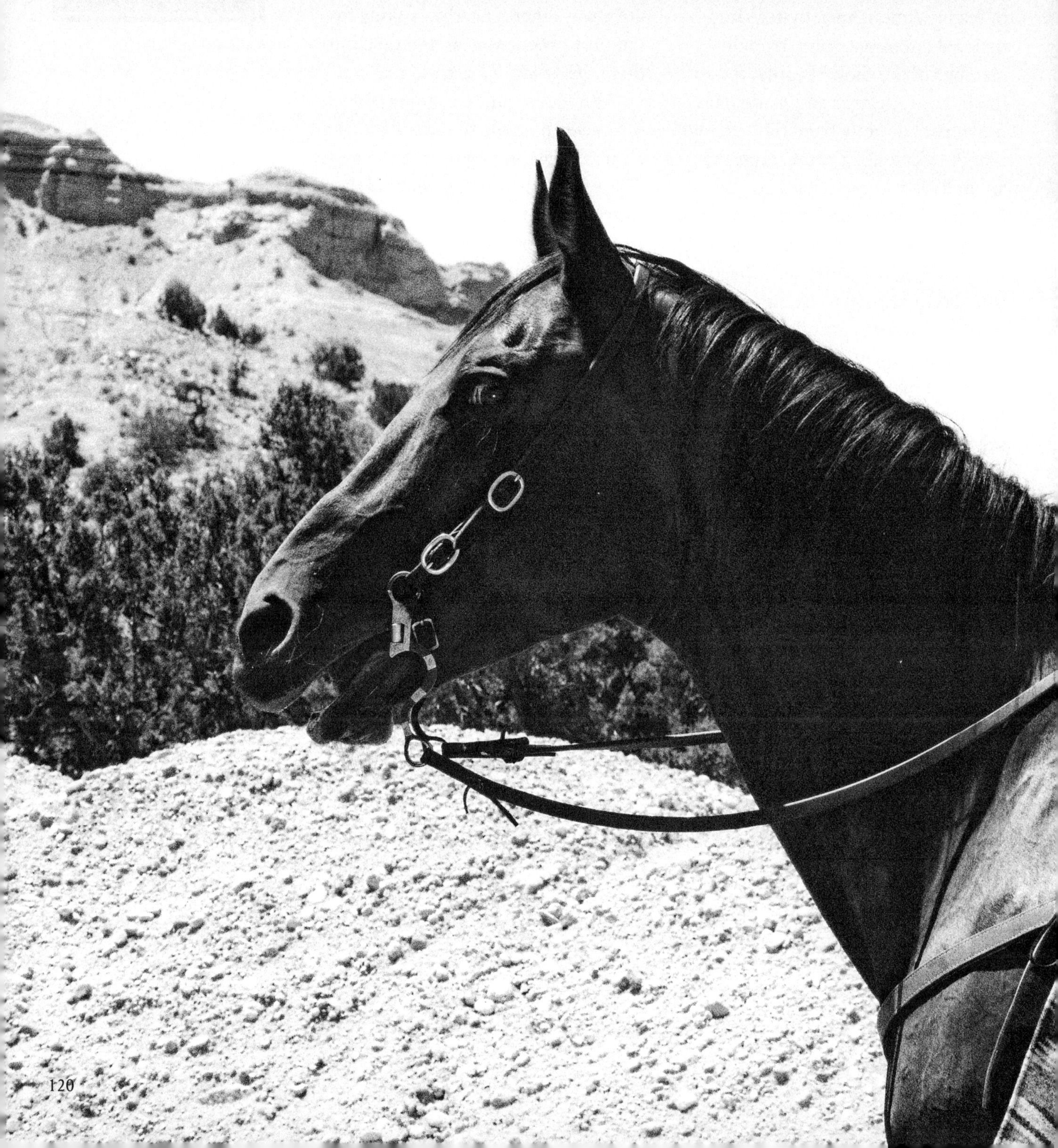

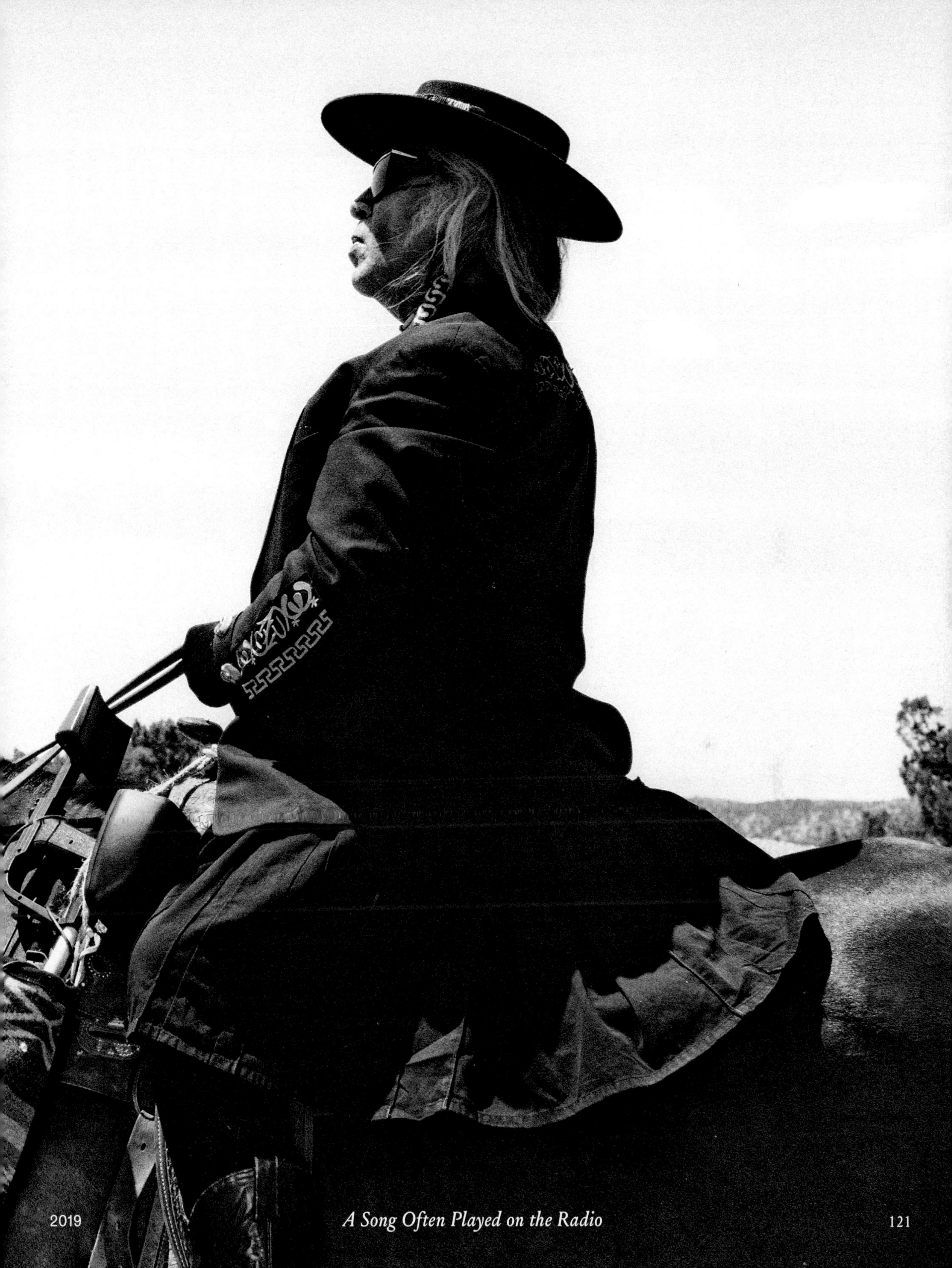

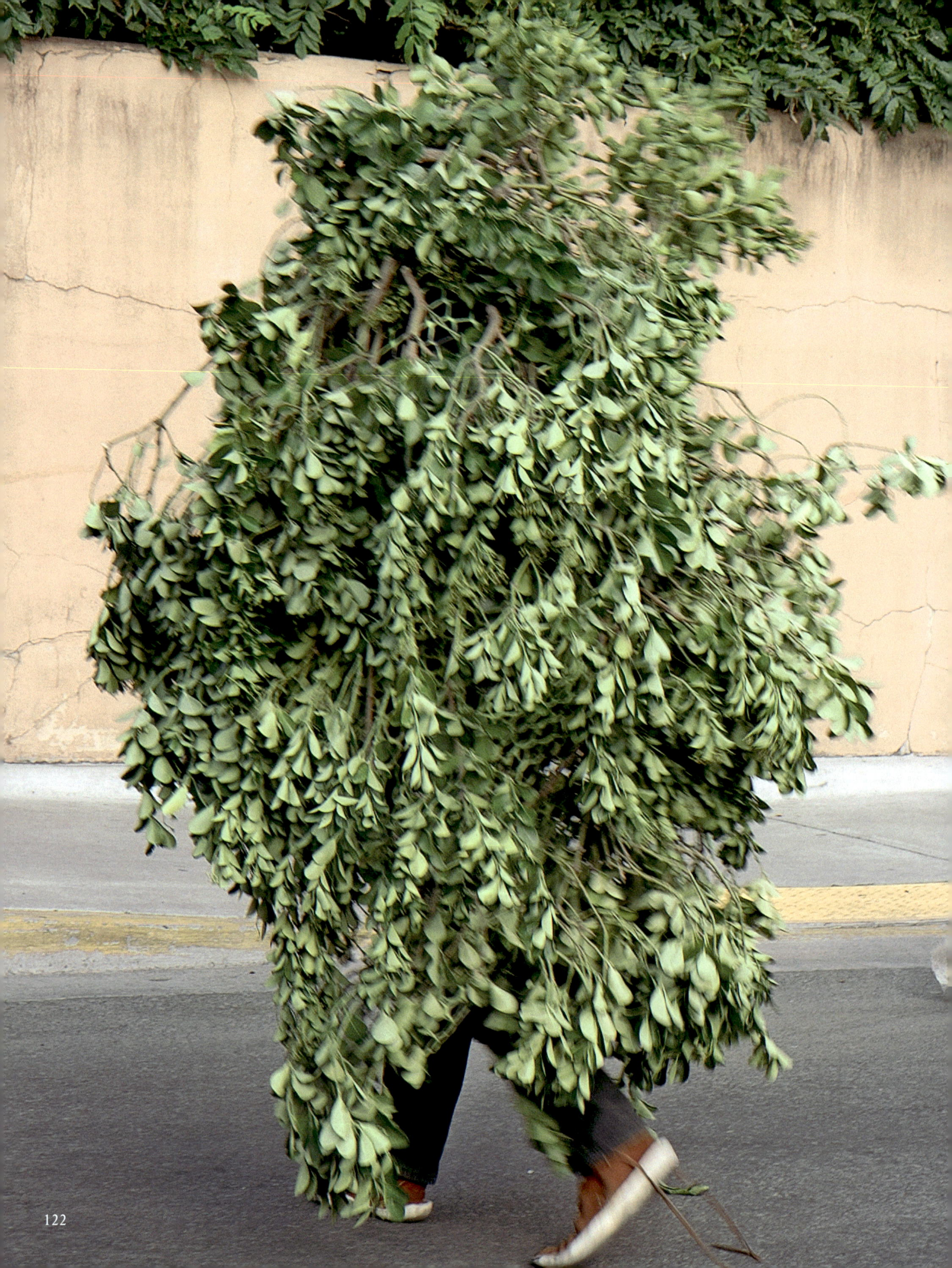

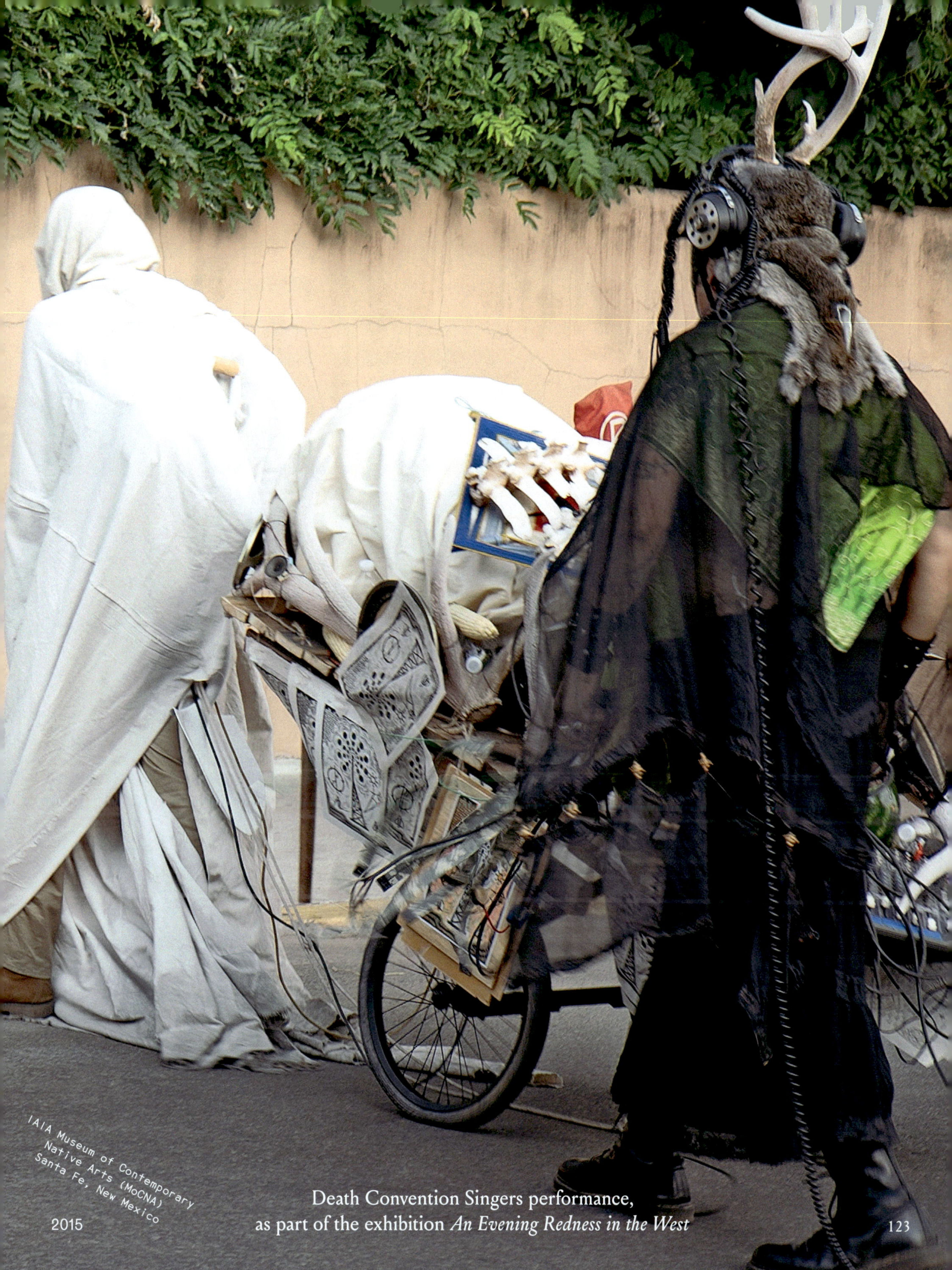

IAIA Museum of Contemporary Native Arts (MoCNA) Santa Fe, New Mexico

2015

Death Convention Singers performance, as part of the exhibition *An Evening Redness in the West*

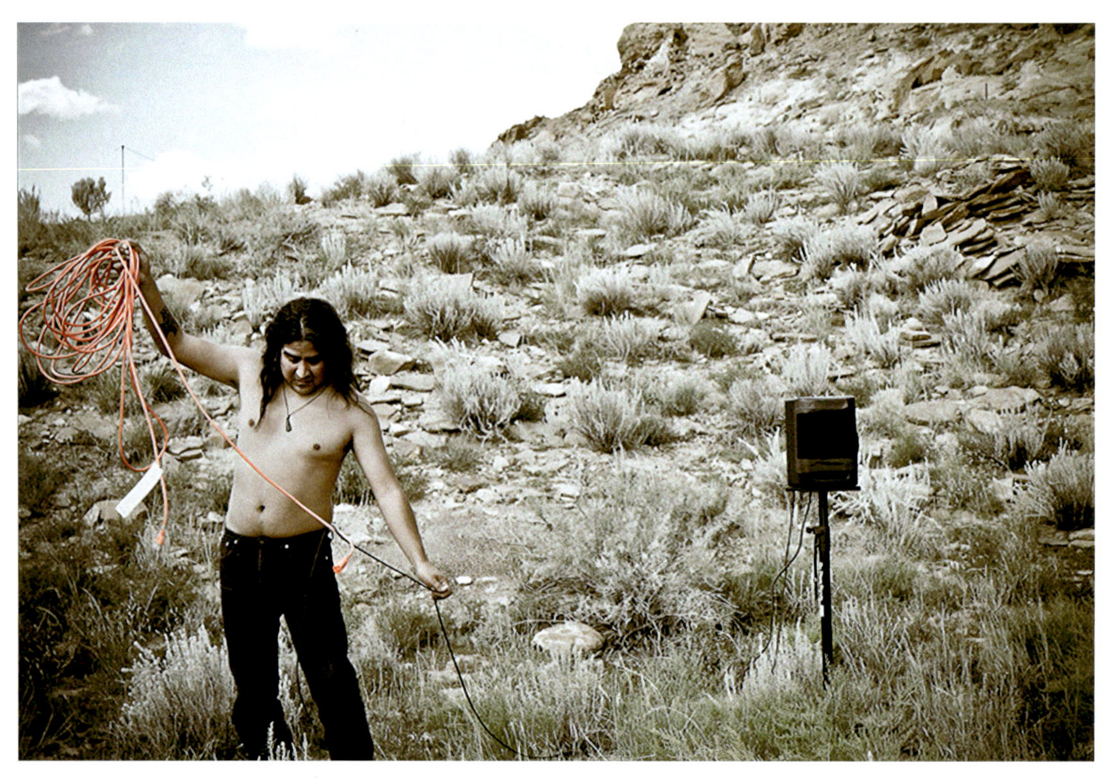

Raven Chacon installing for a moonlight performance
with Robert Henke

Chaco Canyon, New Mexico

2013

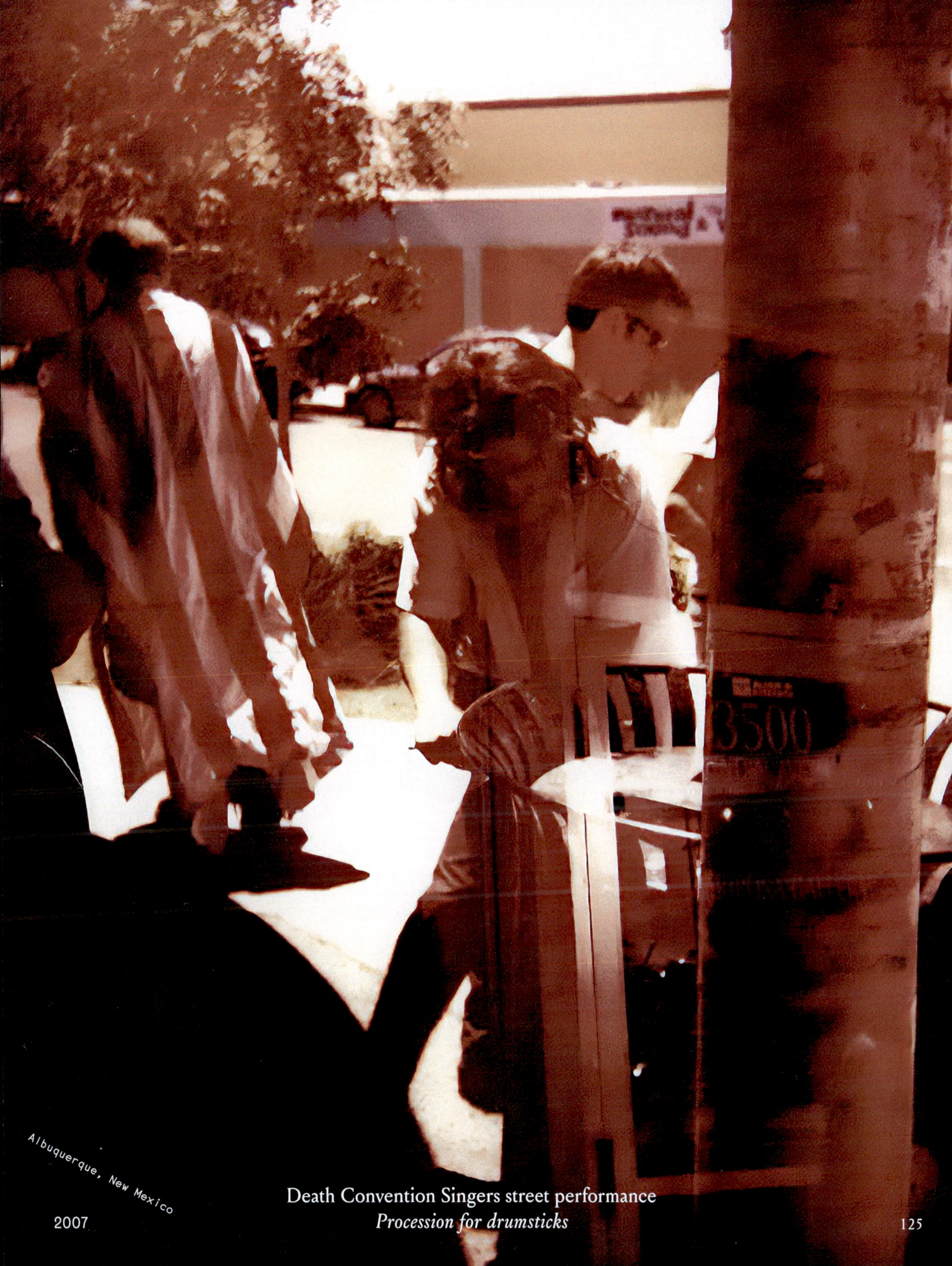

Albuquerque, New Mexico

2007

Death Convention Singers street performance

Procession for drumsticks

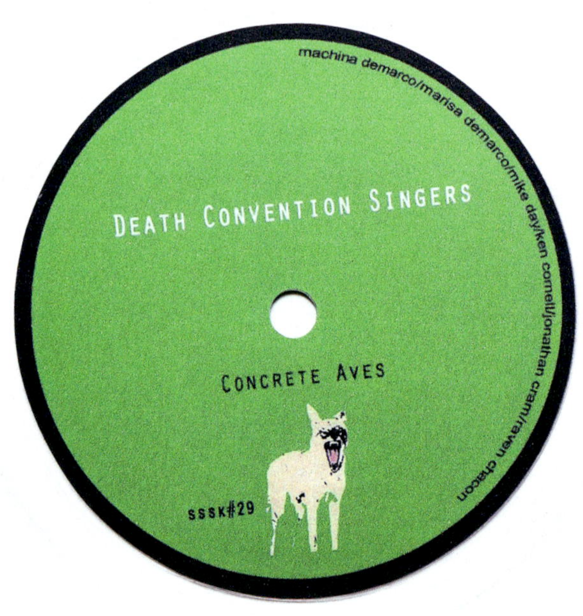

Death Convention Singers + Dirty/Birdies
Split lathe-cut 7" (SSSK #29)

2007

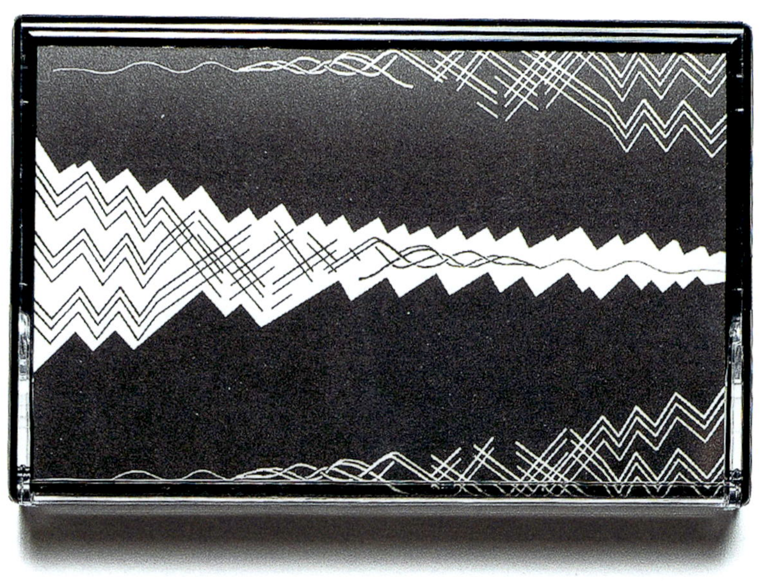

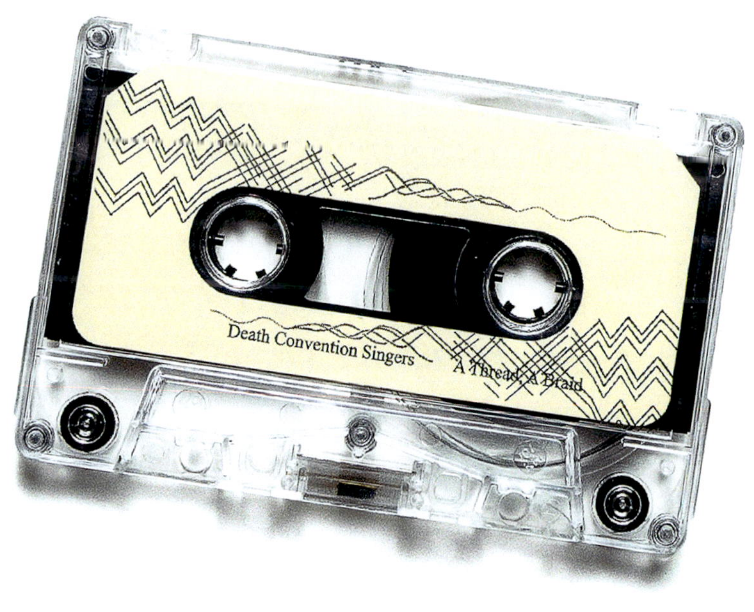

Death Convention Singers
A Thread, A Braid cassette (SSSK #71)

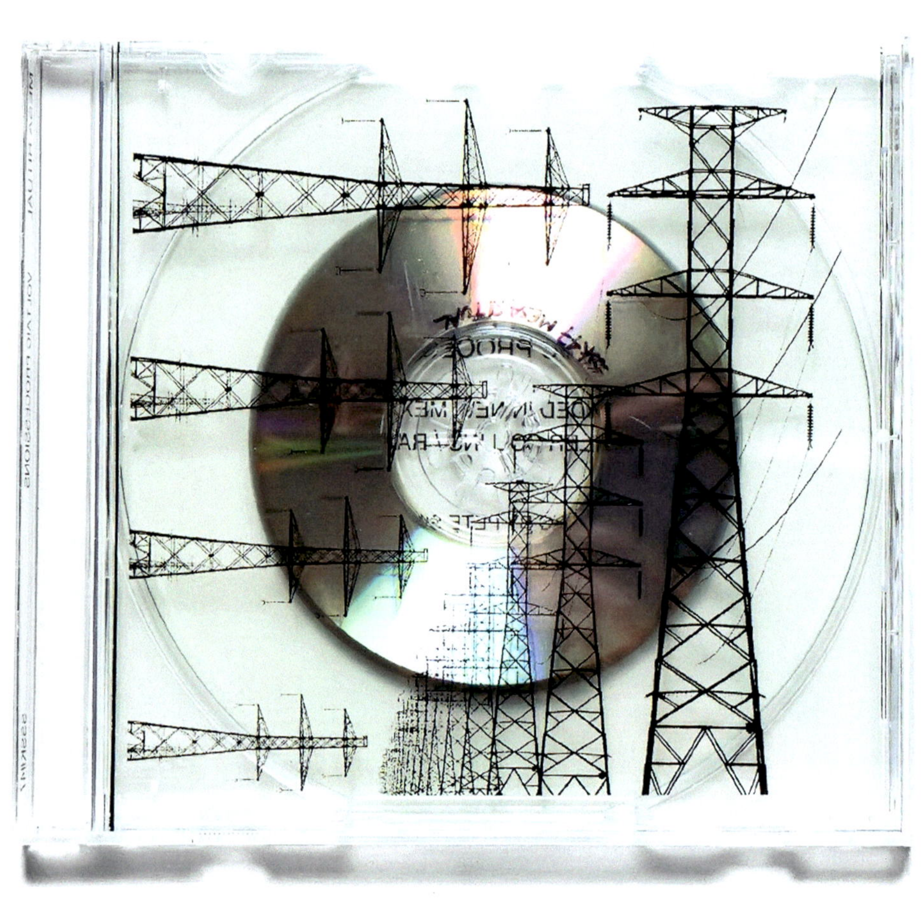

Mesa Ritual
Voltaic Processions mini-CD (SSSK #47)

2007

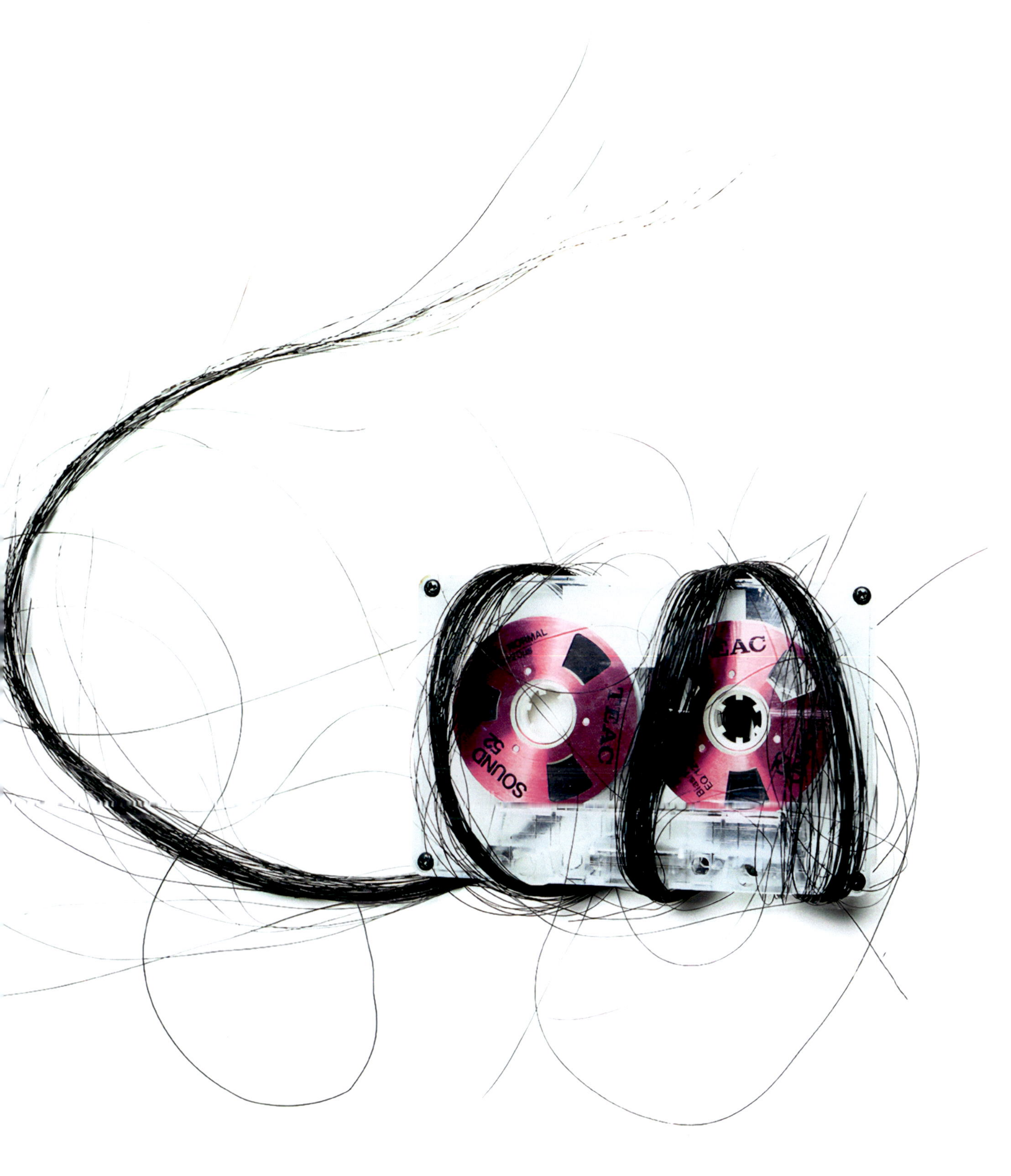

Horse Thief
2013 *Ethnic/Cleansing* cassette (SSSK #62)

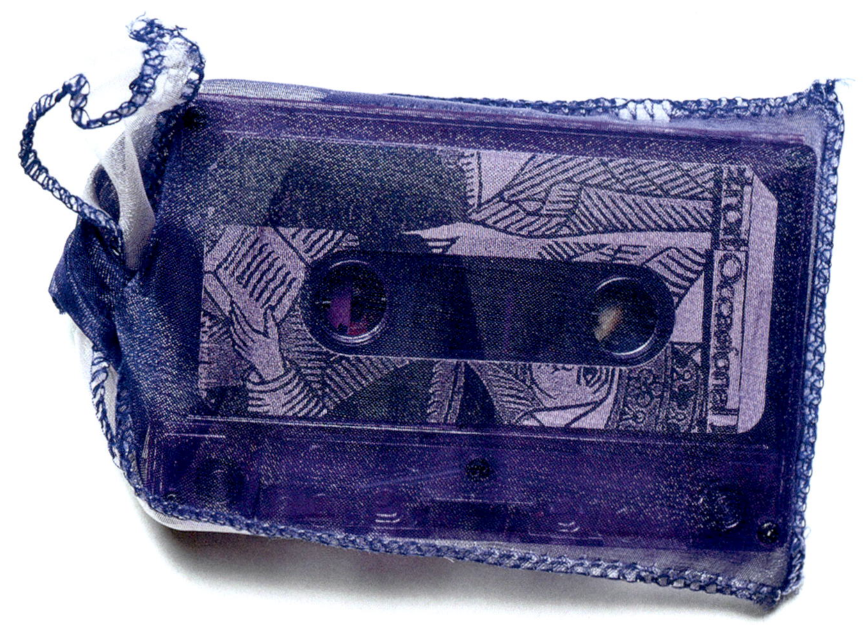

Occasional Detroit
Prayer Packages (SSSK #35) 2008

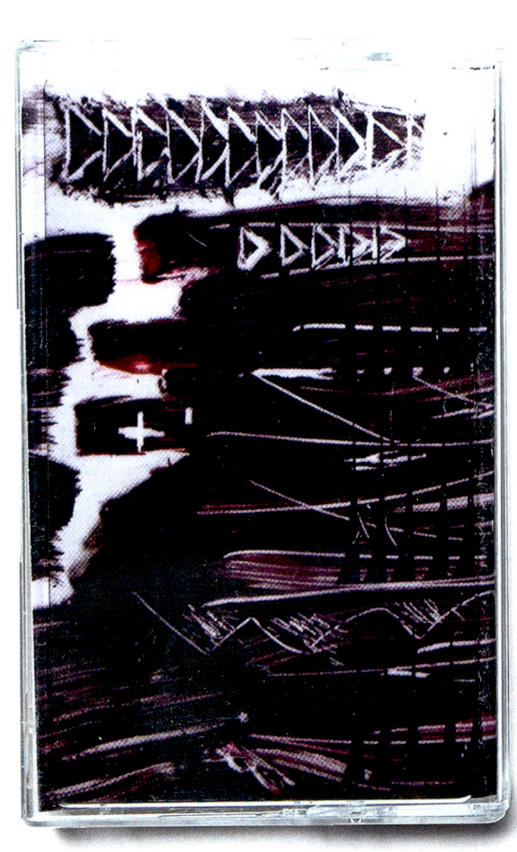

Raven Chacon
Black Streaked Hum 2009

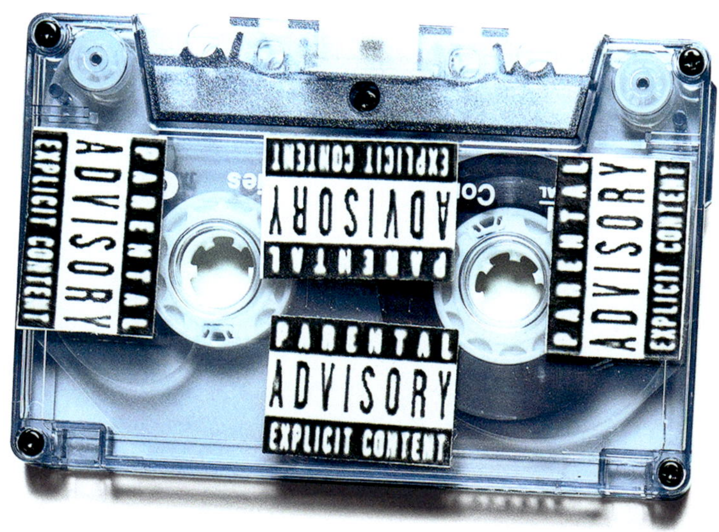

2001 The Kleptones
Sample/All rights reversed cassette (SSSK #3)

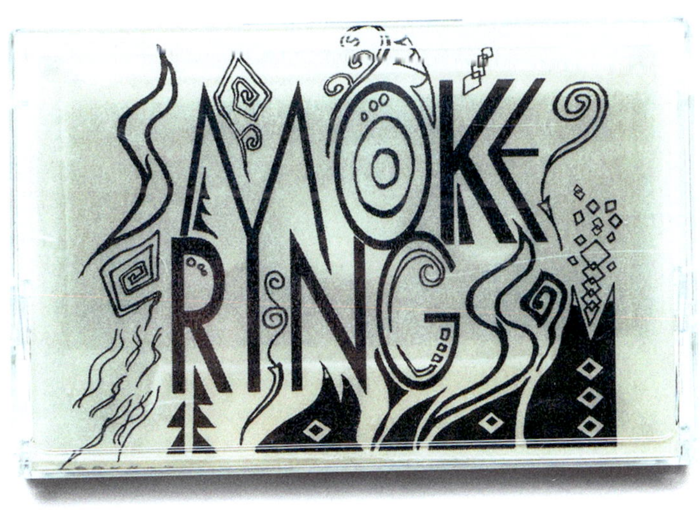

2008 Smoke Rings
Smoke Rings cassette (SSSK #43)

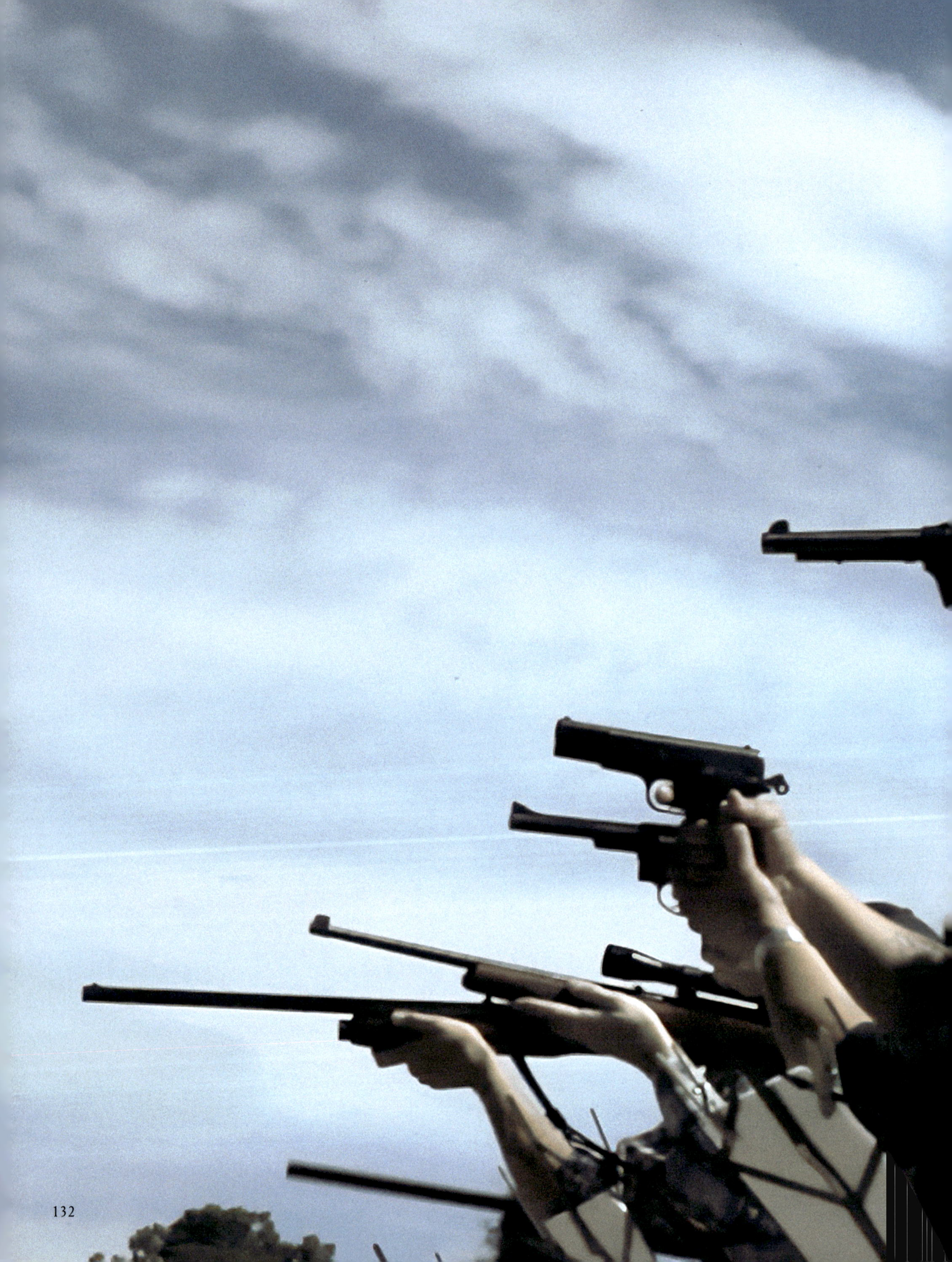

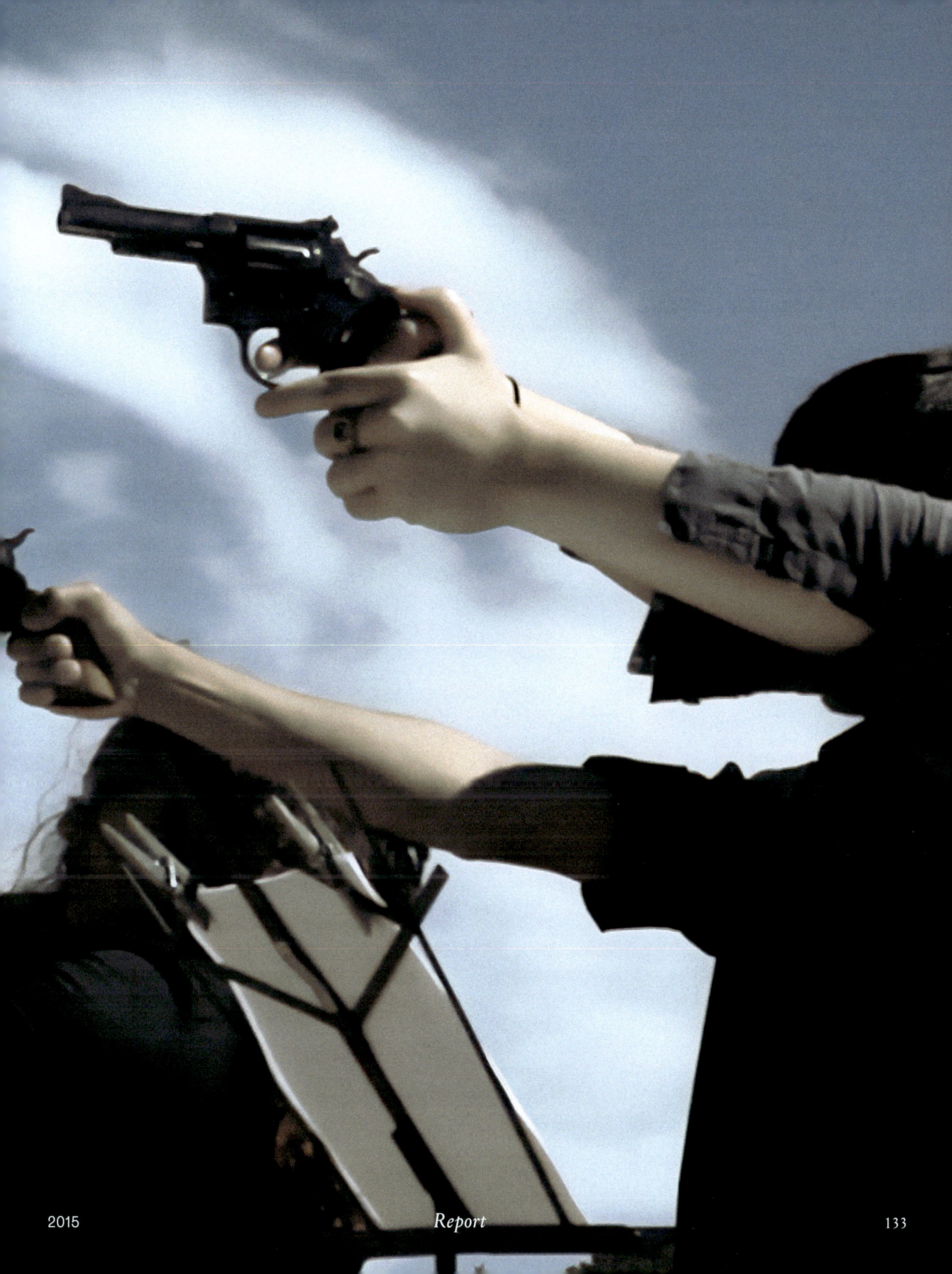

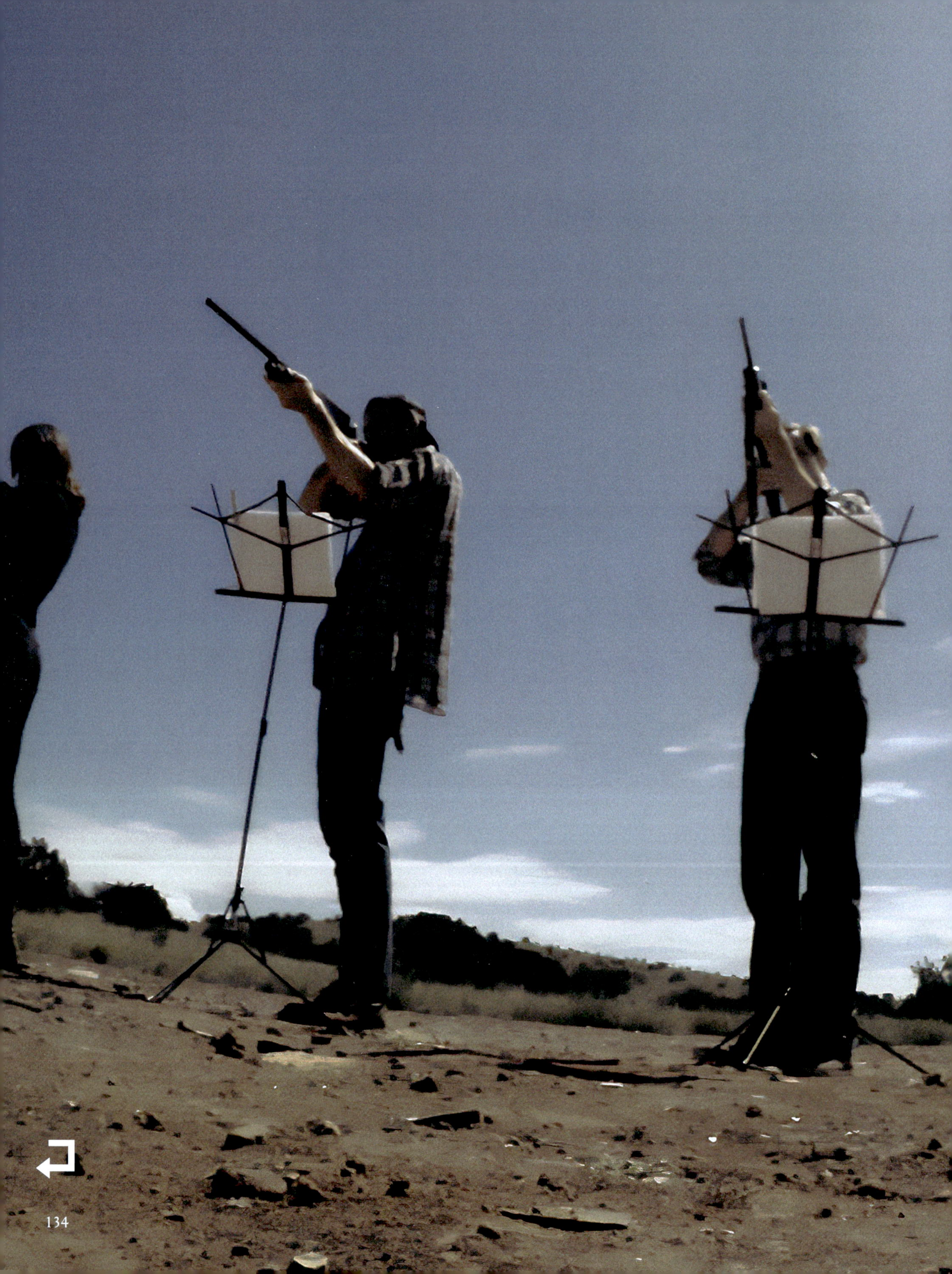

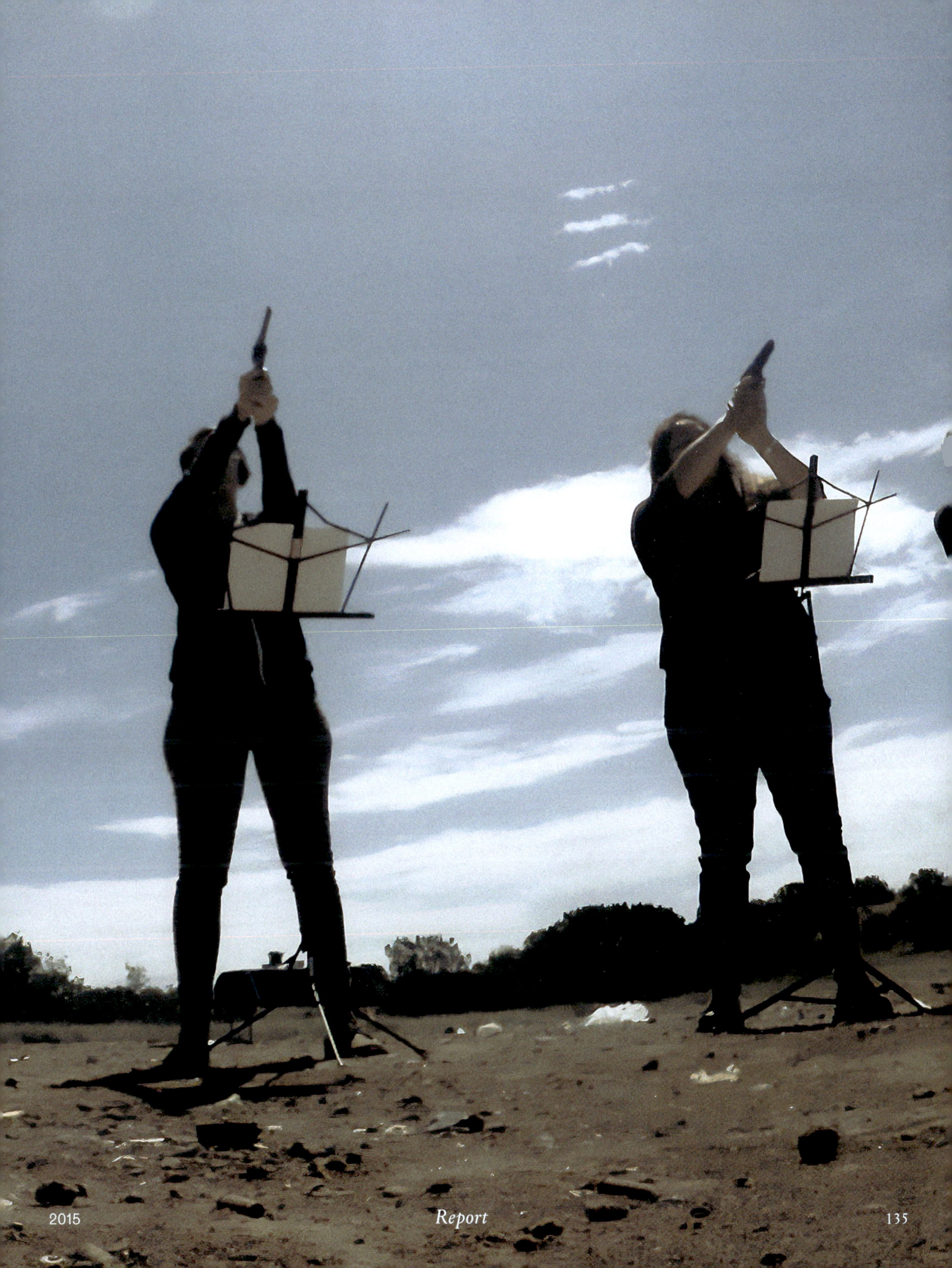

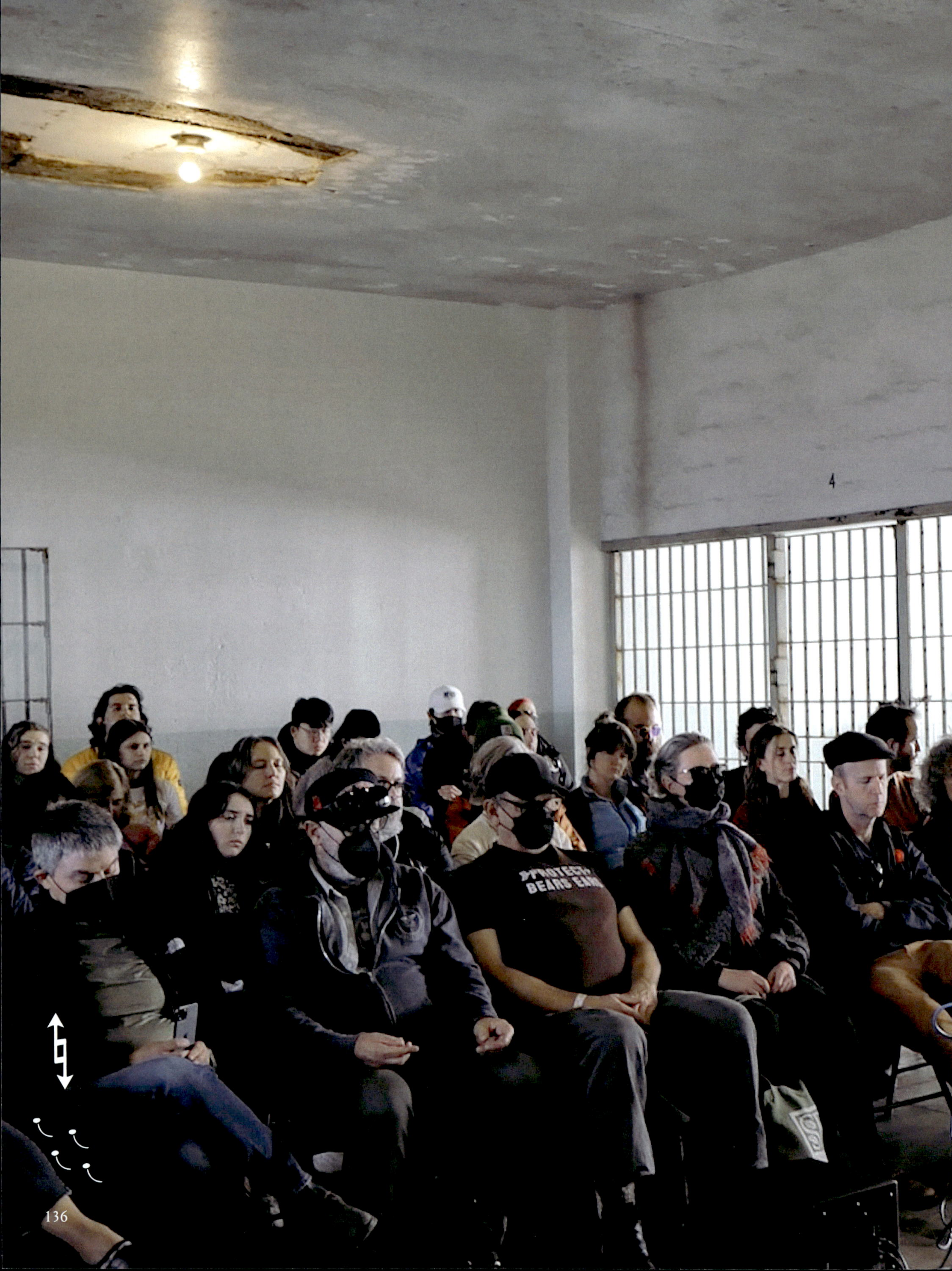
4
PROTECT
BEARS EARS

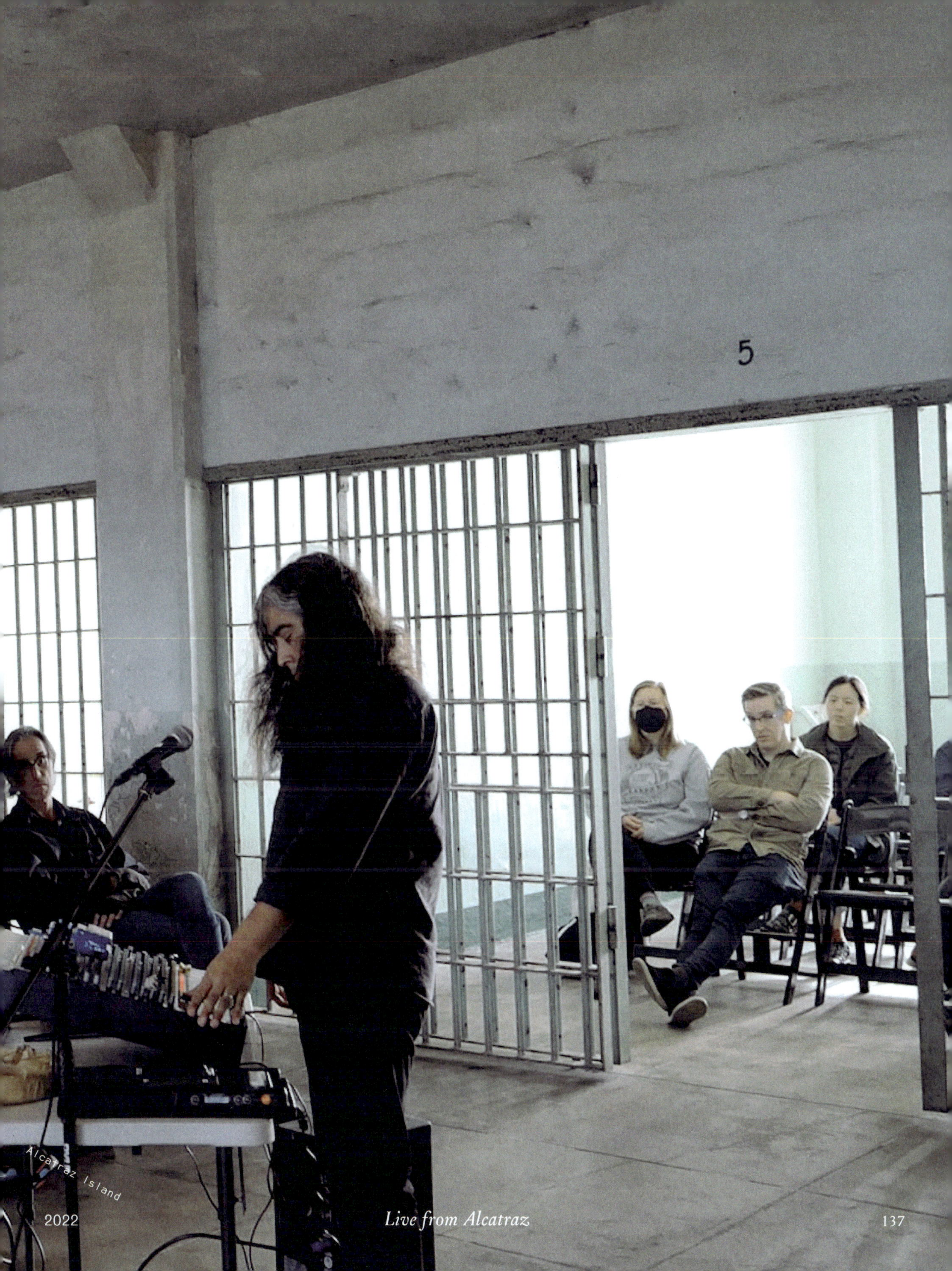

Alcatraz Island

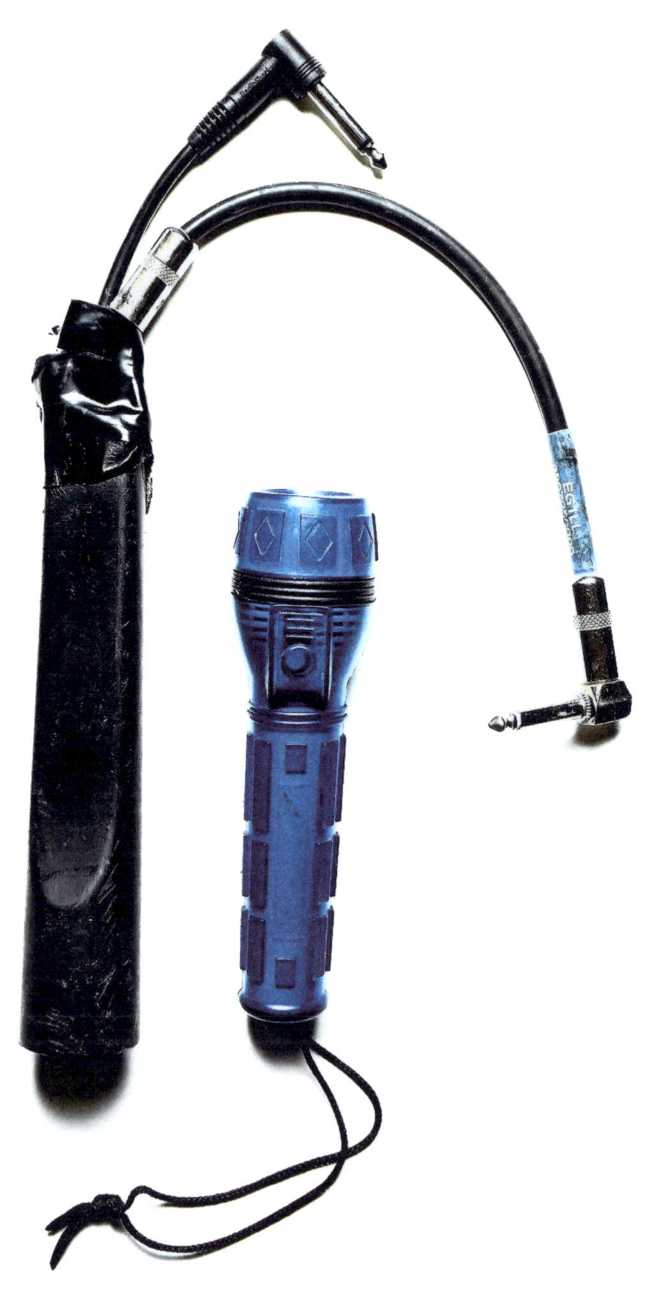

Light Drum

2008

Lou Cornum

The Moon Again

They never made it back to that moon. Once the only one, it gave the category by which all others would be known. This moon, the Moon, was imagined as a world, then as the desecration of a world, then as the incubator for another world, and then abandoned.

In the beginning decades of the twenty-first century, the space race took off again, driven by fierce rivalries and mass injections of cash. NASA was the minor player now, holding on to its relevance through military and private industry connections. The agency announced its return to the moon not as an end in itself but as the jumping-off point for mankind's next great leap: the move to Mars. They never got to either.

Like the deserts of the Southwest United States, the lunar surface is strewn with the remains of boom-and-bust schemes and lingering projections from wealthy tycoons. In the 2020s, Yusaku Maezawa poured a fraction of his billions into trying to artwash the moon. First there was the dearMoon mission. Maezawa had hand selected a crew of artists, musicians, and performers to board the first *Space X* civilian mission to the moon. It was a test of the viability for space tourism dressed up in the usual megalomania of the super-rich. Maezawa claimed the journey to the moon would provoke and inspire new creative works and forms from the crew upon their return. After years of launch setbacks, half of the group dropped out and the other half fell from their niche of fleeting fame so as to make the whole mission objective null. Still, he kept at it.

One ride would not be enough. As the crises of liberal institutions rippled across the so-called democracies of the world, the technocrats teamed up with the venture capitalists to take higher education to a whole new level of meaning. Like the artistic premise of dearMoon, their for-profit education project launched under the premise of cultural production. Built entirely by the lunar robotics crew of *Space X* and inhabited not by living beings but digital avatars of Maezawa and the remaining acolytes of his initial mission, the Lunar Art Institute, first school on the moon, is in shambles. Dust to dust.

Instead of settling the moon, the most the United States could do was a big floating ball. MetaEarth—the dystopian version of Buckminster Fuller's vision of geodesic dome cities floating over the earth like inhabited clouds. The MetaEarth dome was above the clouds, past the atmosphere. A joint venture of Meta and Space XYZ, the space commode was eventually pronounced "meh" by the various millionaires and billionaires who spent a season living off-Earth. Another rip-off in the great space scam of the twenty-first century.

The makers of this second moon had destroyed at least one universal law: that which goes up must come down. In the case of MetaEarth, what goes up cannot physically come down except through an act of chaotic catastrophe (meteor strike, nuclear weapon, etc.). It is suspended there, not far from the decommissioned international space station and the floating battleships of multiple nations. ME is the only civilian-populated celestial body to date.

But now that the moon is alone once again, the shining disk of solitude, can we begin to know the moon again? The question itself is still plagued by a certain hubris. Perhaps instead we embrace the inability to know the moon, accept its radical alterity to meet it not as world but as Other. Let the moon be moon.

The Navajo have protocols for the time of lunar eclipse. During this time, we are meant to stay inside and steer our gaze away from the sky phenomenon. Let the moon be. In this, what I read as a gesture of deference, are we relating to the moon as relative or as stranger? The moon is the earth's oldest companion and yet they remain now forever locked at a distance. To be relative to the stranger: this is the compact and the promise and the undertaking of the earthly lunatics.

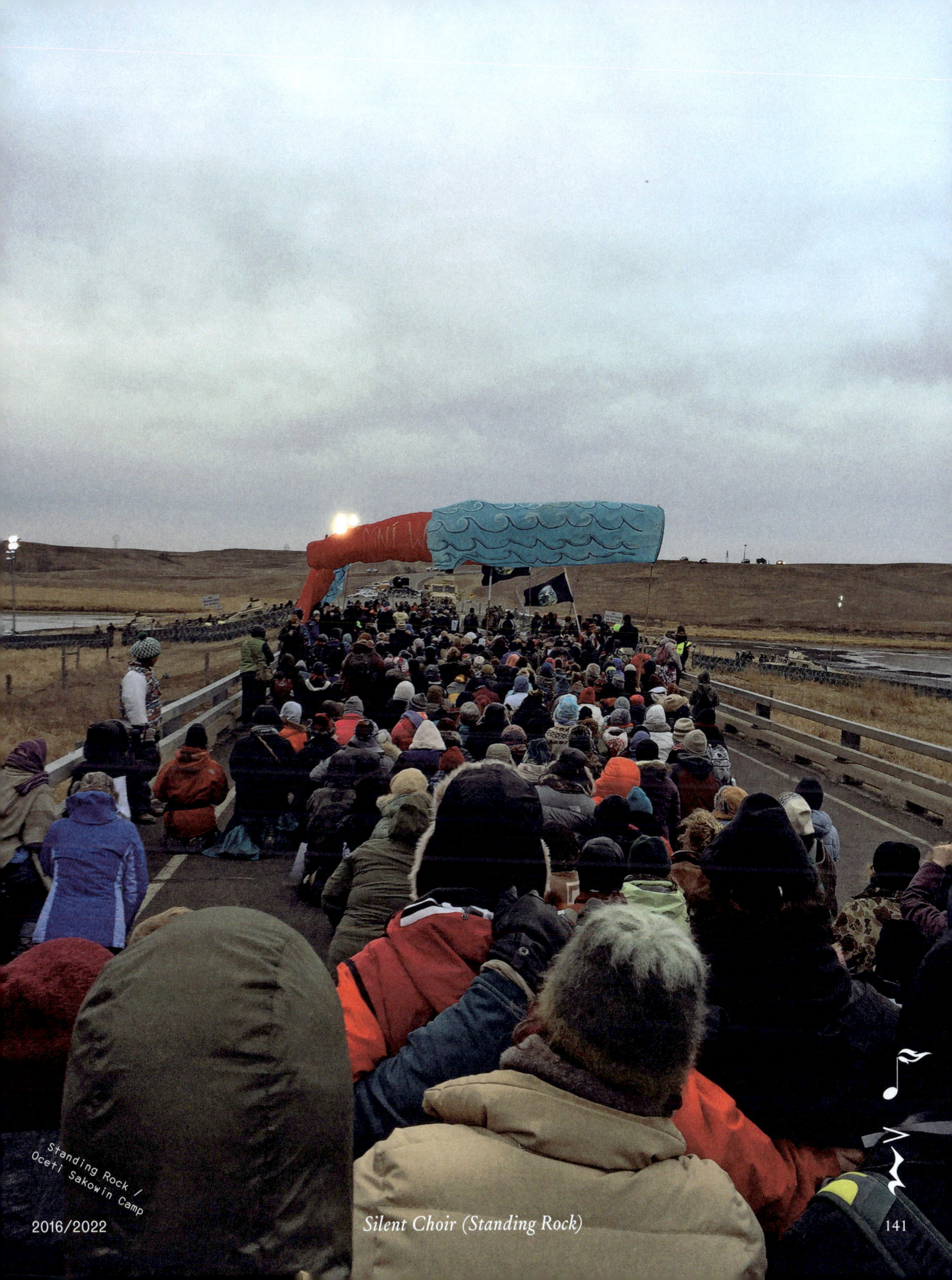

Silent Choir (Standing Rock)

Marja Bål Nango

Stolen

Stolen drums
Stolen winds
Stolen land
Stolen tongues
Stolen
Stolen stolen

They stole our language
Stole our thoughts
They stole our gods
Stole our drums
They stole our land
Stole our winds

All for something
That is true

Power drums, power lines, power to the people from the people

Trading land
For trauma
Sorrow
And
Grief

Traded land for trauma
Wiped our tears with golden coins
Replaced our gods with booze

Power to the people from the people

But we were never your people

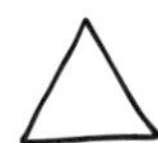

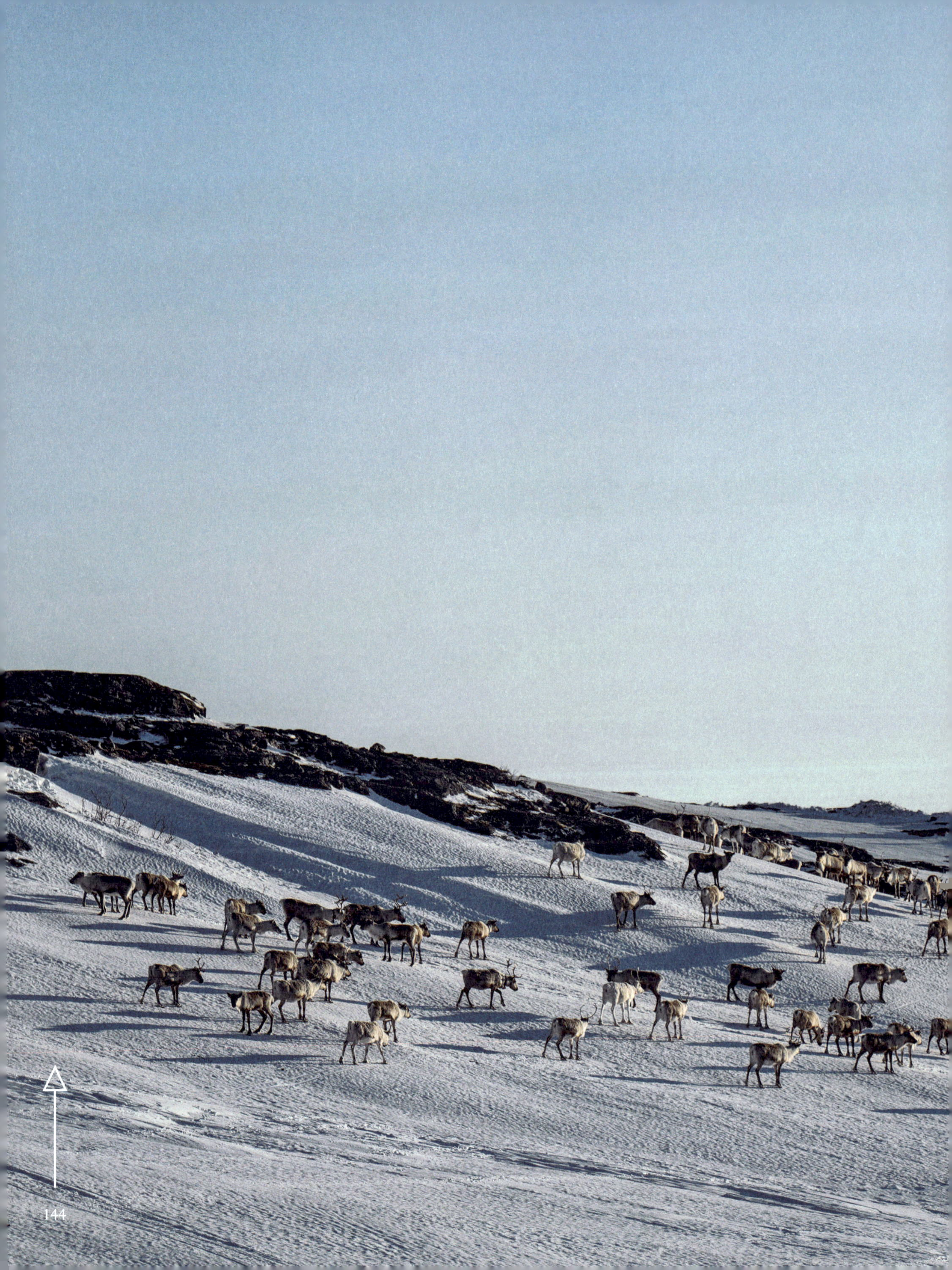

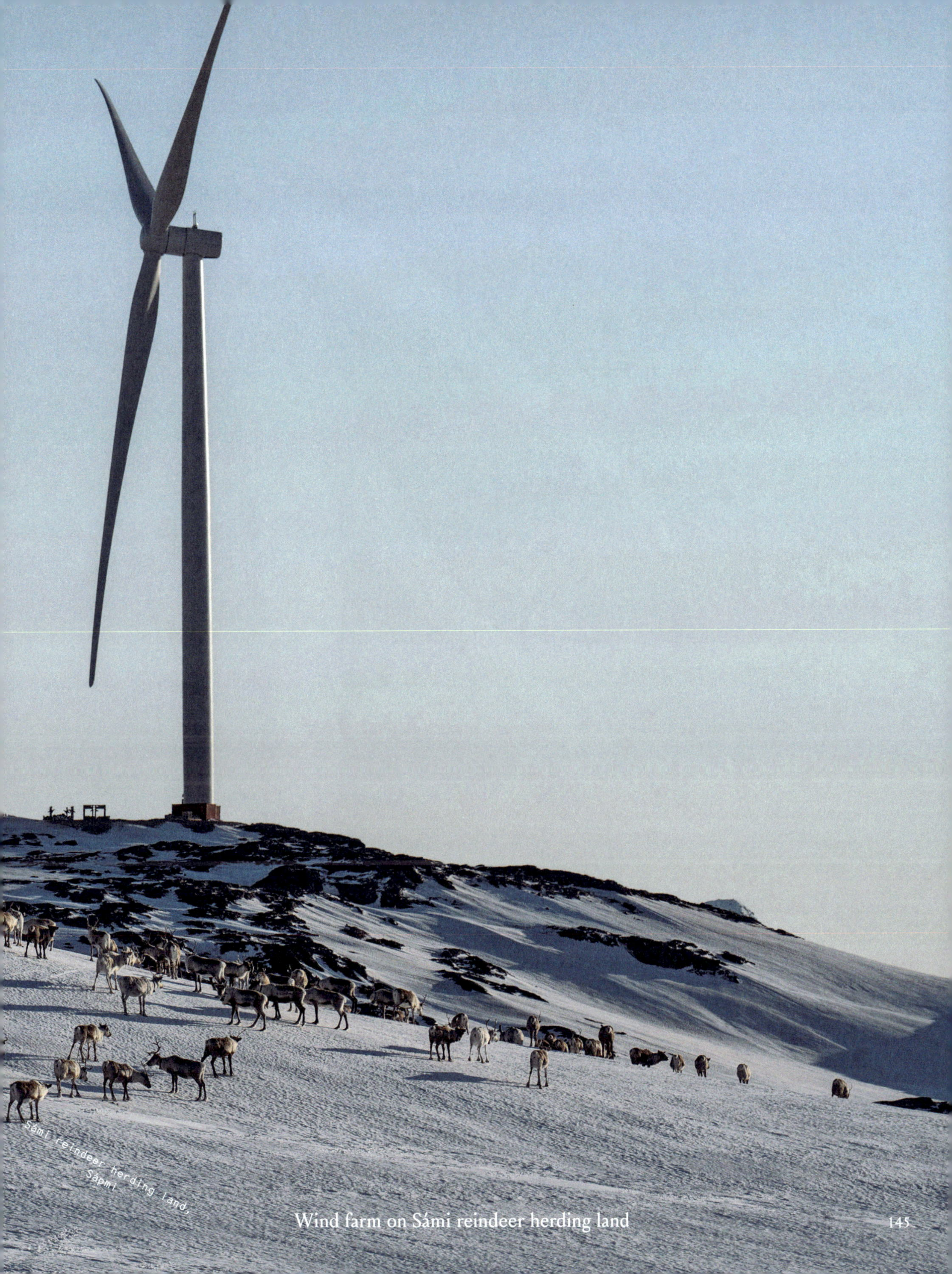

Wind farm on Sámi reindeer herding land

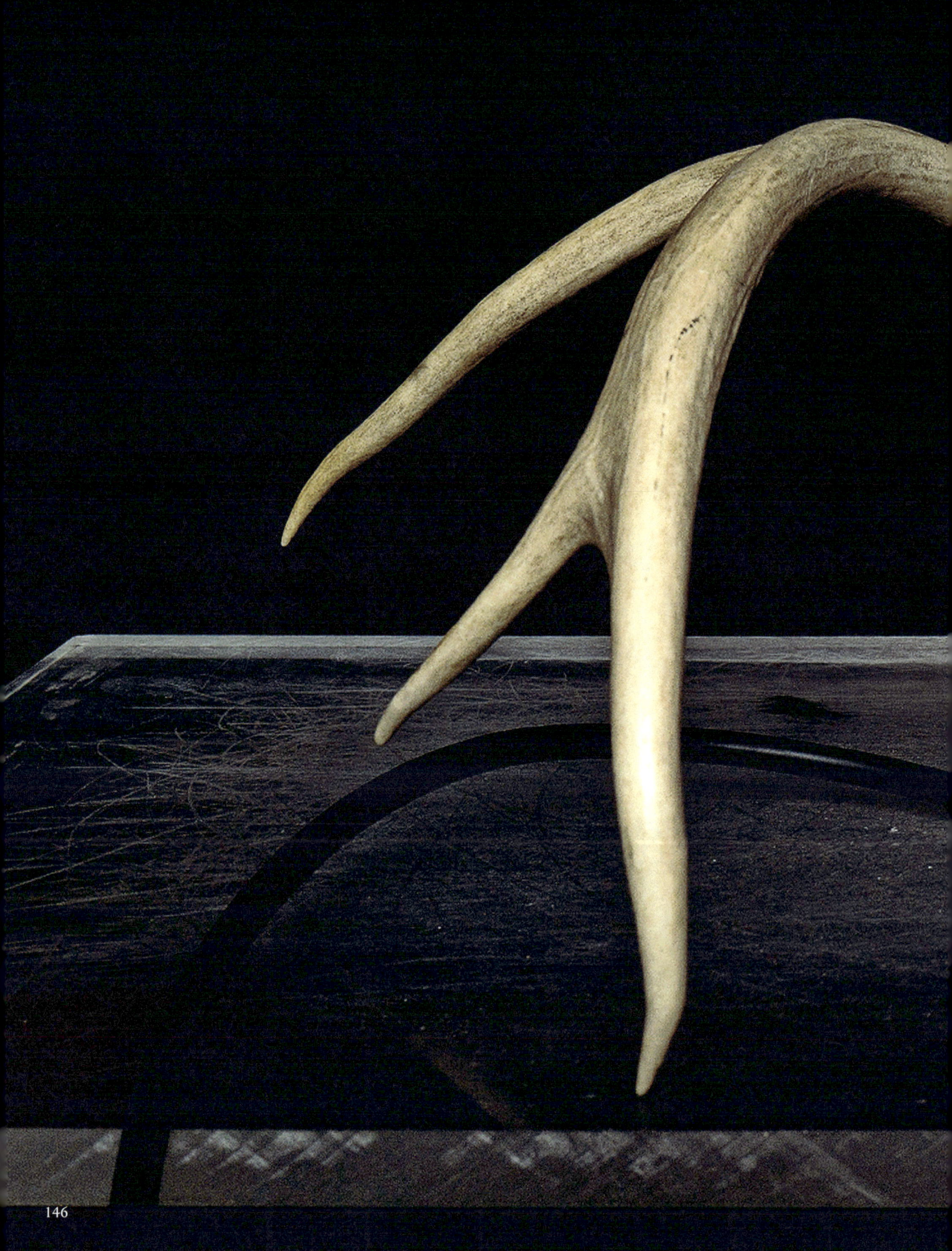

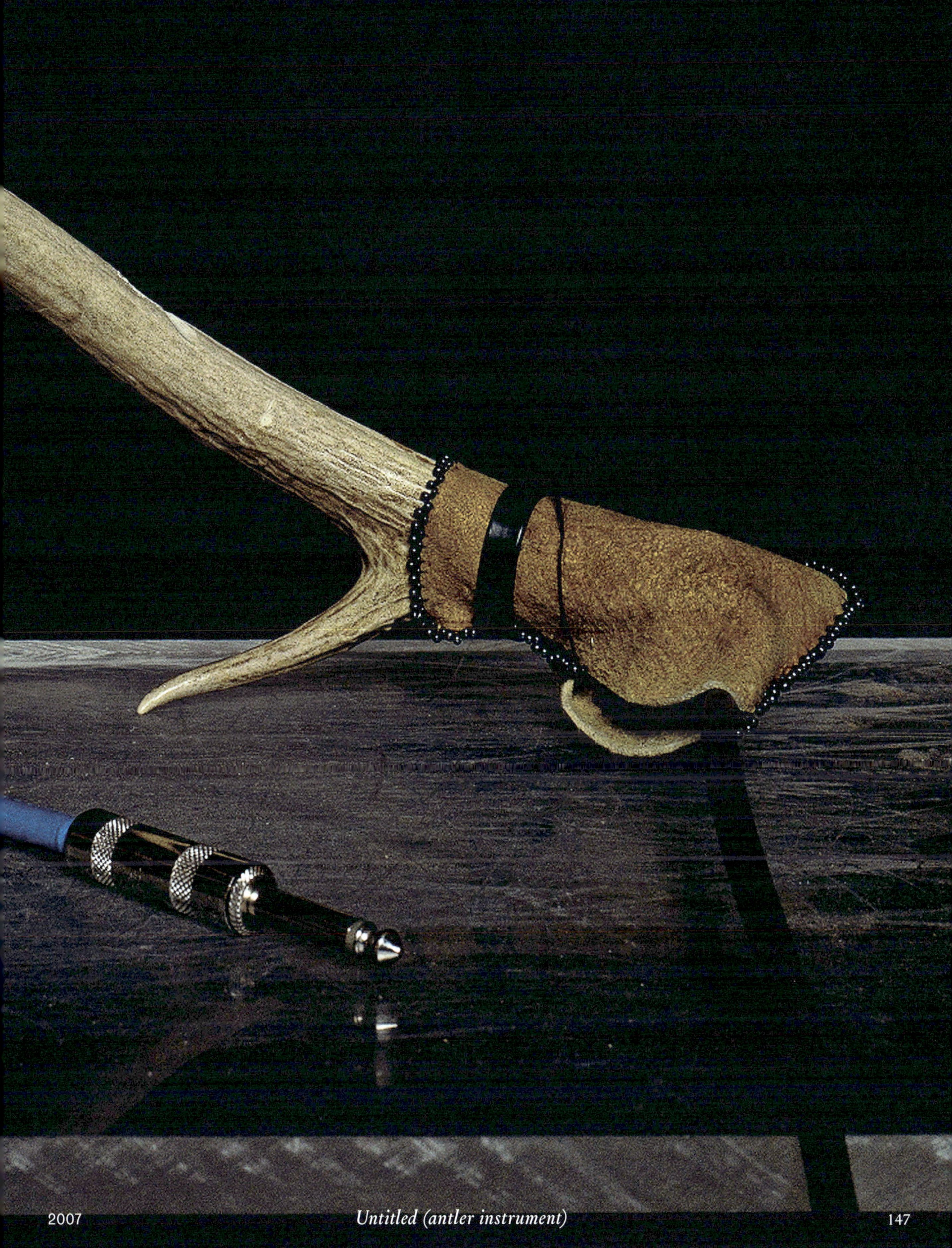

2007 *Untitled (antler instrument)*

Smávot Ingir

The Map

We look at the map together. This is all deserted, you say.

Index finger tracing the riverbed, following the migratory route, up toward the calving land.

Our voices are tired, quivering. Don't you *see* our words?

This is not deserted. Don't you *see* us?

In a language that we were forced to learn to survive, we draw on the map lying on the table in the meeting room. The use of the site, every little scree and patch of snow, is valuable, even the herding qualities of mosquitoes is something we show them.

In between the rocky mounds grow small plants that you never see, but the reindeer find their way to them. The annoying mosquito herds the animals upward to the patches of snow in the heat of summer. The rivers that you want to enclose in pipes are our natural fences.

Why is it that you always want to be in the best places?

Where the ground is bare early in spring, where reindeer find food after a harsh winter, where calves are born. Why should the construction roads go through mating land, migratory routes, why do you think that the wind turbines should be placed where the best winter food for our animals is?

You're blind.

Norway's laws do not protect reindeer herding, when the state and developers are allowed to roam freely in the name of the green shift, while wiping out the country's Indigenous peoples and our traditional lives. No wonder we are tired, for generations we have given, piece by piece, for the benefit of society at large. Now there is nothing more to give on our part. If we are now forced to give you the last remnants of the reindeer's traditional areas, we draw our last breath and become the living dead, wandering between our father and mother, sun and earth.

But you don't give a shit about that.

A dead Sámi is a good Sámi.

Something that has been, something you can exhibit in museums. You wear our dead bodies like jewelry, look what we've preserved for posterity. In the end, the Norwegianization project of the state was carried out, our total annihilation.

Your new skin starts to itch, vibrate, what's going on? So you didn't know that we Sámi never die. Even if we disappear from this time in this life.

Our bodies suffocate you, as you feverishly try to undress, but we burn ourselves into your skin, your soul, your being, and all your sins. No one escapes. We spit you out of our bodies, our land. You're banished, with your moneybag.

Leave and never come back.

We will preserve the land forever.

For us, the reindeer, and our descendants.

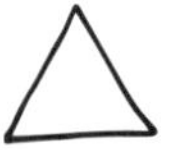

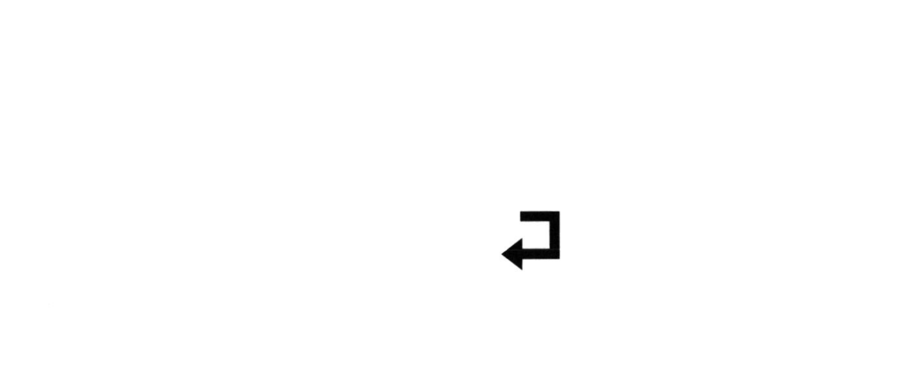

INT. - DAY

UNNAMED INDIGENOUS ARTIST

My tribe walks counterclockwise when we enter a room. The clock is a colonial tool.

ANT

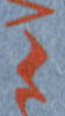

Sigbjørn Skåden

Birds I've heard close to home

Bird sound transcriptions by ear and according to English orthography. These birds are heard in and around Láŋtdievvá/Planterhaug (68.537216 north, 16.7530003 east). The list is not exhaustive.

Along the fences and fields

Tseetsoo-tweetweetweetwee-yessir
– Čáhčče
Grrrgrrr-grraaah-grrrgrrr-grraaah
– Garjá
Whahahahahaha-whahahahahaha
– Skire
Geddege-geddege-geddege-ge-geeeh
– Almmigáica
Greeeee-greeee-greeee-greeee
– Stearra

Around the yard

Wibit-gouweet-gouweet-gouweet-gouweet
– Láđđospálfu
Wee-weescree-weescree-weescree-weescreeeee
– Dálgaheasta
Twoo-twootwoo-trrree-twootwoo
– Ruoivil
Ouioui-ouioui-oui
– Seaibevuohttán
Kwreeeh-kwreeeh-kwreeeh
– Skáhpeloddi
Tweeweeweeweeweeweeweeh-tweeweeweeweeweeh
– Alitgaccet

In the woods

Hoooooo-hoorooroorooroo
– Idjaskuolfi
Deereedeedeereedeedeereedee
– Hábat
Who-who-who-who-who-who
– Huikeloddi
Hoohoo-hoohoo-hoohoo
– Giehka
Drrrrrrrrrrrrrr-drrrrrrrrr-drrrr
– Čáihni
Glgh-glghglghglgh-grrtgrrtgrrt
– Čukča
Whoooh-Whoooh
– Lidnu
Kweetreetree-kweetreetree-tweetwaa-tweetwaa-tsirrick-tsirrick-bwooee-tsipptsipptsipptsipp-bwooee-tsipp-twootwee-twoo-twoo-bweeptrrp
– Čirggás

Down in the marshes

Bwooooweeeee-bwooooweeeee-bwooooweeeee
– Jeaggeloddi
Reereereereereereereereereeree
– Čuovži
Gwoooo-gwoooo-gwoooo-gweeee-gweeee-gweeee
– Guške

On the waters

Goooo-goooo-gooowiaaaah-gooowiaaaah
– Gáhkkor
Gwaaa-gwaaa-gwaaa-gwaaa-gwaaa
– Rakču
Eeeep-aeeeep-eeep
– Njuokča
Gwahgah-gwahgwahgwaaahgaaaah-gwahgwahgaa
– Ránesčuonjá
Kreeeekrk-trwee-tweetweetwee-dree-dree
– Čierit

Circling the cliffs

Rooah-rooah-rooah-rooah
– Ruŋká

In the mountains

Gweeeh-gweeeh-gweeeh
– Boaimmáš
Gwah-gw-gw-gw-gw-gwah
– Rievssat
Twotwee-tweetreetreetweetree
– Állat

Might be lost?

Aaoooo-aaoooo-aaoooo
– Hávda
Goooah-goooah-gwah-
gwah-gwah-gwah-gwah
– Gáiru
Tawee-tawee-tawee-
tawee-tawee
– Cagan

Appendix – Bird names in translation

Láđđospálfu – Barn swallow
Dálgaheasta – Great tit
Ruoivil – Bullfinch
Seaibevuohttán – White wagtail
Skáhpeloddi – Bohemian waxwing
Alitgaccet – Blue tit
Čáhčče – Wren
Garjá – Hooded crow
Skire – Magpie
Almmigáica – Snipe
Stearra – Starling
Idjaskuolfi – Tawny owl
Hábat – Northern goshawk
Huikeloddi – Boreal owl
Giehka – Cuckoo
Čáihni – Woodpecker
Čukča – Western capercaillie
Lidnu – Eagle-owl
Čirggás – Song thrush
Jeaggeloddi – Golden plover
Čuovži – Dunlin
Guške – Curlew
Gáhkkor – Red-throated loon
Rakču – Mallard
Njuokča – Whooper swan
Ránesčuonjá – Greylag goose
Čierit – Arctic tern
Ruŋká – Raven
Boaimmáš – Rough-legged buzzard
Rievssat – Willow ptarmigan
Állat – Snow bunting
Hávda – Eider
Gáiru – Great black-backed gull
Cagan – Oystercatcher

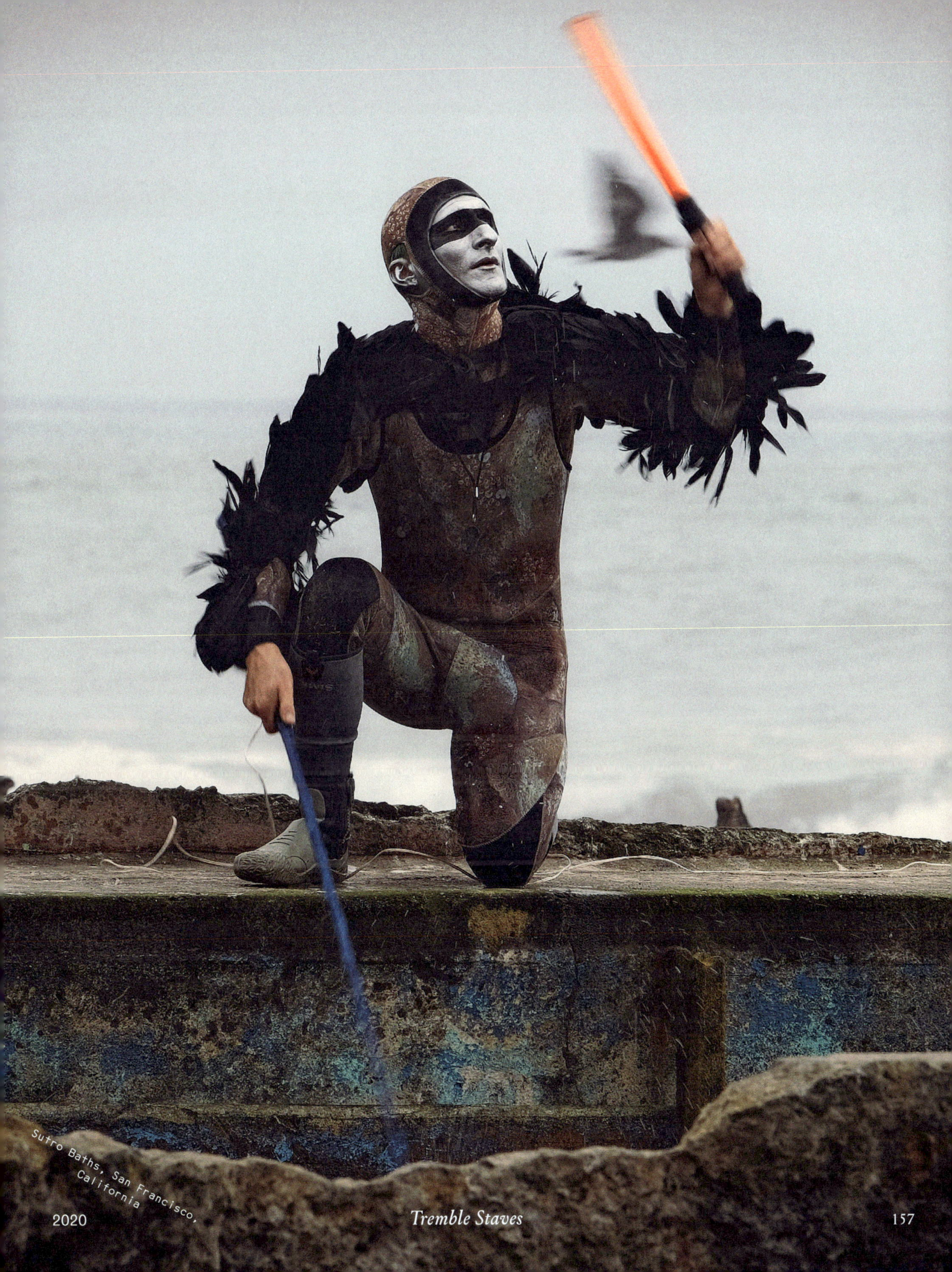

Sutro Baths, San Francisco, California

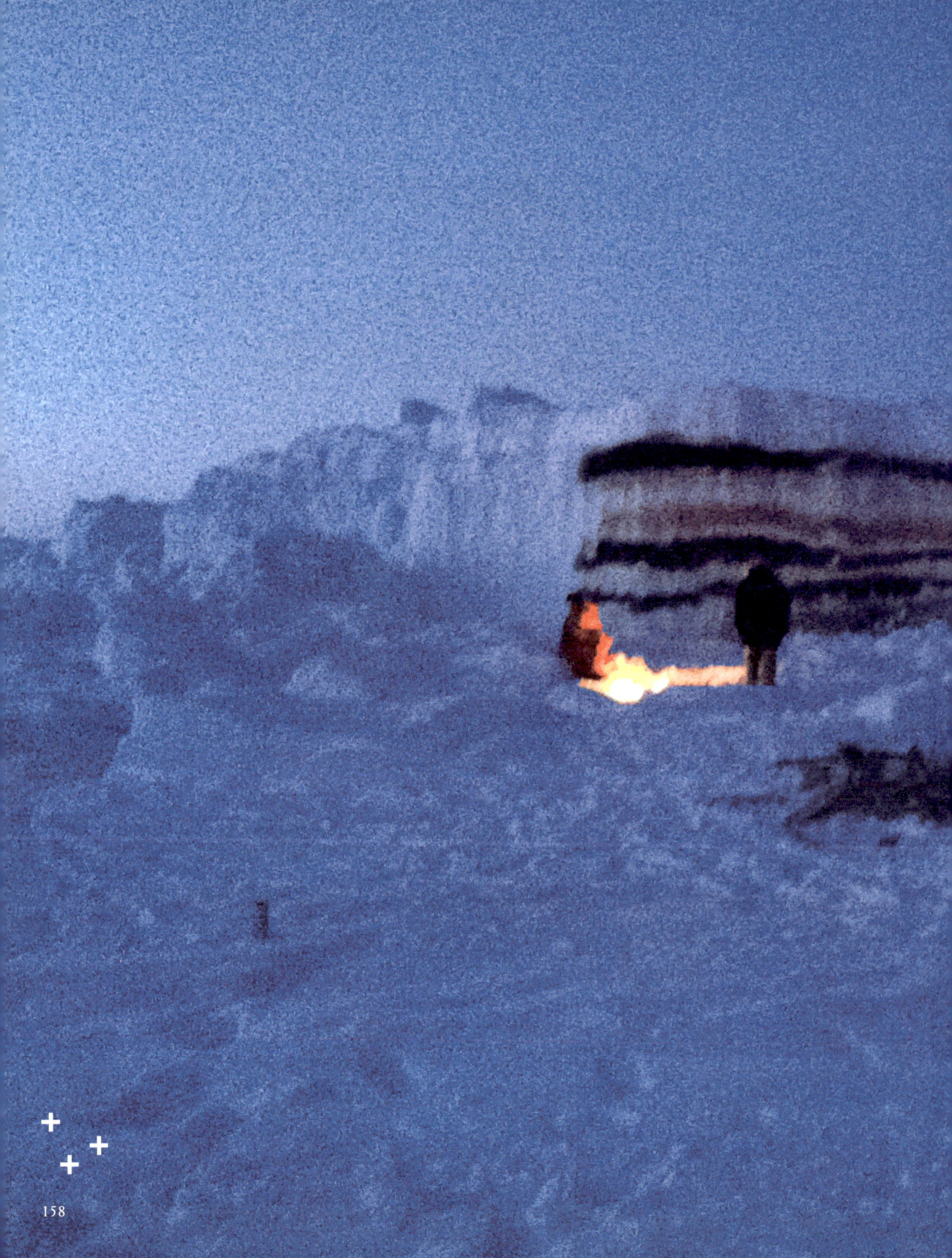

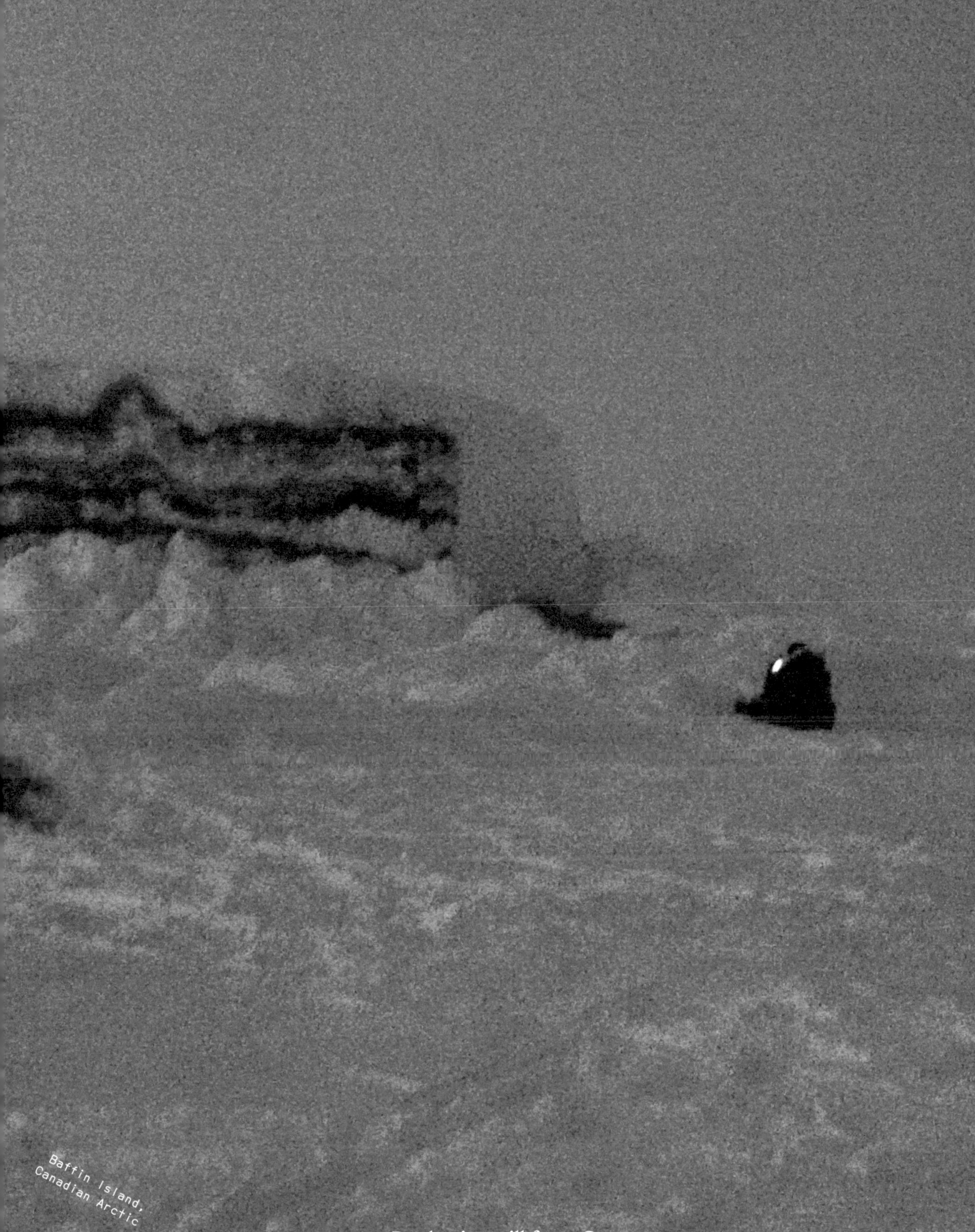

2013–15 Production still from *Gauge*

Candice Hopkins

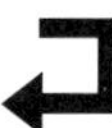

An archive of sound

Howl.

Careening down a valley of sandstone cliffs
where Navajo Nation borders Hopi. The car
window rolls down, raw air rushes in. Just then
a recorder captures the high pitch of hot wind.
The window rolls up again. Thin red dust settles
on the car's dashboard. We watch the cliffs
in silence.

Years later, listening amid a sweaty noise set
in Albuquerque, I think I hear this pitch again.
I open my eyes and see that it's the screech of
a whistle, one cast from an ancient instrument
carved from the leg bone of an eagle. Bone
and hide were the first instruments. From their
rhythms came the first music. Before that was
the wind. At least in these parts.

Hiss.

Three images:

A deep valley, its sandy bottom specked with green cut by trails of dry arroyos. High walls streaked with ochre. A single rock towers in the middle like the sole remainder.

Dry yellow land recedes into deep purples. Light and shadow move in tandem up the face of the mountain range. The sky, a shock of radiating pink.

A single arching rock. In its ruddy center a perfect circle worn by millennia of wind and grit pictures the sky beyond.

A record needle drops. The image begins to spin. Field recordings of each place—Spider Rock, the Sandia Mountains, Window Rock—captured during the quietude of daybreak and dusk are turned to their maximum volume. Out of the grooves comes a dry hiss.

Scrape.

A shrill note pierces the dense air amid a crush of overlapping sounds. A deer antler is scraped hard against glass, each pass leaving thin streaks of marrow. The marrow blunts the shrill; the antler's tips intensify it. The tone's sharp edges pierce the rafters. They hold an archive of sound.

Raven says music is beauty aligning with other beauty. At other times, it is nature misaligning with machines. That thin trace of marrow on glass is evidence of those alignments and misalignments. Meanwhile, music is found in the remains.

Song.

Mid-set, the faint voice of a man singing is played from a small tape deck. His chorus emanating as though from the pit of another Earth. Held in its reverb are generations of familial songs, passed from Cheii to Cheii. The singing is stretched to accommodate ancient ears.

Songs sung in ceremony transit along the inner edge of earthen walls. Recorded on tape, they become a citation sedimented beneath other recordings. An origin repeated, they are the foundation of all songs, including this one.

Roar.

A motley assortment of items fashioned into other instruments to make new music. The end of a length of dark plastic tube is wound with black electrical tape. Two cables emerge from one end. One plugs into an amp, the other input leads to a photosensitive trigger.

During the set, the venue goes dark. Darkness has a way of concentrating sound. A small flash-light switches on. Each time the light passes the end of the plastic tube, it triggers a portal of noise that roars in rhythm with each swing. This is a drum; the drumstick is light itself.

Trill.

A collection of ancient whistles. Most made from clay. Some are in the shape of small birds; others, tiny people. Many of the people are crafted with their mouths open, as though captured mid-note. Seeing them is a reminder of how these Puebloan instruments live in collections—made amid song and ceremony, theirs is now a profoundly silent world.

Their faint music is tucked among the thresholds of the exhibition space, where one door leads to another, and hidden in the ceiling above the vitrines. In this new ensemble, the whistles are sounding again. Their chirps, their trills, their minor timbres shape a soundscape that tethers their time with ours. They carry this with them on return to their shelves and their boxes. Their waiting now an expectant pause.

Gust.

A slow build. First one layer, then another. The nearly imperceptible changes that drones embody. A mass witnessing for a crowd of hundreds. In time, these layers encompass the cavernous room. Starting low, near the floor, they rise in the space, nestling among steel beams, along high metal doors, industrial cables, and giant pulleys.

Later a multitude of tiny brass bells chime, like a predawn awakening. Their light tone pricks the heavy brick walls.

The player then lies down, a directional speaker in each hand. The wail of wind emerges from each, beaming the recording around the room. People, unsure of the origin of the sound, sit up in disbelief as the gust washes over them. They think their ears have deceived them.

Lexicon   Raven Chacon

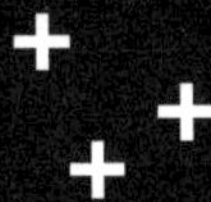

Stars

In *Compass* [p. 79], this symbol signifies the right-hand or left-hand hammer-on any three notes, one at a time, letting each sustain before tapping the next. In *American Ledger No. 1* [pp. 38–39], a single cross signifies any percussive sound.

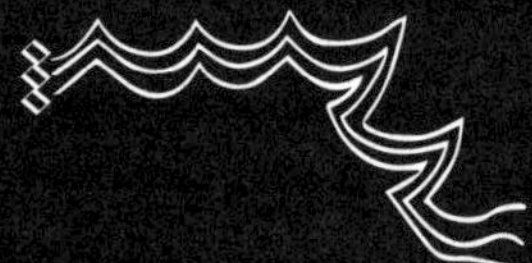

Learning a melody

This symbol is the main shape in *Whistle Quartet* [p. 57], and also appears in *Double Weaving* [p. 188]. It represents the learning of melody, where those learning must sing along with the teacher to learn the phrase. It represents a song that is sung all night, perhaps in a ceremony. In *Compass* [p. 79], the same symbol is used to indicate that the guitarist's right hand slide three fingers along three strings (over the fretboard) to produce harmonic glissandos.

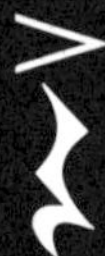

Accented rest

This symbol appears in many of my compositions. It is a marker of time; a beat of a pulse that is a silence more felt than heard (or not-heard).

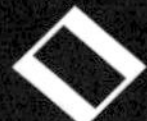

Diamond

The diamond is not necessarily an artificial harmonic, but rather meaning to lightly touch the most resonant part of the instrument. In addition to the cross/stars, this often represents the night sky and those who live above us.

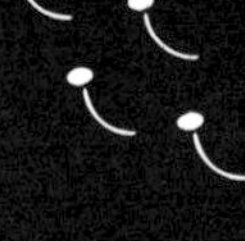

Pre-bend

Mostly for use on the guitar, this signifies an action of the left-hand pre-bent string to be plucked and slowly released while another finger prepares another pre-bend to be played next. This gesture represents the passing on of knowledge from one who is no longer living to the living. [*Compass*] [p. 79]

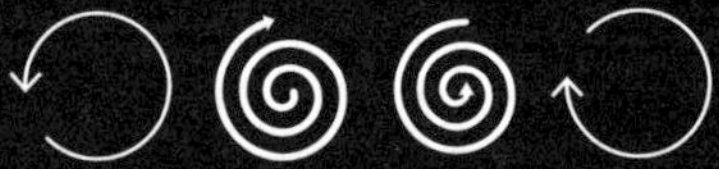

Circular bowings

On a stringed instrument, clockwise or counterclockwise bowing patterns per slurred passage. Bow position, speed, and number of the cycles may also be indicated. These also indicate any circular movement to be performed in a score (walking through a space, rubbing a material on a drum head). It also represents temporal patterns, or of someone losing their way, getting lost, possible spiraling into the ground or into the sky.

↑

High arrow

This signifies the highest pitch possible on any instrument. When notated for a singer, it asks that they sing higher than they ever had before. When it appears in a composition, it is often referencing the sky or a future that is in the sky.

Pressured bow stroke

On a stringed instrument, a sudden attack with heavy bow pressure, then with less pressure as the bow runs out, or vice versa. Although the effect of a normal crescendo and decrescendo is to increase volume, these only indicate an increase or decrease in distortion.

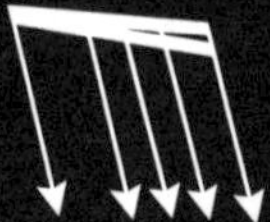

Rain

Quick exhalations from the mouth, as if crying. Used in *Ella Llora*.

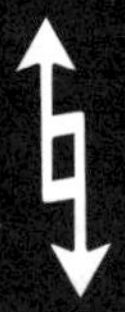

Off-tone

Two musicians start on the same pitch then slowly drift apart. When this appears in a narrative composition, it often symbolizes inequity between two groups.

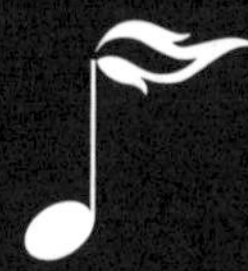

Flame match

Indicates to light a match in front of a microphone. Used in *American Ledger No. 1* [pp. 38–39].

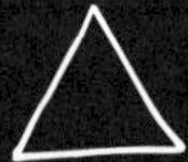

Reverse scream

For a singer to inhale while screaming, with an effect as if the scream is returning into the body. It is a quick swallow of the horror, so as to not burden the rest of the world with it.

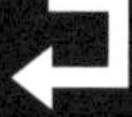

Reload

Used in *Report* [pp. 132–35] to indicate the reloading of the guns.

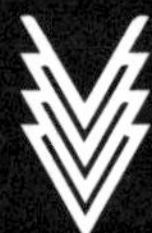

Realign

When the preceding section allows players to play out of time or sync, the *guide* cues the quartet to play on the downbeat of the indicated measure to re-sync.

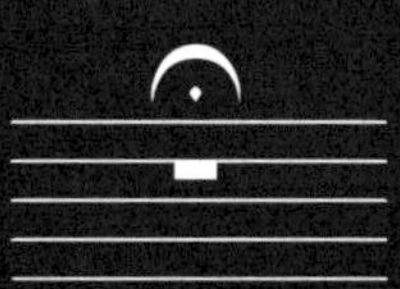

A sunrise

A fermata often represents more than a prolonged pause. It signifies a sun rising over a horizon, marking the passing of days (or any long time value) in the narrative of the piece.

Selected Works 1999–2024

Selected Compositions

p. 83
Duet 2000
Composition
For two musicians not making any sound

piano 2000
Composition
For noise electronics

Niltsa' Bi'áád Hooltil (Female Rain Approaching) 2001
Composition
For chamber ensemble

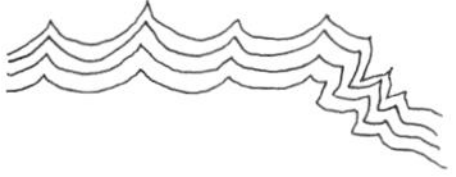

III + IV ENTER TOGETHER WHEN READY. REPEAT UNTIL THE END. IMPROVE WITH EACH REPEAT UNTIL MATCH THE ABILITIES OF THE LEADER(S). LEADER I MAY TAKE A BREAK WHEN DESIRED NEEDED

p. 57
Whistle Quartet 2001
Composition
For dog whistles

Whistle Quartet replicates the way one (or ones) might learn a song from an elder or leader; how one (or ones) become part of a group, and how one (or ones) become leaders when their leader is no longer there.

Pointillisimo 2001
Composition
For string quartet

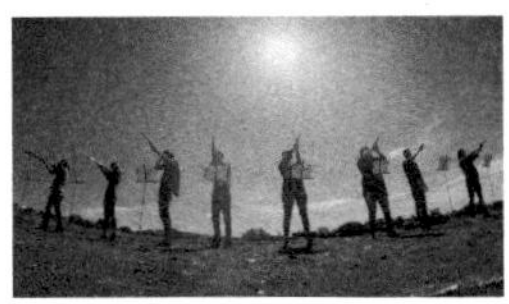

pp. 132–35
Report 2001/2015
Composition, video
For a firearm ensemble

The sonic potential of revolvers, handguns, rifles, and shotguns is utilized in a tuned cacophony of percussive blasts interspersed with voids of timed silence. In the piece, guns—instruments of violence, justice, defense, and power—are transformed into mechanisms for musical resistance. The composition was performed and recorded as a video in 2015.

Octet (dando la vuelta) 2002
Composition
For mixed ensemble

Octet (dando la vuelta) is an exercise in clockwise and counterclockwise motion and accidental harmony.

Ella Llora 2002
Composition
For female voice

This composition originated from a found cassette on the streets of Albuquerque of a woman giving recorded court testimony or deposition. A large portion of the audio recording comprises the woman in a state of sorrowful crying. The crying was transcribed into standard Western music notation for a soprano to perform. The original audio cassette has since been destroyed.

(+) cello 2003
Composition
For looped cello and interrupter

A 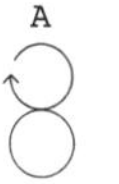 B 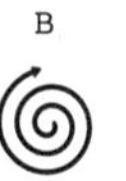 C 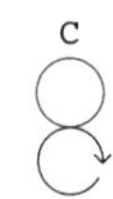 D 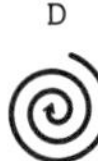

Performer #1: B C D A
Performer #2: C D A B
Performer #3: D A B C
Performer #4: A B C D

Music for Voice 2003
Composition
For 4 tam-tams

Each performer rubs on a tam-tam with a superball, while mouthing the heard "words" of the sounds produced by the gestures indicated. The audience or viewer infers their own version of what is being said.

Atsiniltlish' iye 2003
Composition
For flute, clarinet, bassoon, cello, and percussion

In *Atsiniltlish' iye*, every gesture is in the shape of a lightning zigzag.

Beesh Naalnishi 2003
Composition
For chamber orchestra

Beesh Naalnishi is composed of 24 inversions of a 24-note quarter-tone cluster.

Bilagáana ádin 2003
Composition
For solo flute and backing ensemble

Naakishchiin ana'i 2004
Composition
For flute and marimba
Commissioned by Kim Turney

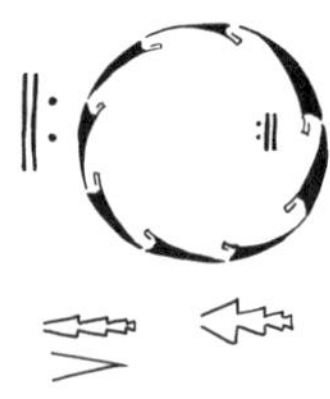

pp. 58-59
... lahgo adil'i dine doo yeehosinilgii yidaaghi 2004
Composition, performance
For chamber ensemble
This is a purely graphic notation score where the burden of creating "Indigenous music" is put upon the ensemble.

Mute Nonet 2004
Composition
For electric guitars and 8-channel mixer using the mute buttons

Lats' aadah 2004
Composition
For solo violin
Written for Mark Menzies

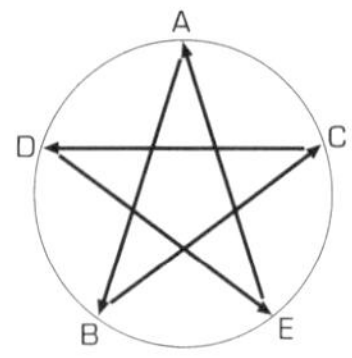

4th insert, verso
Mirror Quintet 2004
Composition
For 5 like strings
This is a teasing game.

Echo Contest 2005
Composition, performance
For 2 people to find each other in a feedback loop of mimicry

Scream Out of Each Window 2005
Composition, performance
For a family to perform in a very tall building

Solo for Guitar 2006
Composition
A prolonged song for guitar
Written for Gabriel Ayala

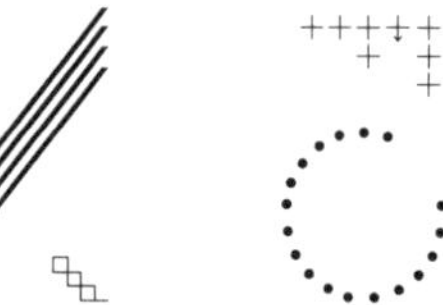

Adiits'a'ii 2006
Composition, performance
Trans. (from Navajo), "loud interpreter"
Similar to *... lahgo adil'i dine doo yeehosinilgii yidaaghi* but for nonmusicians.

Hasta'aadah 2006
Composition
For wind ensemble
Commissioned by the University of Mary Washington, Fredericksburg, VA
The conductor helps the group learn the piece but is not present for the performance.

Taa'go Deza (Three Points) 2007
Composition
3 songs for singing cellist
Commissioned by Dawn Avery

Nihikeedoo' yinaal 2007
Composition
For mixed ensemble and electronics
Commissioned by Contemporary Music Forum / VERGE Ensemble, Washington, DC
This work is a rare instance where Chacon has incorporated his noise instruments into a chamber composition.

Round 2007
Composition
For a turntable and many performers playing the same groove of a 12" record with amplified wooden skewers

Nilchi' Shada'ji Nalaghali 2008
Composition
For overly amplified feedback piano
Commissioned by Emanuele Arciuli
The performer's only action is to depress the keys slowly so as to allow the strings to resonate.

Whisper Trio 2008
Composition
A learning piece for 3 performers whispering a poem in an endangered language

Biyán 2011
Composition
For flute, clarinet, violin, cello, and percussion
Commissioned by the Chatter Ensemble of Albuquerque, New Mexico

Double Weaving 2014
Composition
For string quartet
The string quartet ETHEL commissioned *Double Weaving* in 2014, during the quartet's tenth and final year working with Chacon as part of the Native American Composers Apprenticeship Project. Chacon describes *Double Weaving* as an accumulation of techniques he learned from both ETHEL and his students during their workshops together.

Song for Voice, Drum, and Shadowing Voice 2015
Composition
A solo commissioned by Ruby Kato Attwood

pp. 54-56
The Journey of the Horizontal People 2016
Composition
For string quartet
Commissioned by the Kronos Quartet

The Journey of the Horizontal People is a future creation story, telling of a group of people traveling from west to east across the written page, contrary to the movement of the sun, but involuntarily and unconsciously allegiant to the trappings of time. With their bows, these wanderers sought out others like them, knowing that they could survive by finding these other clans who resided in the east, others who shared their linear cosmologies. It is told that throughout the journey, in their own passage of time, this group became the very people they were seeking.

Asdzaa Nadleehe & Yoolgai Asdzaa 2016
Composition
For soprano, mezzo-soprano, and instruments
Commissioned by Arizona Opera

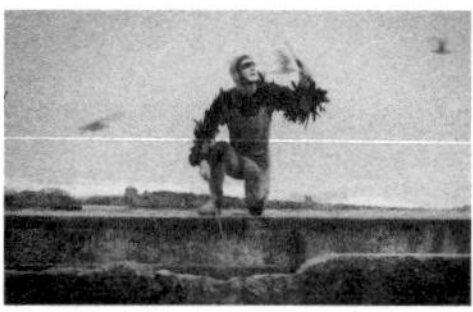

pp. 100–103, 157
Tremble Staves 2017–19
Composition, performance
Movements: *Estuary*, 2019; *Tributary*, 2017; *Delta*, 2019; *Channel*, 2019; *Distributary*, 2018; *Sound*, 2019
Commissioned by the Living Earth Show
Originally performed among the collapsed ruins of the failed Sutro Baths in San Francisco's Lands End, but can be performed by any ruins near a large body of water. Instruments include quarter-tone guitar, bathroom sink, floating cello, dowsing rods, bird calls, amplified tile, stirred broken mirrors, amplified fishing rod, homemade feedback ukulele, oxygen tank, student guitarists, thirteen-plus percussionists, and a narrator who tells the history of the acceleration of the site's ruins and waters.

Invisible Arc 2017
Composition
For solo cello
Written for Rhonda Rider

Tá́á'ts'áadah 2018
Composition
For solo trumpet
Commissioned by Delbert Anderson

p. 69
Quiver 2018
Composition
For solo cello
Commissioned by Michelle Kesler
Following *Taa'go Dez'a* (2007) and *Invisible Arc* (2017), *Quiver* is the third part in a trilogy of conceptual works for solo cellist on the subject of hunting and its traditional protocols. This final section of the larger work examines patience and waiting, precision of technique, and navigations around the will of nature.

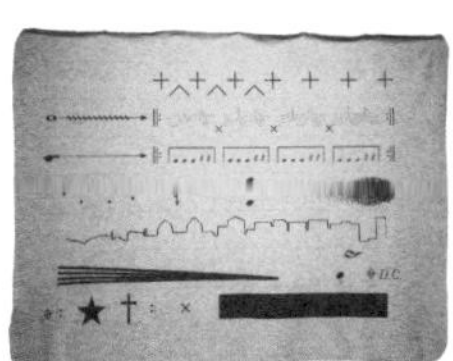

pp. 38–39
American Ledger No. 1 2018
Composition
Unique army blanket, digital print
American Ledger No. 1 is a narrative score for performance, telling the creation story of the founding of the United States of America. In chronological descending order, moments of contact, enactment of laws, events of violence, the building of cities, and erasure of land and worldview are mediated through graphic notation, and realized by sustaining and percussive instruments, coins, axe and wood, a police whistle, and a match. The score is to be displayed as a flag, a wall, a blanket, a billboard, or a door.

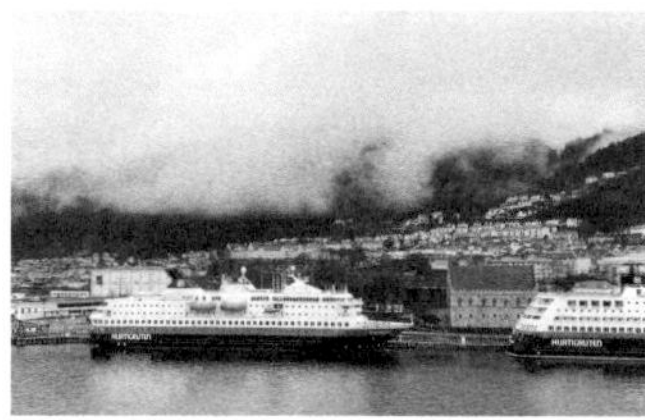

Chorale (for 4–8 docked ships with foghorns) 2018
Composition
The piece, which lasts five minutes, is written for four to eight foghorns, and is performed by the crew of each ship.

American Ledger No. 2 2019
Composition
Commissioned by Atomic Culture
American Ledger No. 2 is a site-specific score for the city of Tulsa, Oklahoma, and surrounding areas. Through its symbology and subsequent sound, the score recounts episodes of the region's forced migrations, both into and out of the city, and violence toward Black and Native communities. To be performed by many people walking a circular path, *American Ledger No. 2* utilizes drums, whistles, megaphone, trumpet, mallet percussion, and matchsticks, in an unstable system of equity and exchange. The score can be presented as a flag, a billboard, railroad debris, or any pyrographed object sourced from the region.

(Bury Me) Where the Lightning [Will] Never Find Me 2019
Composition
For bass clarinet, percussion, violin, and cello
Commissioned by Arraymusic
(Bury Me) Where the Lightning [Will] Never Find Me is a continuation of ideas from *Atsiniltlish' iye* (2003).

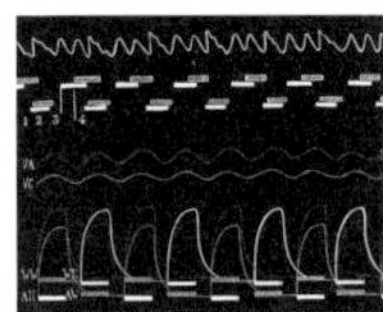

p. 81

Horse Notations 2019
Composition
For flute, string quartet, and 2 hand drums
Commissioned by Oregon East Symphony

The composition utilizes an 1874 *Popular Science* article titled "The Paces of the Horse" and its analysis of horse gaits—the walk, trot, canter, and gallop—as source material for rhythms, drum patterns, bow pressures, and volume arcs. Graphic representations from the article appear in the score as notations for the drum(s) and any instruments that learn from the drum. *Horse Notations* is a look at the speed of the day, a perspective of tempo throughout one's life, and a view of the momentum of shared human and animal history.

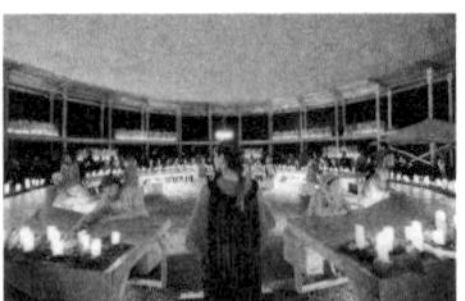

pp. 106-9

Sweet Land 2020
Composition
Co-composed with Du Yun, libretto by Aja Couchois Duncan and Douglas Kearney
Commissioned and produced by The Industry

Sweet Land is a Manifest Destiny opera that erases itself while weaving together several narratives simultaneously, opening with the arrival of settler-colonial visitors in the homelands of an Indigenous civilization. As the story unfolds, past scenes are left behind and erased, emulating the whitewashing of dissent against dominant historical narratives.

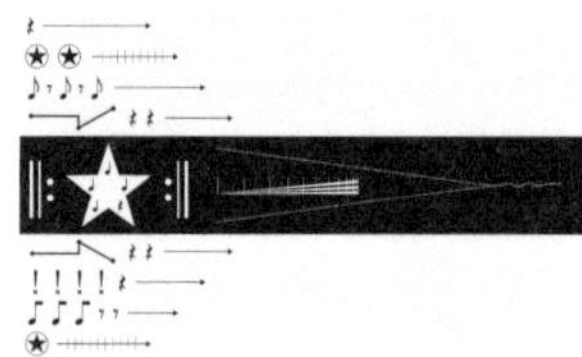

American Ledger No. 3 (In All Its Phases ...) 2020
Composition
For 2 women's choirs, 2 glockenspiels (or other metallophone), 2 drums, and coins
Dedicated to Ida B. Wells
Commissioned by the Renaissance Society

This is a score presented as a flag and newspaper telling the story of historical as well as recent lynchings in the United States of America, its acceptance in the South, and the complacency of the North. *American Ledger No. 3* is a negotiation of viewpoint, the navigation around noise, and the revealing of truth through voice.

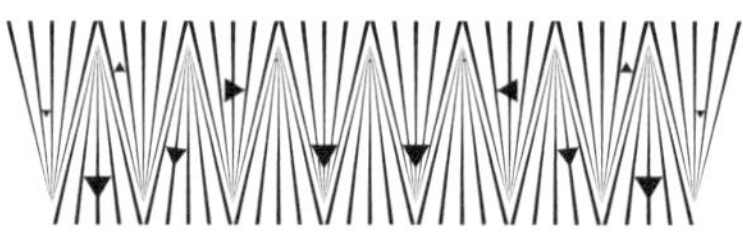

pp. 24, 44-45

Plainsong 2020
Composition
For many musicians with sustaining instruments
Commissioned by AKA Artist-Run Centre

Plainsong is a large-format outdoor score displayed on the side of a building, presenting musical staves and noteheads of various sizes. While producing long-sustaining tones on any instrument, musicians move to discrete near or distanced positions in order to navigate through the score. *Plainsong* does not have clear beginnings or endings; a performance of tones appearing as a slow-paced interruption in the day.

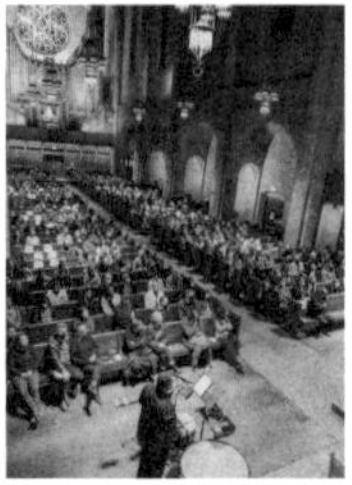

pp. 74-75

Voiceless Mass 2021
Composition
For pipe organ and large ensemble
Commissioned by WI Conference of the United Church of Christ, Plymouth Church UCC, and Present Music

Voiceless Mass is a Pulitzer Prize-winning large ensemble work composed specifically for the Nichols & Simpson organ at the Cathedral of St. John the Evangelist in Milwaukee, Wisconsin, but can be performed in any space of worship with high ceilings and a pipe organ. This work considers the spaces in which we gather, the history of access to these spaces, and the land upon which these buildings sit. Though "mass" is referenced in the title, the piece contains no audible singing voices, instead using the openness of the large space to intone the constricted intervals of the wind and string instruments. In exploiting the architecture of the cathedral, *Voiceless Mass* considers the futility of giving voice to the voiceless, when ceding space is never an option for those in power.

pp. 76-77

Music for 13 Paths 2021
Composition, sound installation, and performance
For thirteen performers with wind chimes, equally divided within an octave; walking plan adapted to the Benton Park neighborhood of St. Louis, Missouri, in the context of Counterpublic 2023

p. 79
Compass 2021
Composition
For overly amplified guitar
Commissioned by United States Artists
Performed outdoors, the performer takes cues from shadows, wind, insects, clouds, and more to determine the course of musical decisions.

Being Future Being 2021
Composition
For dancers and noise
Commissioned by
Emily Johnson / Catalyst

Owl Song 2021
Composition
For sinfonietta and voice
Commissioned by
Borealis Festival for the
BIT20 Ensemble

Ashdla' 2022
Composition
For string orchestra
Commissioned by
I Musici de Montréal

Call for the Company in the Morning 2022
Composition
For a variety of 8 trumpets
Commissioned by hcmf
and BBC Radio 3
The trumpet as a signal instrument is investigated in this piece, referencing fox-hunting horn calls to create an open landscape of drones. Its roles in the marking of time passing, of hunting, sport, and ecological balances are explored, its tone corrupted into a timbre of fear.

Old Song 2022
Composition
For English horn, bass clarinet, cello, and percussion
Commissioned by
Chatter New Mexico
Old Song is a continuation of Chacon's exploration of lightning and its zigzag shape that started with *Atsiniłtłish 'iye* (2003) and continued with *(Bury Me) Where the Lightning [Will] Never Find Me* (2019). This third piece in the series acknowledges how the sound of thunder has remained a musical influence throughout human existence.

Wave upon wave 2023
Composition
For 8 hyper-directional voices
Words by Natalie Diaz
Commissioned by the Perelman
Performing Arts Center and thingNY
Wave upon wave tells of the ongoing violence that has occurred in the surrounding area of Manahatta, where it was performed, even while it continues to be a site of refuge for many.

Artworks

Field Recordings 1999
Sound installation
Headphones, audio,
photographs, and text

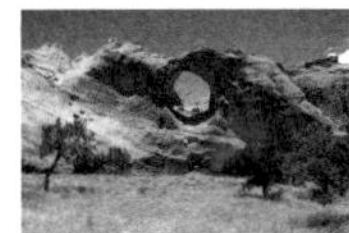

p. 27 *Window Rock, 4:00 a.m*

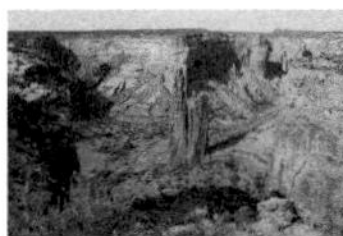

p. 29 *Canyon de Chelly, 10:00 a.m.*

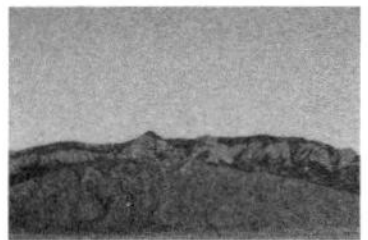

p. 30 *Sandia Mountains, 11:00 p.m.*

Three field recordings of places in the Southwest, captured during quiet times of day or night, are then amplified to their maximum volume. While seemingly reduced to noise, the recordings magnify revealing colors and patterns, giving new information about the essence of each location.

Meet the Beatless 2003
Sound work, album
Meet the Beatless is an album of ten songs composed using audio shards from 140 Beatles songs. Samples of the original records were chosen for their chord progression, tempo/time signature, lyrical content, harmonic (non)compatibility, and retrograde inversion possibilities.

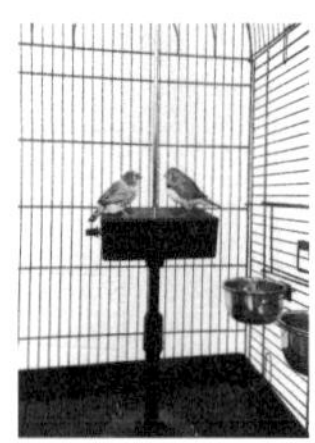

While Contemplating Their Fate in the Stars, the Twins Surround the Enemy 2003
Installation
Live finches, cage, pitch theremin, and speakers

A pair of zebra finches interact with a pitch theremin instrument while situated in a cage. The instrument, being the center of the birds' home, becomes an encroaching presence that the birds realize can be manipulated over time. Over the course of the installation, the birds change the pitch with the placement of their bodies while harmonizing with the instrument by matching their chirps with its pitch.

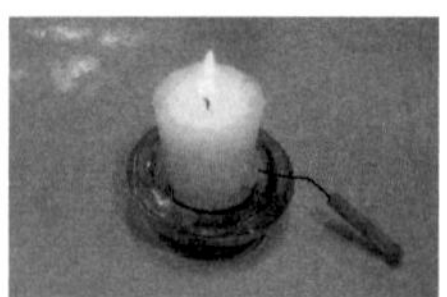

Still Life (0) 2004
Installation
300–400 custom candle-firecrackers

This is the first installation in a series that speaks to long-form American Indian history, from creation stories to the contemporary world. It is a site-specific work, recognizing each year of encroachment and colonial occupation in a North American location. When each candle burns down, a firecracker is ignited and sounded, representing cumulative generational trauma and subsequent actions of resistance.

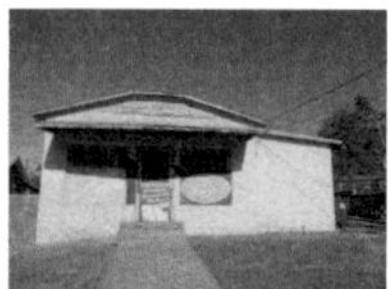

Ofrendas de Luz 2008
Installation
Headphones, audio, photographs, and text

An anonymous chain letter becomes an invitation to anonymous recording sessions in pitch-black abandoned buildings in Albuquerque, New Mexico.

Drum Grid 2010
Community collaboration, performance, score, and video

A broken telephone game composition for numerous drummers, each positioned on a street corner. Beginning with a single drum hit from one player, subsequent drummers imitate the sound of the previous drummer down the block, with the gesture being misinterpreted and evolving as it travels around the neighborhood.

Still Life No. 1 2011
Sound installation
Mirrors, analog timers, strobe lights, and photo sensor

Still Life No. 1 is a full-room installation version of the *Light Drum* (2008).

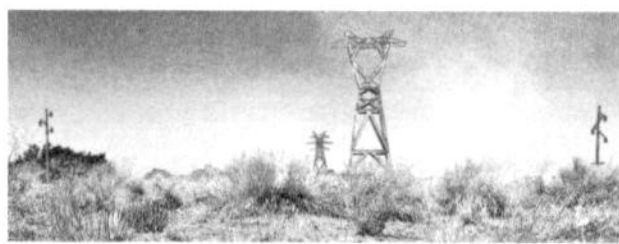

pp. 14–15

Singing Toward the Wind Now / Singing Toward the Sun Now 2012
Sound installation
4 stainless steel sculptures, speakers, piano wire, solar panels, oscillators, and amplifiers

Installed at Canyon de Chelly National Monument / Visitors Center, Chinle, Arizona, in 2012, *Singing Toward the Wind Now / Singing Toward the Sun Now* is an arrangement of four metal sculptures that function as musical instruments played by the natural elements. Electrical utility towers span that Navajo Nation; here they are incorporated with Navajo geometries that appear in weaving and painting designs. Two of the towers function as harps, their strings activated by the blowing wind and sand, producing a quiet singing drone. The other two are solar-powered oscillators, producing a faint and subtle electronic beating sound. Representing the Talking Gods, this council of holy people speaks to visitors to the canyon.

Still Life No. 2 2012
Sound installation

Still Life No. 2 is constructed of single drumbeats composed from the shards of found sounds and field recordings of both the natural and the mechanical world. These beats are stretched across an unstable timeline to approximate the unpredictability of linear time, measuring the inconsistencies and unsteadiness of the day, whether within a minute, an hour, or a twenty-four-hour cycle. Recorded in Morley, Alberta; Albuquerque, New Mexico; Mora, New Mexico; and Tuba City, Arizona.

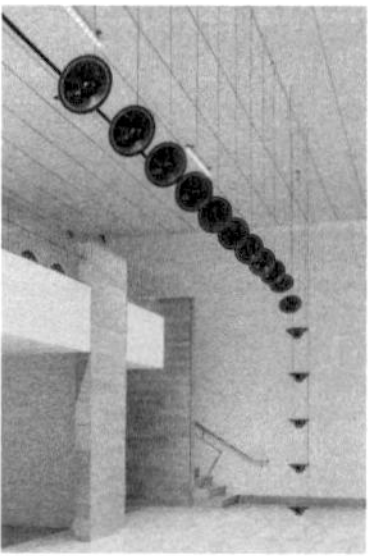

pp. 35–37

Still Life No. 3 2015
Sound installation
Speakers, text, and timed lights

This work retells the Diné Bahane'—the Navajo story of creation and emergence into the current world. Using timed audio and delay systems, the speech of a woman telling the story in Navajo language is transferred through a series of connected speakers activating future and past parts of the same story, revealing instances when long history repeats itself. As words emanate from the speakers, voices overlap, blurring the linearity of the story.

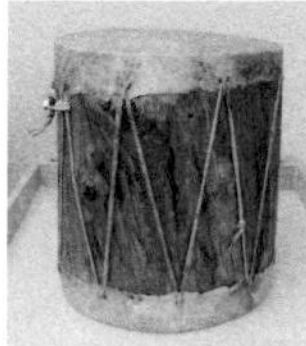

Still Life No. 4 2017
Sound installation
Reclaimed sound

Still Life No. 4 is a recording of an old Pueblo drum stewarded in the Colorado Springs Fine Arts Center collection. The location and date of the drum's origin are not known. A single drum hit was captured and inserted repeatedly into multiple accelerated audio timelines, allowing the instrument to align with the "speed of life" of other living beings in the building.

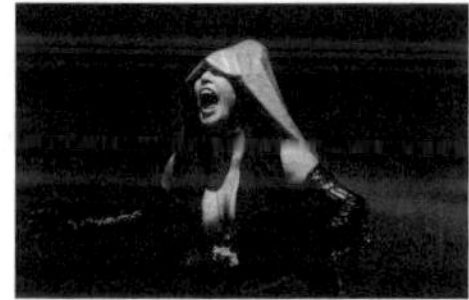

pp. 91, 110–12
For Zitkála-Šá 2017–20
Score series:
For Autumn Chacon
For Carmina Escobar
For Joy Harjo
For Candice Hopkins
For Suzanne Kite
For Barbara Croall
For Cheryl L'Hirondelle
For Ange Loft
For Laura Ortman
For Heidi Senungetuk
For Olivia Shortt
For Jacqueline Wilson

For Zitkála-Šá is a series of graphic scores dedicated to contemporary American Indian, First Nations, and Mestiza women working in music performance, composition, and sound art. Chacon envisioned the scores as portraits of the women and how they navigate the twenty-first century. The title of the series refers to the Yankton Dakota composer and musician Zitkála-Šá, who lived from 1876 to 1938. In the early twentieth century Zitkála-Šá was known as a composer, writer, editor, teacher, and political activist. Several of her works chronicled her early struggles with identity; as an orator, many of her speeches brought awareness to the systemic oppression of Native people.

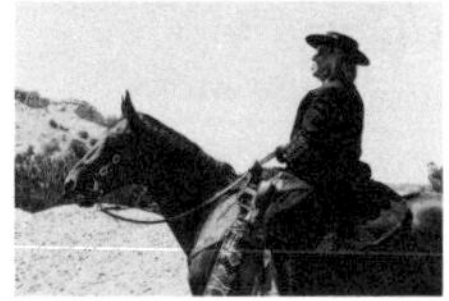

pp.120–21
A Song Often Played on the Radio 2019
Video, color, 16:9 stereo or 5.1 surround sound
22 minutes
Written and directed by Raven Chacon and Cristóbal Martínez
Featuring Guillermo Gómez-Peña and Nacha Mendez

In a search for the mythological Cities of Cibola, a horseman finds himself in a race against another rogue seeking the valuable metals of the New Mexican desert. Spurred by the justification of moralistic "dichos," the rival explorers come to learn about what truly brought them to this land, understanding their true identities, and finding that they were only stealing from themselves.

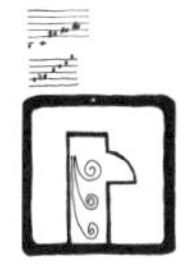

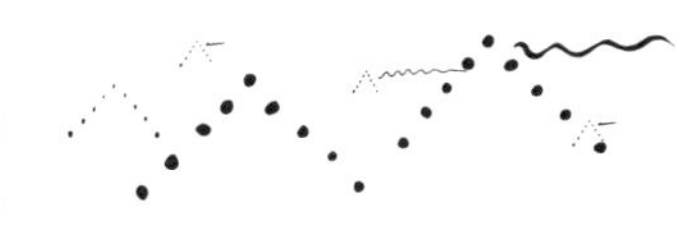

pp. 70–73
Mouth Piece (for a collection of objects) 2020
Score, sound installation
Digital print, audio files

Mouth Piece is a grouping of seven songs composed from sounds and pitches of Pre-Columbian whistles, flutes, and ocarinas in LACMA's Art of the Ancient Americas collection. Performed by Alethia Lozano, principal flutist of the National Symphony Orchestra of Mexico, the songs were presented as beams of directionalized sound, introducing visitors to the exhibition spaces, telling the stories of other non-sounding objects in the exhibition, and inviting the listener to align their own voice with the cumulative activity in the gallery.

Decrescendo/Crescendo 2021
Sound installation
Sound, music composition, and built materials

Decrescendo/Crescendo is composed of a 40-foot-long corridor with a 7-foot opening on both sides slowly narrowing toward the center. As a listener walks toward a small gap in the center of the corridor, a field recording of the grounds of a detention center reproduces a contradictory soundscape of isolation and reduced freedom. Reflecting on the dilemma of whether justice is served through incarceration, the sound installation expresses this predicament in the architectural form of an incarcerated space, finding points of resolution but also echoing where we as a society have stalled, unsure of how to solve issues of punishment and justice.

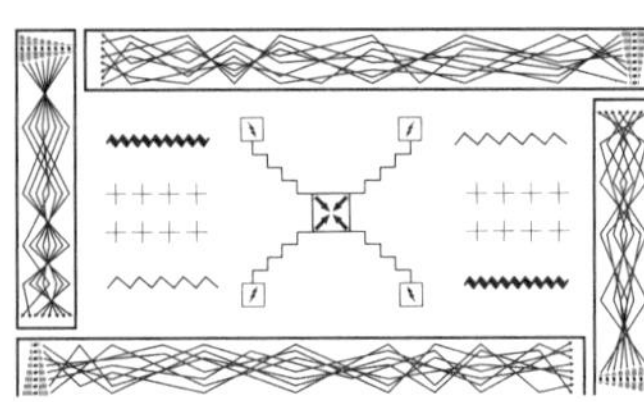

Storm Pattern 2021
Score, sound installation
Textile, 8-channel
hyper-directional sound

This work consists of isolated field recordings of flying drones at the 2016 Standing Rock Oceti Sakowin camp, Thanksgiving weekend, tuned to A440.

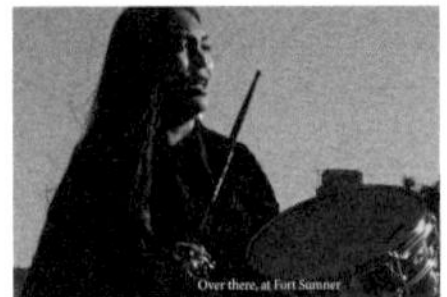

pp. 104–5
Three Songs 2021
3-channel video installation

American Indian women sing the history of a landscape, including its present, past, and future, where a conflict, displacement, or massacre of their tribe took place. The songs reference the Navajo Long Walk, the Trail of Tears and resulting drownings in the Arkansas and Mississippi rivers, and the removal of the Seminole people from their homelands. Chacon describes: "These songs of resistance, with only a snare drum as accompaniment, become a sonic testimony, an acknowledgment of shared survival, and a healing call in their mother tongues."

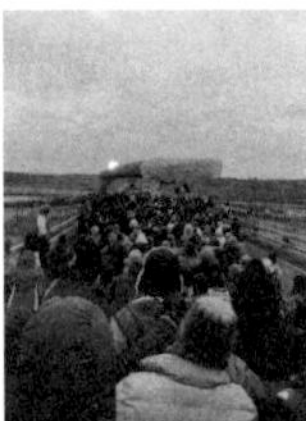

p. 141
Silent Choir (Standing Rock) 2016/2022
Field recording, printed digital image
Inkjet on vinyl
Variable dimensions

This is a field recording of a moment on the Backwater Bridge barricade near the NODAPL Water Protector encampment at Standing Rock. On Thanksgiving weekend, 2016, the women leaders of the camp led hundreds of protesters in a silent confrontation of pipeline security officers and North Dakota state police stationed on the bridge. It is an audio capture of dense silence; the field recording holds power, instilling in the listener knowledge of the women's sonic resistance.

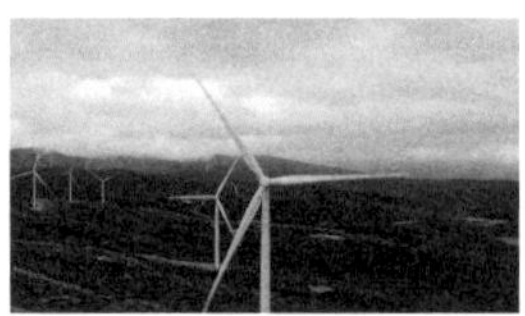

p. 16
Maneuvering the Apostles 2024
2-channel video installation with sound

This close-up drone footage of the Kvitfjell Raudfjell wind farm in the traditional homelands of the Sámi, along with a soundtrack of tremolo-effected bird recordings, considers the encroachment of green energy into the spaces of our horizontal and vertical neighbors.

pp. 22, 31, 49
... the sky ladder 2024
Sound installation

A turntable in the attic of the Nordnorsk Kunstmuseum, Northern Norway/Sápmi plays drilling sounds from the processing of the planks at Lásságámmi.

p. 34
Sketch for *... the sky ladder* 2024
Sculptural score composed of wooden planks, hand drilled by members of the Bål Nango family at Lásságámmi, Sápmi

p. 21
For Four (River Valley) 2024
4-channel video installation
Performance and video documentation from Gálggojávri, Sápmi

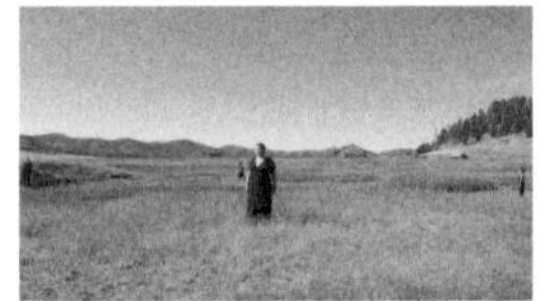

pp. 46–47
For Four (Caldera) 2024
4-channel video installation
Performance and video documentation occurred at Valles Caldera, New Mexico

These two video works document a musical round using the contour of the landscape viewed from a valley to sing a site-specific song.

Instruments

p. 95

Feedback Drum 2002
Instrument
Snare drum, guitar pickups, and speakers

The snares on the top of the drum vibrate from the sound of their signal being amplified by guitar pickups and fed back onto the body of the drum. *Feedback Drum* has been activated in solo performances by Raven Chacon and in band tours by KILT (Bob Bellerue, Raven Chacon, and Sandor Finta) between 2004 and 2007.

p. 138

Light Drum 2008
Instrument
Flashlight, vacuum cleaner attachment, cables, and photocell

Raven Chacon records the sounds of the deserts of the Navajo Nation from a moving car at various driving speeds, capturing a range of low-frequency drones, hums, and noises. These sounds pass through the *Light Drum's* cables only when a light activates the photocell. A flashlight is used as a "drum beater" to create a low round tone.

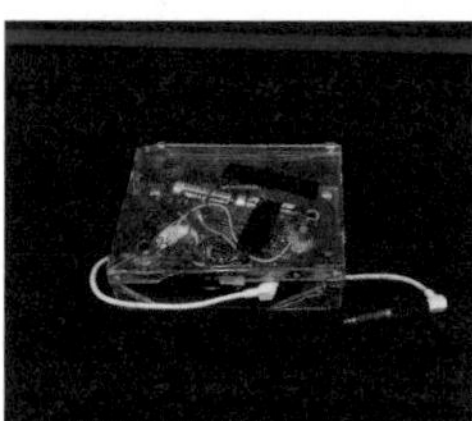

Untitled (distortion box) 2005
Instrument

This is a Sony Walkman that was found smashed in the middle of a street in Albuquerque, New Mexico. The tape head has been replaced with an input jack.

p. 98

Untitled (circuit bent sleep machine) 2006
Instrument

This instrument combines sounds that do not naturally go together. For example, whale sounds are blended with desert sounds, and sounds from the beach are mixed with those from a rainforest.

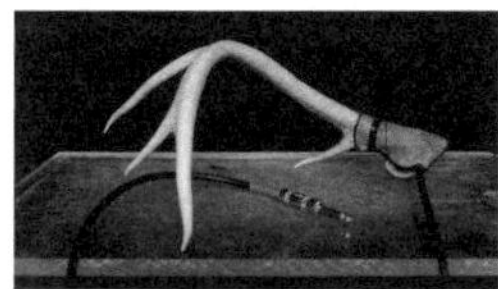

pp. 146–47

Untitled (antler instrument) 2007
Instrument
Deer antler, embedded with piezo microphones

Shrill chords are produced by scraping the instrument on glass, plexiglass surfaces, and/or tiles.

Selected Works from Postcommodity

Raven Chacon was a member of the Indigenous artist collective Postcommodity from 2009 to 2018, contributing his knowledge of sound, music, and performance toward coauthoring twenty-two installations and three full-length albums with the group. Other members of the collective since its founding include Cristóbal Martínez, Kade Twist, Steven Yazzie, and Nathan Young.

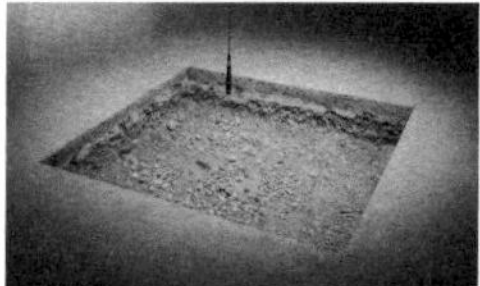

Do You Remember When? 2009
Site-specific intervention, mixed-media installation
Cut concrete, exposed earth, light, and sound

Worldview Manipulation Therapy 2009
Multichannel video, sound, and mixed-media installation
12 hours

It's My Second Home, but I Have a Very Spiritual Connection with this Place 2010
2-channel video installation with sound
30 minutes

If History Moves at the Speed of Its Weapons, then the Shape of the Arrow Is Changing 2010
3D sound sculpture
9 audio channels, loudspeakers, and gold acrylic paint

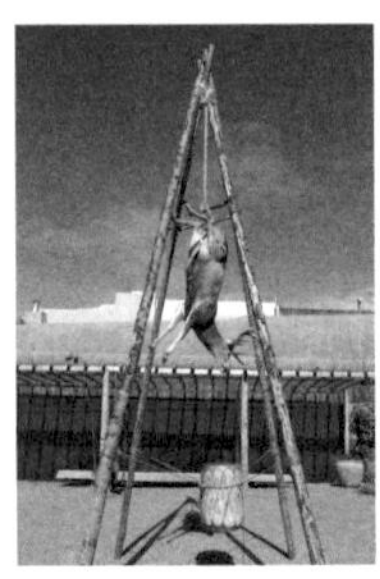

My Blood Is in the Water 2010
Mixed-media installation,
sculpture with sound
Mule deer taxidermy, wood poles,
water, amplifier, and drum

Repellent Eye (Winnipeg) 2011
Land art installation and intervention
10-foot-diameter vinyl sphere,
acrylic paint

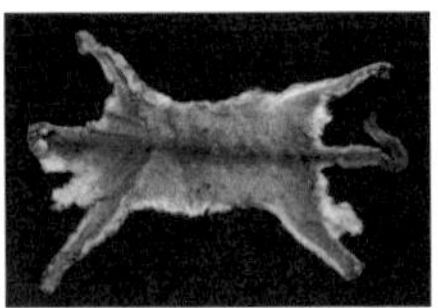

pp. 96–97, 99
Mother, Teacher, Destroyer 2011
4-channel video, mixed-media
sculpture
Wood, deer antler, deer hide,
boar bladder, turnbuckles, fishing
swivels, and found materials

Promoting a More Just, Verdant and Harmonious Resolution 2011
Interactive 4-channel video
and sound installation
Infinite duration

Radiophonic Territory (Nocturne) 2011
Sound installation, social
collaboration, and performance
Stereo FM transmitter,
radio receiver, audio transducers,
and natural-fiber rope
12 hours

The Night Is Filled with the Harmonics of Suburban Dreams 2011
Sound and mixed-media installation
Splash pool, 3/4 hp pool pumps,
PVC pipe, piezo microphones, bass
transducers, and instrument amplifiers

Gallup Motel Butchering 2011
Multichannel video
9 minutes 5 seconds

With Salvage and Knife Tongue 2012
Generative 4-channel video
and sound installation
Infinite duration

Game Remains 2014
Interactive video game
and sound performance

People of Good Will 2014–15
Collaborative event space
and performance series
Heritage Hall, Guelph, Ontario, Canada

Pollination 2015
Immersive installation

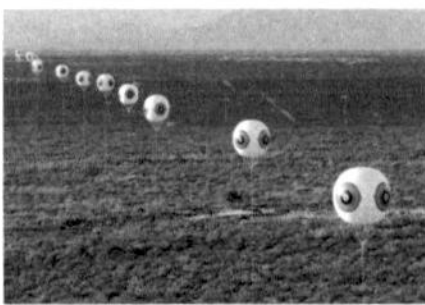

pp. 40–43
Repellent Fence/Valla Repelente 2015
Land art intervention
Installation view at US/Mexico
Border, Douglas, Arizona/
Agua Prieta, Sonora

A Very Long Line 2016
4-channel video with sound
Infinite duration

Coyotaje 2017
Inflatable sculpture,
closed-circuit night-vision video,
sound, and photograph

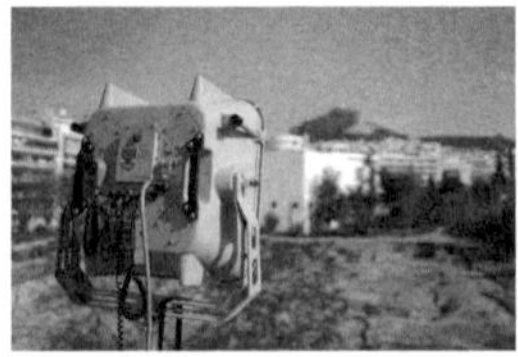

The Ears between Worlds Are Always Speaking 2017
2 LRADs, 2-channel hyper-directional
sound work
8 hours daily

Blind/Curtain 2017
Hyper-directional speakers emitting
pink noise

In Memoriam 2017
Performance of *In Memoriam* by
Robert Ashley, and *In Memoriam … Mary Cecil, Victoria Callihoo (née Belcourt), and Eleanor (Helene) Thomas Garneau* by Postcommodity,
Ocicwan, Alex Waterman, and
Will Holder
Compositions performed and recorded at Banff Centre for Arts and Creativity, Banff, Alberta, and the Windspear Centre for Music in Edmonton, Alberta.

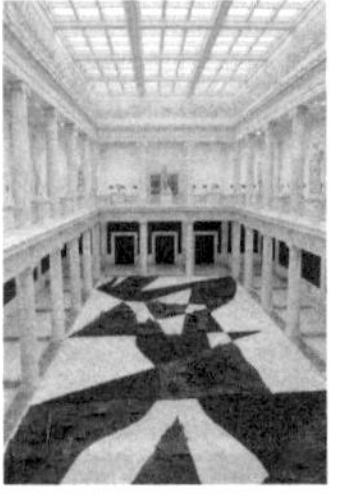

p. 48
From Smoke and Tangled Waters We Carried Fire Home 2018
Sculptural graphic score
for solo jazz performance
Steel, coal, and glass, 3,200 sq. feet

Selected Performances

Between 1995 and 2023, Raven Chacon performed over 700 concerts as a solo artist or with his collaborators, bands, collectives, and ensembles.

p. 125
Death Convention Singers' street performance (*Procession for drumsticks*), in Albuquerque, New Mexico 2007

p. 124
Raven Chacon installing for a moonlight performance with Robert Henke, at Chaco Canyon, New Mexico 2013

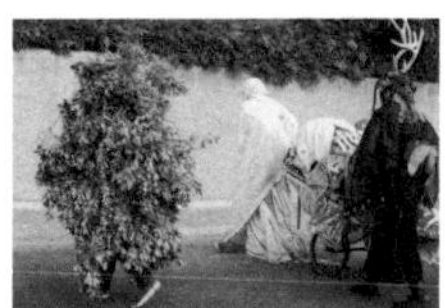

pp. 122–23
Death Convention Singers' performance, as part of the exhibition *An Evening Redness in the West* at the IAIA Museum of Contemporary Native Arts (MoCNA), Santa Fe, New Mexico 2015
On the left, Raven Chacon walks as a bush.

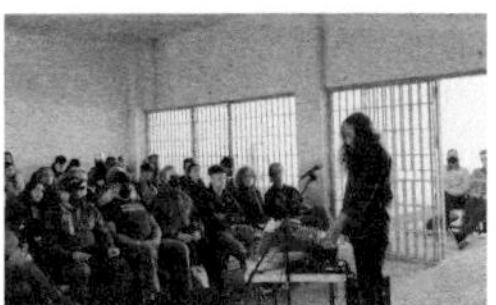

pp. 136–37
Live from Alcatraz 2022
Performance
As part of *Undoing Time: Art and Histories of Incarceration* at ASU Art Museum in Tempe, Arizona, Raven Chacon debuted a new sound work on Alcatraz Island on November 6, 2022. The work is a sonic meditation on the histories of Alcatraz and its occupation for nineteen months beginning in November 1969 by the group Indians of All Tribes to protest the unjust treatment of Indigenous people by the US government. The sound piece draws upon many sources, including archival sound footage of Radio Free Alcatraz, which broadcast news of the occupation from the island every weeknight for most of the first year of the protest.

Collaborative Works

Raven Chacon, Mely Mitchell, and Rob Valdez
Be'eldiildaahsinil/Abduction Song 2001
Video on surveillance monitor
An oral account, relayed by Chacon's grandfather, Frank Dineyazhe, telling a family story in the Navajo language. As a teenage girl, Chacon's great-great-grandmother was kidnapped by a Mexican man and taken from her home at Dinetah (Navajo homelands) to what is now Albuquerque, New Mexico (Bee'eldiildaahsinil).

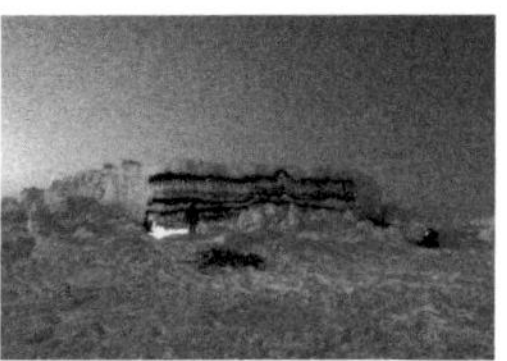

pp. 158–59
Erik Boomer, Raven Chacon, Alexa Hatanaka, Eric McNair-Landry, Sarah McNair-Landry, Danny Osborne, and Patrick Thompson
Gauge 2013–15
3-channel sound and video installation, 5.1 surround audio
14 minutes
Created on Baffin Island in the Canadian Arctic, this extreme ice-painting and graffiti project employs the natural forces of time, extreme temperatures, and the ever-changing environment to dictate process on a grand scale. Rather than making a permanent site-specific work, the ice is used as a temporary canvas that is submerged in the frozen sea, occasionally re-emerging with the tides. Color is sprayed through fire extinguishers and other nontraditional art-making tools on the monumental ice walls as the tides cause them to rise and fall upward of ten meters.

These short-lived works are subjected to the friction of ice, the ocean beneath, and the changing temperatures which in time erase the paintings, washing the natural charcoal and food-grade dyes from memory. *Gauge* exists as an immersive installation with an audio soundtrack composed from hundreds of on-site field recordings of the shifting ice, wildlife, modern tools, and the harsh, overwhelming environment.

Raven Chacon and Candice Hopkins
Score for Marginal Objects 2014
Score, performance

Raven Chacon and Candice Hopkins
Nuestro día viene 2018
For choir
Commissioned for a larger work by Szu-Han Ho

A song in the style of a corrido: words, sentences, fragments, and thoughts were borrowed from interviews with migrants who have traversed the US/Mexico border. In some cases different people used the same words to describe their experiences or had the same experiences but used different words.

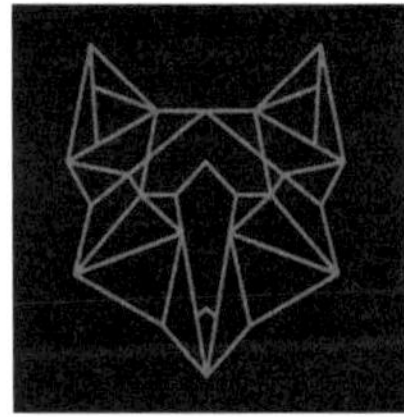

Raven Chacon and John Dieterich, in collaboration with Vancouver New Music and an endless pool of musicians
Parallel 03 2020
Web instrument

The web instrument *Parallel 03*, designed by Endlings (John Dieterich and Raven Chacon) and six Vancouver musicians and sound artists, utilizes a variety of cross-platform and anonymous methods for composition and improvisation. Composed, recorded, and arranged over four months of isolation in 2020, the eight collaborators became generators, translators, mistranslators, and filters for contributions fed into an incalculable feedback loop of expansive processes. The instrument is designed to receive new content from other contributors, allowing for a constant stream of unique, ephemeral music.

Parallel 03 collaborators thus far are: Parmela Attariwala, Adrian Avendaño, John Brennan, Raven Chacon and John Dieterich (Endlings), Elisa Ferrari, Marina Hasselberg, Alanna Ho, and Joel Schuman.

pp. 61–66
Raven Chacon and Candice Hopkins
Dispatch 2020
Score adapted as a script

Dispatch is either a transcription of events around the 2016 DAPL encroachment at Standing Rock, a prompt for an ecological oral future, or, at the very least, a critique of the privilege of meditative Deep Listening. This score can be realized as a performance or as a series of imagined events. It can also be enacted in the real world. The players, the prompts, and the schematics are derived from an analysis of the surface dynamics and organization of the Water Protectors in defense of Standing Rock during the #noDAPL movement, not glossing over the miscommunication, profiteering, and injustices. In an increasingly fractured society, new paths and new formations are needed to refocus our attention in an attempt to find truth. Participating in this score may produce sonic or visual artifacts; these are as important as the actions.

Raven Chacon and Candice Hopkins
Rift Transcription 2020
Digital video with sound

Raven Chacon and Rob Thorne
Earth Mother/Father Sky 2021
Digital video with sound

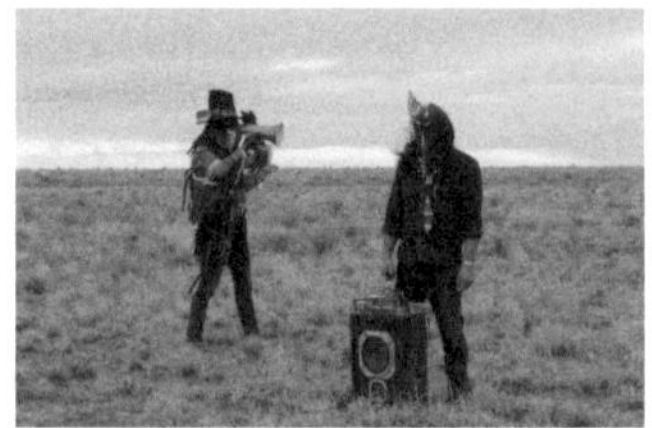

Raven Chacon and Cannupa Hanska Luger
Wathéča :: Ch'iyáán Yiskáago 2022
Digital video with sound

Select Discography

p. 131
The Kleptones
Sample / All rights reversed cassette
(SSSK #3) 2001
Released by Sicksicksick Distro

p. 126
Death Convention Singers +
Dirty/Birdies
Split lathe-cut 7" (SSSK #29) 2007
Released by Sicksicksick Distro

p. 130
Black Streaked Hum 2009
3" CDR and digital
Independent release

p. 128
Mesa Ritual
Voltaic Processions mini-CD
(SSSK #47) 2010
Released by Sicksicksick Distro

p. 127
Death Convention Singers
A Thread, A Braid
cassette (SSSK #71) 2021
Released by Sicksicksick Distro

Partial Discography

Solo:
- *An Anthology of Chants Operations* 12" LP (Ouidah, 2020)
- *At the Point Where the Rivers Crossed, We Drew Our Knives* 12" LP (Anarchymoon Records, 2010)
- *Black Streaked Hum* EP 3" CD/cassette (Lightning Speak/Featherspines, 2009)
- *Music for Flute, Electric Guitar, and Outdoor Sine Wave* CDR (Easydiscs, 2009)
- *Overheard Songs* CD (Innova, 2006)
- *still/life* EP 3" CDR (SSSK, 2004)
- *Beesh Naalnishi* CD (SSSK, 2004)
- *x-x-x-x-x* CDR (SSSK, 2000)

Endlings (duo with John Dieterich):
- *Human Form* 12" LP (Whited Sepulchre Records, 2021)
- *Endlings* LP/CD (SSSK/Lightning Feet, 2017)
- "Summer Assassins"/"Creeping of the Foul" digi single (Deathbomb Arc, 2012)

Postcommodity:
- *In Memoriam ... Mary Cecil, Victoria Callihoo (née Belcourt), and Eleanor (Helene) Thomas Garneau* 12" 3LP (Ociciwan, 2021)
- *We Lost Half the Forest and the Rest Will Burn This Summer* 12" LP (PCP/SSSK, 2015)
- *Your New Age Dream Contains More Blood Than You Imagine* 12" LP (Anarchymoon Recordings, 2011)
- "Excerpt from Piles of Cougar Pelts," track on *Sound + Vision: Beyond Reason* 12" LP (VZW Contour, 2011)

Death Convention Singers (aka Cobra//group):
- *A Thread, A Braid* cassette (SSSK, 2020)
- *Death Convention Singers* CD (SSSK, 2012)
- *Corrido* cassette (SSSK, 2008)
- *Brujas* CD (SSSK, 2008)
- Split lathe-cut 7" with Dirty/Birdies (SSSK, 2007)
- *The Covers EP* CDR (SSSK, 2007)
- *Locas* CDR (SSSK, 2006)

Mesa Ritual (duo with William Fowler Collins):
- *Mesa Ritual* 12" LP (SIGE Records, 2014)
- *Voltaic Processions* EP Minimax CDR (SSSK, 2010)

KILT (trio with Bob Bellerue and Sandor Finta):
- *She's got the devil in her heart* cassette (Fabrica Records, 2014)
- *Culos Asados* cassette (Obsolete Units, 2013)
- *Santa Muerte* 12" LP (Anarchymoon, SSSK, Universal Consciousness, 2012)
- *Into the Red, into the Black* cassette (Banned Productions, 2012)
- *Kitchen Sorcery* CD (Prison Tatt Records, 2011)
- *Chrome Bellows* cassette (Peyote Tapes, 2009)
- *Vaya Con Nada* 3" CDR (Small Doses, 2009)
- *Snow White in Hell* 12" LP (Anarchymoon, Bastardised, SSSK, 2007)
- *sharp dark love* 3" CD (EMR, 2006)
- *KILT / Dead Wolf Black* split cassette (Bastardised, 2006)
- *Dead Wolf Black / KILT* split CDR (Bastardised, 2006)

Splits, collaborations, and compilations:
- Wolf Eyes, *Difficult Messages Volume Four* 7" (2022)
- Chacon/Nakatani/Santistevan Trio, *Inhale/Exhale* 12" LP (Other Minds, 2022)
- *White People Killed Them* 12" LP (SIGE, 2021)
- Grey Plumes, "Niso"/"Peyak" 7" (EHEPIK, 2018)
- OVO + Raven Chacon, *Crisalide Fossile* (Bronson Recordings / Weird Tapes, 2015)

- *Novasak / Raven Chacon*, split and collaborative 2CDR (Sycophantide, 2008)
- Black Drink, s/t cassette (SSSK, 2008)
- *50 BPM or Less Vol. 2*, compilation CD (Canned Beef Records, 2007)
- Christ with Braces, *Nuestra Señora la Reina de los Ángeles* 3" CDR (SSSK, 2007)
- *Swamp Comp Vol. 3*, compilation CDR (Swamp of Pus, 2006)
- *Corral Comp* 2CD (Anarchymoon Recordings, 2006)
- *L.A. Noisescape*, compilation CD (Bastardised, 2006)
- Jeff Gburek/Raven Chacon, *Jesus Was a Wino* CDR (Herbal Records, 2006)
- Raven Chacon/Torturing Nurse, *The Incredible 17000 KM Split* CDR (8kMob, 2006)
- *ABQ=/=LAX*, 5-way split 7" (Hype Machine/SSSK, 2006)
- Alchemical Burn + Raven Chacon, *Bachelors, Even* 2CDR (SSSK, 2006)
- *Redglaer / Raven Chacon*, split cassette (Stentorian Tapes, 2005)
- *Raven Chacon / Redglare*, split tour cassette (Anarchymoon Recordings, 2005)
- The Kleptones, *Meet the Beatless* CDR (SSSK, 2003)
- The Kleptones, *Sound Bites for Audiophiles* CDR (SSSK, 2002)
- Los Subliminados, *Backward Messages* cassette (SSSK, 2001)

Additional Selected Projects

Sicksicksick Distro 2001–ongoing
Record label

Since 2001, Raven Chacon's Sicksicksick Distro record label has been documenting the quietest loudness in the Southwest US.

p. 115
Collaboration with NACAP
2004–ongoing

Since 2004, Raven Chacon has served as composer-in-residence for the Native American Composer Apprentice Project (NACAP), mentoring over three hundred high school Native composers in the writing of new string quartets.

p. 130
Occasional Detroit
Prayer Packages (SSSK #35) 2008
Packaging made by Raven Chacon, cassette in a purple silk sleeve
Released by Sicksicksick Distro

p. 131
Smoke Rings
Smoke Rings cassette (SSSK #43) 2008
Packaging made by Raven Chacon
Released by Sicksicksick Distro

p. 116
1Kind / Unkind / Rio Grande
Satanical Gardens 2009
Hand-drawn flyer by Raven Chacon for a concert at a venue he cofounded in Albuquerque, New Mexico

p. 129
Horse Thief
Ethnic/Cleansing
cassette (SSSK #62) 2013
Packaging made by Raven Chacon
Released by Sicksicksick Distro

Biographies

Raven Chacon was born at Fort Defiance, Navajo Nation, in 1977, grew up in Chinle, also on the Navajo Nation, and later lived in Albuquerque, New Mexico, with his parents and sisters. There, as a young person, he studied classical piano and began building his own instruments, eventually playing with as many musicians as possible, from rock bands to mariachi groups, while studying music theory and composition, film, and art at the University of New Mexico.

Chacon relocated to Los Angeles for graduate studies in composition with James Tenney at the California Institute of the Arts, and remained in Los Angeles for six years, while also touring the United States with various solo and group projects, composing chamber works, and developing a curriculum for the Native American Composer Apprentice Project, an education initiative to mentor young composers on the Navajo, Hopi, and Salt River Pima reservations.

In 2009, Chacon joined the collective Postcommodity and cocreated twenty-two art installations with the group, including the two-mile-long land art installation *Repellent Fence / Valla Repelente* (2015). While a member of the collective, the group exhibited at the Whitney Biennial, New York; Documenta 14, Athens and Kassel; Carnegie International, Carnegie Museum of Art, Pittsburgh; and the Biennale of Sydney.

As a solo artist, Chacon has exhibited at the Los Angeles County Museum of Art; the Whitney Biennial, New York; and the Renaissance Society, Chicago, among others. He has performed, or had works performed, at the San Francisco Electronic Music Festival; Borealis Festival, Bergen, Norway; the Perelman Performing Arts Center, New York; Holland Festival, Amsterdam; Ostrava Festival, Ostrava, Czech Republic; and Huddersfield Contemporary Music Festival, UK, in addition to hundreds of concerts over twenty-five years.

In 2022, Chacon received the Pulitzer Prize for Music for his composition *Voiceless Mass*; in 2023, he was awarded a MacArthur Fellowship.

Ingir Bål Nango is a screenwriter. She previously worked as a scriptwriter and host for Sámi children's television at NRK TV. She is from a reindeer-herding family in the Bassevuovdi / Holywood reindeer district of Skibotn. Nango was educated at the Norwegian Children's Book Institute in Oslo and studied scriptwriting at the ISFI × Alma × Netflix Writing Academy. Nango's "Liane's Adult Monologue" was published in the monologue *She Said* by Transit Forlag. She wrote and codirected *Hilbes biigá*, which screened at nearly thirty film festivals, and *The Tongues*, winner of four awards, three of them at Oscar-qualifying film festivals. She cowrote *Guođoheaddji* (*The Herder*), currently in development through Sundance Screenwriters Lab 2022.

Marja Bål Nango is a film director, scriptwriter, and producer. She is from a reindeer-herding family in the Bassevuovdi/Holywood reindeer district of Skibotn, and studied directing at Nordland College of Art and Film, and film producing at the International Sámi Film Institute/ Sámi University. Additionally, she studied scriptwriting at the ISFI × Alma × Netflix Writing Academy. Nango has made several award-winning short films; her latest, *The Tongues*, won Best International Short Film at the 2020 Palm Springs International Shortfest, Best Director at the 2020 Rhode Island International Film Festival, and academy-qualifying Best Live Action Short at the 2020 ImagineNative Film Festival. At the 2021 Sundance Film Festival, Nango was named a Merata Mita Fellow, with her feature film *Guođoheaddji* (*The Herder*) selected for yearlong support. She is currently developing *Guođoheaddji* (*The Herder*) through Sundance Screenwriters Lab 2022.

Lou Cornum is a writer and academic based in New York City. They were born in Chandler, Arizona, in 1989 and are an enrolled member of the Navajo Nation. Their research interests broadly encompass Indigenous cultural studies with particular attention to Indigenous futurism, nuclear landscapes, and the politics of Native American Studies. Cornum's public writing on Indigenous literature, art, film, and politics can be found in *Triple Canopy, Social Text Online*, and *Frieze*, among other publications, and their scholarship has been published in the journals *Critical Ethnic Studies* and *History of the Present*. They are a founding editorial collective member of *Pinko: A Magazine of Gay Communism* and former senior editor of *The New Inquiry*.

Aruna D'Souza is a writer and critic based in New York / Manhatta, the homeland of the Lenape (Lenapehoking). Her work appears regularly in *4Columns*, where she is a member of the editorial advisory board, and she is a contributor to the *New York Times*. Her book, *Whitewalling: Art, Race, & Protest in 3 Acts* (Badlands Unlimited), was named one of the best art books of 2018 by the *New York Times*. Recent editorial projects include Linda Nochlin's *Making It Modern: Essays on the Art of the Now* (Thames & Hudson, 2022) and Lorraine O'Grady's *Writing in Space, 1973–2018* (Duke University Press, 2020); she cocurated the retrospective of O'Grady's work, *Both/And*, which opened in March 2021 at the Brooklyn Museum. D'Souza is the recipient of a 2021 Rabkin Prize for art journalism and a 2019 Andy Warhol Foundation Art Writers Grant. She delivered the Distinguished Critics Lecture for AICA (the International Association of Art Critics) in 2019, and was appointed the Edmond J. Safra Visiting Professor at the National Gallery of Art, Washington, DC, in 2022, and the William Wilson Corcoran Visiting Professor of Community Engagement at the Corcoran School of the Arts & Design, George Washington University, in 2022–23.

Candice Hopkins is a citizen of Carcross / Tagish First Nation and lives in Red Hook, New York. Her writing and curatorial practice explore the intersections of history, contemporary art, and Indigeneity. She is the executive director of Forge Project, Taghkanic, NY. She curated *Indian Theater: Native Performance, Art, and Self-Determination since 1969* for the Hessel Museum of Art at Bard College, Annandale-on-Hudson, NY, and co-curated (with Raven Chacon and Stavia Grimani) *Impossible Music* for the Miller ICA at Carnegie Mellon University, Pittsburgh, PA, and the touring exhibitions *Soundings: An Exhibition in Five Parts* (with Dylan Robinson) and ᑕᑯᒃᓴᐅᔪᒻᒪᑎᒃ *Double Vision*, featuring textiles, prints, and drawings by Jessie Oonark, Janet Kigusiuq, and Victoria Mamnguqsualuk. She was the senior curator for the 2019 and 2022 editions of the Toronto Biennial of Art, and part of the curatorial team for the Canadian Pavilion at the fifty-eighth Venice Biennale, featuring the work of the media collective Isuma; documenta 14, Athens and Kassel; and *Sakahàn: International Indigenous Art*, National Gallery of Canada, Ottawa. Her essays include "The Gilded Gaze: Wealth and Economies on the Colonial Frontier," in the *documenta 14 Reader*; "Outlawed Social Life," in *South as a State of Mind*; and "The Appropriation Debates (or The Gallows of History)," in *Saturation: Race, Art, and the Circulation of Value* (New Museum / MIT Press, 2020).

Anthony Huberman is a curator and writer based in New York. He is currently the artistic director of GPS (Giorno Poetry Systems), a nonprofit organization founded in 1965 by the artist John Giorno, where artists, poets, and musicians reflect on the work of other artists, poets, and musicians. Previously, he was the director of and a chief curator at the Wattis Institute for Contemporary Arts in San Francisco, the founding director of the Artist's Institute in New York, a curator at Palais de Tokyo in Paris and SculptureCenter in New York, and the director of public programs at MoMA PS1 in New York. He has also curated exhibitions at Kunst-Werke in Berlin, the Institute of Contemporary Arts in London, Culturgest in Lisbon, and Secession in Vienna, and co-curated the 2014 Liverpool Biennial. Major group exhibitions include *Drum Listens to Heart* (2022), *Mechanisms* (2017), *For the blind man in the dark room looking for the black cat that isn't there* (2009), and *Grey Flags* (2006). Recent publications he has edited, coedited, or contributed to include *Cecilia Vicuña: Word Weapons* (2023), *What Happens Between the Knots?* (2022), *Where Are the Tiny Revolts?* (2021), *Abbas to Yuki: Writing Alongside Exhibitions* (2019), and *Today We Should Be Thinking About* (2016). Huberman has taught curatorial studies at Hunter College and the California College of the Arts, and is currently a visiting professor at the Center for Curatorial Studies at Bard College.

Patrick Nickleson is an Assistant Professor of Musicology at the University of Alberta. His work narrates what contemporary experimental and popular musics have to teach us about disputed histories of ownership and theft, property and dispossession. He has published in the *Journal of the Royal Musical Association*, *Twentieth-Century Music*, *Perspectives of New Music*, *Intersections*, *The Affect Theory Reader 2*, and *Aural Poetics*, and is the author of *The Names of Minimalism: Authorship, Art Music, and Historiography in Dispute*, and coeditor of *Rancière and Music*. Nickleson lives in amiskwacîwâskahikan (Edmonton, Alberta) with his partner, Laura, and their dog, Gammon.

Eric-Paul Riege uses a rich array of natural and synthetic materials to create his signature woven sculptures that reflect on the Diné (Navajo) philosophy of hózhó. Hózhó, as a practice in everyday life as well as in Riege's own artistic practice, is a worldview that encompasses the values of beauty, balance, and goodness in all things physical and spiritual. For Riege, hózhó lives in the continuation of the Indigenous weaving and jewelry-making traditions inherited within his own family history, particularly from his maternal ancestors. Often displaying these intricate objects as suspended looms, and activating them through video and performance, Riege uses space, sound, and gravity like any other material manipulated by the artistic hand. What results are sensorial installations built in homage to cosmology, craft, and inherited knowledge, where the spiritual and physical realms of memory are bridged as one. Riege has had solo institutional exhibitions at the Institute of Contemporary Art, Miami, in 2019 and the Hammer Museum, Los Angeles, in 2022. He has also shown at the Toronto Biennial of Art 2022; the Contemporary Arts Center, New Orleans, as part of *Prospect.5: Yesterday we said tomorrow* (2021–22); and the SITElines.2018 Biennial, Santa Fe, New Mexico. He earned a BFA in Studio Art and Ecology from the University of New Mexico, Albuquerque, in 2017.

Dylan Robinson is an Associate Professor in the School of Music at the University of British Columbia, Vancouver, Canada. As a member of the Skwah First Nation, his scholarship, art, and writing seek to affirm Stó:lō epistemology. His book, *Hungry Listening: Resonant Theory for Indigenous Sound Studies*, examines Indigenous and settler-colonial practices of listening, and was awarded Best First Book by the Native American and Indigenous Studies Association, Royal Musical Association, and the Society for Music Theory. He coedited *Music and Modernity among First Peoples of North America* and *Arts of Engagement: Taking Aesthetic Action In and Beyond the Truth and Reconciliation Commission of Canada*. As co-chair of the Indigenous Advisory Council for the Canadian Music Centre, he is currently leading a process for the reparation and redress of music that appropriates Indigenous song and misrepresents Indigenous cultures. In his current research project, "Caring for Our Ancestors," he works with Indigenous artists to reconnect kinship with Indigenous life incarcerated in museums.

Sigbjørn Skåden is a Sámi writer from Láŋtdlevvá/Planterhaugen in North Norway. He writes in both Indigenous Sámi language and Norwegian, and has, since his debut in 2004 with the epic long poem *Skuovvadeddjiid gonagas*, published another book of poetry, three novels, and a children's book, in addition to writing numerous works for the stage and interdisciplinary art projects. Skåden has been the Young Artist of the Year at Riddu Riđđu Festival, the prologue writer for the Arctic Arts Festival, and a profile author for the European poetry platform Versopolis. He has been nominated for the Nordic Council Literary Award and the Norwegian Broadcasting Listeners' Award, and has received the Havmann Award for best North-Norwegian book published in 2014. Skåden has an MA in English Literature from the University of York and an MA in Sámi Poetry from the Arctic University of Norway in Tromsø. His latest book is the novel *Fugl*, published in 2019.

Ánde Somby hails from a lineage steeped in the traditions of reindeer herding. A proficient Sámi linguist, he is also deeply rooted in the art of yoiking. At the age of twelve, Somby's academic pursuits took him to a boarding school, a departure that deeply impacted him. Confronted with the poignant loss of his familial surroundings, Somby was spurred by two defining resolutions. Firstly, he aspired to acquire a legal education, aiming to safeguard the cultural heritage he held dear (fulfilling this, he now imparts knowledge at the Faculty of Law at UIT, the Arctic University of Norway); simultaneously, he embraced yoiking with fervor. As a teenager, he embarked on a professional journey as a yoiker, touring extensively across the United States, Canada, and numerous other nations. Collaboratively, he has produced records celebrating the resonance of yoik with fellow artists. Notably, he cofounded the renowned record label DAT. For years, Somby's artistic vision was centered on meticulously documenting and delivering yoiks in their most authentic form. He was also instrumental in forming the musical ensemble Vajas, which, in 2006, fused melodious yoiks with electronica. Of late, Somby's craft has evolved to incorporate an avant-garde expressiveness within traditional yoiking renditions.

Founded in 1986, Swiss Institute (SI) is an independent nonprofit contemporary art institution dedicated to promoting forward-thinking and experimental art-making through innovative exhibitions, education, and programs. Committed to the highest standards of curatorial and educational excellence, SI serves as a platform for emerging artists, catalyzes new perspectives on celebrated work, and fosters appreciation for under-recognized positions. SI is committed to being an organization that is diverse, equitable, accessible, and environmentally conscious in its work, structure, and programming. Open to the public free of charge, SI seeks to explore how a Swiss context can be the starting point for international conversations in the fields of visual and performing arts, design, and architecture.

SI Programming is made possible in part with public funds from Pro Helvetia, Swiss Arts Council; the New York State Council on the Arts, with the support of Governor Kathy Hochul and the New York State Legislature; and the New York City Department of Cultural Affairs in partnership with the City Council. Main sponsors include LUMA Foundation, Friends of SI, the Andy Warhol Foundation for the Visual Arts, and the Horace W. Goldsmith Foundation. Exhibitions are made possible in part by the SI Artist Vision Fund, with leadership support provided by the SI Board of Trustees, Ghislaine Brenninkmeijer, the Kevin Wendle Foundation, and the Freedman Family Foundation. *Spora* is made possible by Teiger Foundation. SI gratefully acknowledges Swiss Re as SI ONSITE Partner, Vitra as Design Partner, Crozier Fine Arts as Preferred Shipping Art Logistics Partner, and SWISS as Travel Partner.

Critical operating support was provided to SI in 2023 as part of a collective fundraising effort with CANNY (Collaborate Arts Network New York). We thank the following supporters: Andrew W. Mellon Foundation, Arison Arts Foundation, Helen Frankenthaler Foundation, Imperfect Family Foundation, and The Jay DeFeo Foundation.

Nordnorsk Kunstmuseum (NNKM)/Davvi Norgga Dáiddamusea serves the regions of Troms, Finnmark, and Nordland, in Northern Norway/Sápmi, as well as the Svalbard Archipelago. This extensive region of the Arctic is on Sámi Indigenous land and is home to diverse and complex communities. The museum plays a significant role in Norway, Sápmi, the Nordic and Circumpolar regions, and the international art world, through relevant exhibitions and public programs. Central to the museum is the care, research, mediation, and activation of a collection of over 2,225 works by artists from the 1600s to the present day. There is a growing presence of Sámi daiddars and duojárs in our collection. We are committed to social, and climate, justice and transformation. Our institutional values are: openness, relevance, and cocreation.

In the Svalbard Archipelago, the museum has programming responsibility for the Nordover Art Centre, and is a key partner in the artist residence Artica Svalbard, which makes NNKM exceptional when it comes to operating so close to the North Pole. NNKM Bodø will open in 2024. We are also working toward a new building in Tromsø, housing the museum and the Arctic Philharmonic.

STAFF

Veronica Aasgrav Evertsen (Deputy Director)
Asmae Armand (Social Media Coordinator)
Rebecca Bayram (Conservator)
Liv Brissach (Curator)
Lise Dahl (Curator)
Ylva Foss Valde (Mediation Coordinator)
Katya García-Antón (Director and Chief Curator)
Oliver Graney (Producer)
Charis Gullickson (Curator)
Therese Lindseth (Communication)
Mona Lundstedt (Communcation)
Britt Anita Mikkelsen (Administration Advisor)
Øystein Oldervoll (Museum Technician)
Astrid Rotvold Nilsen (Responsible for Mediation)
Kim Skytte (Registrar)
Eva Skotnes Vikjord (Curator)
Mathilde Stubmark (Reception and Shop Manager)

Image credits

pp. 14–15: Demian DinéYazhi; p. 28: Øystein Thorvaldsen, courtesy of Stiftelsen Lásságámmi, Nils-Aslak Valkaepää / Áillohaš; pp. 27, 29–30: Mihio Manus; p. 31: Kim G. Skytte, courtesy of Nordnorsk Kunstmuseum; pp. 32–33: still from video documentation by Christine Cynn; p. 34: designed by MARC&STELLA AS; pp. 35–37: Craig Smith, courtesy of Heard Museum; pp. 38–39: Joel Tsui, courtesy of Institute of Contemporary Art at Maine College of Art & Design; pp. 40–41, 43: Michael Lundgren, courtesy of Postcommodity and Bockley Gallery; pp. 44–45: Derek Sandbeck; p. 48: Bryan Conley, courtesy of the 57th Ed. Carnegie International; p. 51: courtesy of Eric-Paul Riege; pp. 61–66: courtesy of the artist and Candice Hopkins; p. 75: Monica Orozco, courtesy of Museum Associates/ LACMA; p. 81: courtesy of the artist and Crow's Shadow Institute of the Arts (CSIA); pp. 91, 110–12: Paula Court; pp. 95–99, 126–31, 138, 146–47: Hank Henley; pp. 100–101, 157: Roger Jones; pp. 102–3: Jaren Bonillo; pp. 106–109: Casey Kringlen, courtesy of The Industry; p. 115: Clare Hoffman; pp. 122–23: Kade L. Twist; pp. 136–137: still from video documentation by Phil Pinto and Laura Tomaselli; pp. 144–45: Gudmund Sundlisæter; pp. 158–59: Danny Osborne, Alexa Hatanaka, Patrick Thompson, Raven Chacon, Sarah McNair-Landry, Eric McNair-Landry, Erik Boomer

Published on the occasion of the exhibition
Raven Chacon: A Worm's Eye View from a Bird's Beak
at Swiss Institute, New York, January 25 – April 14, 2024;
Nordnorsk Kunstmuseum, Northern Norway/Sápmi,
March 16 – September 1, 2024

Editors: Alison Coplan, Katya García-Antón,
Stefanie Hessler
Copy Editor and Proofreader: Miles Champion
Design: Stoodio Santiago da Silva, Ana Cecilia Breña
Norwegian Translation for *The Map*: Victor Szepessy
Image Processing, Printing and Binding:
DZA Druckerei zu Altenburg, Germany
(Project Management: Jens Sippenauer)
Typefaces: Louize by Matthieu Cortat, Grey by
Aurèle Sack, Superstudio by Jonathan Hares
Papers: Materica, Kamiko Fly, Magno Gloss

Raven Chacon: A Worm's Eye View from a Bird's Beak
at Swiss Institute is supported in part by the National
Endowment for the Arts.

NATIONAL ENDOWMENT for the ARTS
arts.gov

This catalogue is made possible through the support
of the Elizabeth Firestone Graham Foundation,
with additional support from the Leon Polk Smith
Foundation. Support for *Vertical Neighbors* is provided
by the Jacques and Natasha Gelman Foundation.

Raven Chacon: A Worm's Eye View from a Bird's Beak
at Nordnorsk Kunstmuseum, Northern Norway/Sápmi
is realized with the kind support of the Lásságámmi
Foundation.

ISBN 978-1-915609-38-0

Distributed by The MIT Press, Art Data,
Les presses du réel, and Idea Books

Front cover: Raven Chacon, performance at
Coyote Canyon, Navajo Reservation, 2013
Inside front flap: Photo taken by Raven Chacon
off I-40 between Navajo Nation and Albuquerque,
New Mexico
Back cover: Photograph for cassette cover for
OVO + Raven Chacon, *Crisalide Fossile*
(Bronson Recordings / Weird Tapes, 2015)
Inside back flap: Photo of Raven Chacon

Every effort has been made to contact the rightful
owners with regard to copyrights and permissions.
We apologize for any inadvertent errors or omissions.

Published by

Sternberg Press
71–75 Shelton Street
UK–London WC2H 9JQ
www.sternberg-press.com

Swiss Institute
38 St Marks Pl
New York NY 10003
www.swissinstitute.net

Nordnorsk Kunstmuseum
Sjøgata 1, 9008
Tromsø, Norway
www.nnkm.no

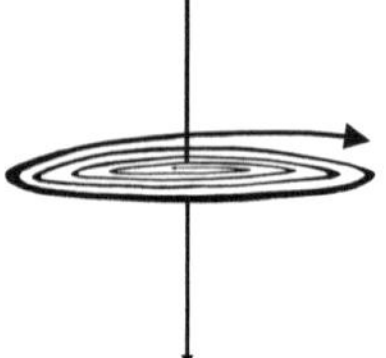